C-3792   CAREER EXAMINATION SERIES

This is your
PASSBOOK for...

Manicurist (Nail Specialty License)

Test Preparation Study Guide
Questions & Answers

COPYRIGHT NOTICE

This book is SOLELY intended for, is sold ONLY to, and its use is RESTRICTED to individual, bona fide applicants or candidates who qualify by virtue of having seriously filed applications for appropriate license, certificate, professional and/or promotional advancement, higher school matriculation, scholarship, or other legitimate requirements of education and/or governmental authorities.

This book is NOT intended for use, class instruction, tutoring, training, duplication, copying, reprinting, excerption, or adaptation, etc., by:

1) Other publishers
2) Proprietors and/or Instructors of "Coaching" and/or Preparatory Courses
3) Personnel and/or Training Divisions of commercial, industrial, and governmental organizations
4) Schools, colleges, or universities and/or their departments and staffs, including teachers and other personnel
5) Testing Agencies or Bureaus
6) Study groups which seek by the purchase of a single volume to copy and/or duplicate and/or adapt this material for use by the group as a whole without having purchased individual volumes for each of the members of the group
7) Et al.

Such persons would be in violation of appropriate Federal and State statutes.

PROVISION OF LICENSING AGREEMENTS – Recognized educational, commercial, industrial, and governmental institutions and organizations, and others legitimately engaged in educational pursuits, including training, testing, and measurement activities, may address request for a licensing agreement to the copyright owners, who will determine whether, and under what conditions, including fees and charges, the materials in this book may be used them. In other words, a licensing facility exists for the legitimate use of the material in this book on other than an individual basis. However, it is asseverated and affirmed here that the material in this book CANNOT be used without the receipt of the express permission of such a licensing agreement from the Publishers. Inquiries re licensing should be addressed to the company, attention rights and permissions department.

All rights reserved, including the right of reproduction in whole or in part, in any form or by any means, electronic or mechanical, including photocopying, recording, or by any information storage and retrieval system, without permission in writing from the Publisher.

Copyright © 2024 by
National Learning Corporation

212 Michael Drive, Syosset, NY 11791
(516) 921-8888 • www.passbooks.com
E-mail: info@passbooks.com

PUBLISHED IN THE UNITED STATES OF AMERICA

PASSBOOK® SERIES

THE *PASSBOOK® SERIES* has been created to prepare applicants and candidates for the ultimate academic battlefield – the examination room.

At some time in our lives, each and every one of us may be required to take an examination – for validation, matriculation, admission, qualification, registration, certification, or licensure.

Based on the assumption that every applicant or candidate has met the basic formal educational standards, has taken the required number of courses, and read the necessary texts, the *PASSBOOK® SERIES* furnishes the one special preparation which may assure passing with confidence, instead of failing with insecurity. Examination questions – together with answers – are furnished as the basic vehicle for study so that the mysteries of the examination and its compounding difficulties may be eliminated or diminished by a sure method.

This book is meant to help you pass your examination provided that you qualify and are serious in your objective.

The entire field is reviewed through the huge store of content information which is succinctly presented through a provocative and challenging approach – the question-and-answer method.

A climate of success is established by furnishing the correct answers at the end of each test.

You soon learn to recognize types of questions, forms of questions, and patterns of questioning. You may even begin to anticipate expected outcomes.

You perceive that many questions are repeated or adapted so that you can gain acute insights, which may enable you to score many sure points.

You learn how to confront new questions, or types of questions, and to attack them confidently and work out the correct answers.

You note objectives and emphases, and recognize pitfalls and dangers, so that you may make positive educational adjustments.

Moreover, you are kept fully informed in relation to new concepts, methods, practices, and directions in the field.

You discover that you are actually taking the examination all the time: you are preparing for the examination by "taking" an examination, not by reading extraneous and/or supererogatory textbooks.

In short, this PASSBOOK®, used directedly, should be an important factor in helping you to pass your test.

MANICURIST

NAIL SPECIALTY WRITTEN EXAMINATION

DUTIES
Gives manicures and pedicures and advises clients on the proper care of nails.

SCOPE OF THE WRITTEN TEST
The written test will be of the multiple choice type and will be designed to test for knowledge, skills, and/or abilities in such areas as: State laws, rules and regulations governing appearance enchancement; license law and safety and health issues; hazardous materials communication; methods of infection control; anatomy and physiology, including body cells, tissues, organs and systems; histology of the skin, bones, muscles and nerves of the hand and arm, and nail structure; infections and infectious agents; nail, skin and foot disorders, and diseases; client consultation and procedures, including color analysis, massage, pedicuring, basic manicure techniques, and advanced techniques including nail tips, wraps, gels and acrylics.

HOW TO TAKE A TEST

I. YOU MUST PASS AN EXAMINATION

A. *WHAT EVERY CANDIDATE SHOULD KNOW*

Examination applicants often ask us for help in preparing for the written test. What can I study in advance? What kinds of questions will be asked? How will the test be given? How will the papers be graded?

As an applicant for a civil service examination, you may be wondering about some of these things. Our purpose here is to suggest effective methods of advance study and to describe civil service examinations.

Your chances for success on this examination can be increased if you know how to prepare. Those "pre-examination jitters" can be reduced if you know what to expect. You can even experience an adventure in good citizenship if you know why civil service exams are given.

B. *WHY ARE CIVIL SERVICE EXAMINATIONS GIVEN?*

Civil service examinations are important to you in two ways. As a citizen, you want public jobs filled by employees who know how to do their work. As a job seeker, you want a fair chance to compete for that job on an equal footing with other candidates. The best-known means of accomplishing this two-fold goal is the competitive examination.

Exams are widely publicized throughout the nation. They may be administered for jobs in federal, state, city, municipal, town or village governments or agencies.

Any citizen may apply, with some limitations, such as the age or residence of applicants. Your experience and education may be reviewed to see whether you meet the requirements for the particular examination. When these requirements exist, they are reasonable and applied consistently to all applicants. Thus, a competitive examination may cause you some uneasiness now, but it is your privilege and safeguard.

C. *HOW ARE CIVIL SERVICE EXAMS DEVELOPED?*

Examinations are carefully written by trained technicians who are specialists in the field known as "psychological measurement," in consultation with recognized authorities in the field of work that the test will cover. These experts recommend the subject matter areas or skills to be tested; only those knowledges or skills important to your success on the job are included. The most reliable books and source materials available are used as references. Together, the experts and technicians judge the difficulty level of the questions.

Test technicians know how to phrase questions so that the problem is clearly stated. Their ethics do not permit "trick" or "catch" questions. Questions may have been tried out on sample groups, or subjected to statistical analysis, to determine their usefulness.

Written tests are often used in combination with performance tests, ratings of training and experience, and oral interviews. All of these measures combine to form the best-known means of finding the right person for the right job.

II. HOW TO PASS THE WRITTEN TEST

A. NATURE OF THE EXAMINATION

To prepare intelligently for civil service examinations, you should know how they differ from school examinations you have taken. In school you were assigned certain definite pages to read or subjects to cover. The examination questions were quite detailed and usually emphasized memory. Civil service exams, on the other hand, try to discover your present ability to perform the duties of a position, plus your potentiality to learn these duties. In other words, a civil service exam attempts to predict how successful you will be. Questions cover such a broad area that they cannot be as minute and detailed as school exam questions.

In the public service similar kinds of work, or positions, are grouped together in one "class." This process is known as *position-classification*. All the positions in a class are paid according to the salary range for that class. One class title covers all of these positions, and they are all tested by the same examination.

B. FOUR BASIC STEPS

1) Study the announcement

How, then, can you know what subjects to study? Our best answer is: "Learn as much as possible about the class of positions for which you've applied." The exam will test the knowledge, skills and abilities needed to do the work.

Your most valuable source of information about the position you want is the official exam announcement. This announcement lists the training and experience qualifications. Check these standards and apply only if you come reasonably close to meeting them.

The brief description of the position in the examination announcement offers some clues to the subjects which will be tested. Think about the job itself. Review the duties in your mind. Can you perform them, or are there some in which you are rusty? Fill in the blank spots in your preparation.

Many jurisdictions preview the written test in the exam announcement by including a section called "Knowledge and Abilities Required," "Scope of the Examination," or some similar heading. Here you will find out specifically what fields will be tested.

2) Review your own background

Once you learn in general what the position is all about, and what you need to know to do the work, ask yourself which subjects you already know fairly well and which need improvement. You may wonder whether to concentrate on improving your strong areas or on building some background in your fields of weakness. When the announcement has specified "some knowledge" or "considerable knowledge," or has used adjectives like "beginning principles of…" or "advanced … methods," you can get a clue as to the number and difficulty of questions to be asked in any given field. More questions, and hence broader coverage, would be included for those subjects which are more important in the work. Now weigh your strengths and weaknesses against the job requirements and prepare accordingly.

3) Determine the level of the position

Another way to tell how intensively you should prepare is to understand the level of the job for which you are applying. Is it the entering level? In other words, is this the position in which beginners in a field of work are hired? Or is it an intermediate or advanced level? Sometimes this is indicated by such words as "Junior" or "Senior" in the class title. Other jurisdictions use Roman numerals to designate the level – Clerk I, Clerk II, for example. The word "Supervisor" sometimes appears in the title. If the level is not indicated by the title, check the description of duties. Will you be working under very close supervision, or will you have responsibility for independent decisions in this work?

4) Choose appropriate study materials

Now that you know the subjects to be examined and the relative amount of each subject to be covered, you can choose suitable study materials. For beginning level jobs, or even advanced ones, if you have a pronounced weakness in some aspect of your training, read a modern, standard textbook in that field. Be sure it is up to date and has general coverage. Such books are normally available at your library, and the librarian will be glad to help you locate one. For entry-level positions, questions of appropriate difficulty are chosen -- neither highly advanced questions, nor those too simple. Such questions require careful thought but not advanced training.

If the position for which you are applying is technical or advanced, you will read more advanced, specialized material. If you are already familiar with the basic principles of your field, elementary textbooks would waste your time. Concentrate on advanced textbooks and technical periodicals. Think through the concepts and review difficult problems in your field.

These are all general sources. You can get more ideas on your own initiative, following these leads. For example, training manuals and publications of the government agency which employs workers in your field can be useful, particularly for technical and professional positions. A letter or visit to the government department involved may result in more specific study suggestions, and certainly will provide you with a more definite idea of the exact nature of the position you are seeking.

III. KINDS OF TESTS

Tests are used for purposes other than measuring knowledge and ability to perform specified duties. For some positions, it is equally important to test ability to make adjustments to new situations or to profit from training. In others, basic mental abilities not dependent on information are essential. Questions which test these things may not appear as pertinent to the duties of the position as those which test for knowledge and information. Yet they are often highly important parts of a fair examination. For very general questions, it is almost impossible to help you direct your study efforts. What we can do is to point out some of the more common of these general abilities needed in public service positions and describe some typical questions.

1) General information

Broad, general information has been found useful for predicting job success in some kinds of work. This is tested in a variety of ways, from vocabulary lists to questions about current events. Basic background in some field of work, such as sociology or economics, may be sampled in a group of questions. Often these are principles which have become familiar to most persons through exposure rather than through formal training. It is difficult to advise you how to study for these questions; being alert to the world around you is our best suggestion.

2) Verbal ability

An example of an ability needed in many positions is verbal or language ability. Verbal ability is, in brief, the ability to use and understand words. Vocabulary and grammar tests are typical measures of this ability. Reading comprehension or paragraph interpretation questions are common in many kinds of civil service tests. You are given a paragraph of written material and asked to find its central meaning.

3) Numerical ability

Number skills can be tested by the familiar arithmetic problem, by checking paired lists of numbers to see which are alike and which are different, or by interpreting charts and graphs. In the latter test, a graph may be printed in the test booklet which you are asked to use as the basis for answering questions.

4) Observation

A popular test for law-enforcement positions is the observation test. A picture is shown to you for several minutes, then taken away. Questions about the picture test your ability to observe both details and larger elements.

5) Following directions

In many positions in the public service, the employee must be able to carry out written instructions dependably and accurately. You may be given a chart with several columns, each column listing a variety of information. The questions require you to carry out directions involving the information given in the chart.

6) Skills and aptitudes

Performance tests effectively measure some manual skills and aptitudes. When the skill is one in which you are trained, such as typing or shorthand, you can practice. These tests are often very much like those given in business school or high school courses. For many of the other skills and aptitudes, however, no short-time preparation can be made. Skills and abilities natural to you or that you have developed throughout your lifetime are being tested.

Many of the general questions just described provide all the data needed to answer the questions and ask you to use your reasoning ability to find the answers. Your best preparation for these tests, as well as for tests of facts and ideas, is to be at your physical and mental best. You, no doubt, have your own methods of getting into an exam-taking mood and keeping "in shape." The next section lists some ideas on this subject.

IV. KINDS OF QUESTIONS

Only rarely is the "essay" question, which you answer in narrative form, used in civil service tests. Civil service tests are usually of the short-answer type. Full instructions for answering these questions will be given to you at the examination. But in case this is your first experience with short-answer questions and separate answer sheets, here is what you need to know:

1) Multiple-choice Questions

Most popular of the short-answer questions is the "multiple choice" or "best answer" question. It can be used, for example, to test for factual knowledge, ability to solve problems or judgment in meeting situations found at work.

A multiple-choice question is normally one of three types—
- It can begin with an incomplete statement followed by several possible endings. You are to find the one ending which *best* completes the statement, although some of the others may not be entirely wrong.
- It can also be a complete statement in the form of a question which is answered by choosing one of the statements listed.

- It can be in the form of a problem – again you select the best answer.

Here is an example of a multiple-choice question with a discussion which should give you some clues as to the method for choosing the right answer:

When an employee has a complaint about his assignment, the action which will *best* help him overcome his difficulty is to
- A. discuss his difficulty with his coworkers
- B. take the problem to the head of the organization
- C. take the problem to the person who gave him the assignment
- D. say nothing to anyone about his complaint

In answering this question, you should study each of the choices to find which is best. Consider choice "A" – Certainly an employee may discuss his complaint with fellow employees, but no change or improvement can result, and the complaint remains unresolved. Choice "B" is a poor choice since the head of the organization probably does not know what assignment you have been given, and taking your problem to him is known as "going over the head" of the supervisor. The supervisor, or person who made the assignment, is the person who can clarify it or correct any injustice. Choice "C" is, therefore, correct. To say nothing, as in choice "D," is unwise. Supervisors have and interest in knowing the problems employees are facing, and the employee is seeking a solution to his problem.

2) True/False Questions

The "true/false" or "right/wrong" form of question is sometimes used. Here a complete statement is given. Your job is to decide whether the statement is right or wrong.

SAMPLE: A roaming cell-phone call to a nearby city costs less than a non-roaming call to a distant city.

This statement is wrong, or false, since roaming calls are more expensive.

This is not a complete list of all possible question forms, although most of the others are variations of these common types. You will always get complete directions for answering questions. Be sure you understand *how* to mark your answers – ask questions until you do.

V. RECORDING YOUR ANSWERS

Computer terminals are used more and more today for many different kinds of exams.

For an examination with very few applicants, you may be told to record your answers in the test booklet itself. Separate answer sheets are much more common. If this separate answer sheet is to be scored by machine – and this is often the case – it is highly important that you mark your answers correctly in order to get credit.

An electronic scoring machine is often used in civil service offices because of the speed with which papers can be scored. Machine-scored answer sheets must be marked with a pencil, which will be given to you. This pencil has a high graphite content which responds to the electronic scoring machine. As a matter of fact, stray dots may register as answers, so do not let your pencil rest on the answer sheet while you are pondering the correct answer. Also, if your pencil lead breaks or is otherwise defective, ask for another.

Since the answer sheet will be dropped in a slot in the scoring machine, be careful not to bend the corners or get the paper crumpled.

The answer sheet normally has five vertical columns of numbers, with 30 numbers to a column. These numbers correspond to the question numbers in your test booklet. After each number, going across the page are four or five pairs of dotted lines. These short dotted lines have small letters or numbers above them. The first two pairs may also have a "T" or "F" above the letters. This indicates that the first two pairs only are to be used if the questions are of the true-false type. If the questions are multiple choice, disregard the "T" and "F" and pay attention only to the small letters or numbers.

Answer your questions in the manner of the sample that follows:

32. The largest city in the United States is
 A. Washington, D.C.
 B. New York City
 C. Chicago
 D. Detroit
 E. San Francisco

1) Choose the answer you think is best. (New York City is the largest, so "B" is correct.)
2) Find the row of dotted lines numbered the same as the question you are answering. (Find row number 32)
3) Find the pair of dotted lines corresponding to the answer. (Find the pair of lines under the mark "B.")
4) Make a solid black mark between the dotted lines.

VI. BEFORE THE TEST

Common sense will help you find procedures to follow to get ready for an examination. Too many of us, however, overlook these sensible measures. Indeed, nervousness and fatigue have been found to be the most serious reasons why applicants fail to do their best on civil service tests. Here is a list of reminders:

- Begin your preparation early – Don't wait until the last minute to go scurrying around for books and materials or to find out what the position is all about.
- Prepare continuously – An hour a night for a week is better than an all-night cram session. This has been definitely established. What is more, a night a week for a month will return better dividends than crowding your study into a shorter period of time.
- Locate the place of the exam – You have been sent a notice telling you when and where to report for the examination. If the location is in a different town or otherwise unfamiliar to you, it would be well to inquire the best route and learn something about the building.
- Relax the night before the test – Allow your mind to rest. Do not study at all that night. Plan some mild recreation or diversion; then go to bed early and get a good night's sleep.
- Get up early enough to make a leisurely trip to the place for the test – This way unforeseen events, traffic snarls, unfamiliar buildings, etc. will not upset you.
- Dress comfortably – A written test is not a fashion show. You will be known by number and not by name, so wear something comfortable.

- Leave excess paraphernalia at home – Shopping bags and odd bundles will get in your way. You need bring only the items mentioned in the official notice you received; usually everything you need is provided. Do not bring reference books to the exam. They will only confuse those last minutes and be taken away from you when in the test room.
- Arrive somewhat ahead of time – If because of transportation schedules you must get there very early, bring a newspaper or magazine to take your mind off yourself while waiting.
- Locate the examination room – When you have found the proper room, you will be directed to the seat or part of the room where you will sit. Sometimes you are given a sheet of instructions to read while you are waiting. Do not fill out any forms until you are told to do so; just read them and be prepared.
- Relax and prepare to listen to the instructions
- If you have any physical problem that may keep you from doing your best, be sure to tell the test administrator. If you are sick or in poor health, you really cannot do your best on the exam. You can come back and take the test some other time.

VII. AT THE TEST

The day of the test is here and you have the test booklet in your hand. The temptation to get going is very strong. Caution! There is more to success than knowing the right answers. You must know how to identify your papers and understand variations in the type of short-answer question used in this particular examination. Follow these suggestions for maximum results from your efforts:

1) Cooperate with the monitor
The test administrator has a duty to create a situation in which you can be as much at ease as possible. He will give instructions, tell you when to begin, check to see that you are marking your answer sheet correctly, and so on. He is not there to guard you, although he will see that your competitors do not take unfair advantage. He wants to help you do your best.

2) Listen to all instructions
Don't jump the gun! Wait until you understand all directions. In most civil service tests you get more time than you need to answer the questions. So don't be in a hurry. Read each word of instructions until you clearly understand the meaning. Study the examples, listen to all announcements and follow directions. Ask questions if you do not understand what to do.

3) Identify your papers
Civil service exams are usually identified by number only. You will be assigned a number; you must not put your name on your test papers. Be sure to copy your number correctly. Since more than one exam may be given, copy your exact examination title.

4) Plan your time
Unless you are told that a test is a "speed" or "rate of work" test, speed itself is usually not important. Time enough to answer all the questions will be provided, but this does not mean that you have all day. An overall time limit has been set. Divide the total time (in minutes) by the number of questions to determine the approximate time you have for each question.

5) Do not linger over difficult questions

If you come across a difficult question, mark it with a paper clip (useful to have along) and come back to it when you have been through the booklet. One caution if you do this – be sure to skip a number on your answer sheet as well. Check often to be sure that you have not lost your place and that you are marking in the row numbered the same as the question you are answering.

6) Read the questions

Be sure you know what the question asks! Many capable people are unsuccessful because they failed to *read* the questions correctly.

7) Answer all questions

Unless you have been instructed that a penalty will be deducted for incorrect answers, it is better to guess than to omit a question.

8) Speed tests

It is often better NOT to guess on speed tests. It has been found that on timed tests people are tempted to spend the last few seconds before time is called in marking answers at random – without even reading them – in the hope of picking up a few extra points. To discourage this practice, the instructions may warn you that your score will be "corrected" for guessing. That is, a penalty will be applied. The incorrect answers will be deducted from the correct ones, or some other penalty formula will be used.

9) Review your answers

If you finish before time is called, go back to the questions you guessed or omitted to give them further thought. Review other answers if you have time.

10) Return your test materials

If you are ready to leave before others have finished or time is called, take ALL your materials to the monitor and leave quietly. Never take any test material with you. The monitor can discover whose papers are not complete, and taking a test booklet may be grounds for disqualification.

VIII. EXAMINATION TECHNIQUES

1) Read the general instructions carefully. These are usually printed on the first page of the exam booklet. As a rule, these instructions refer to the timing of the examination; the fact that you should not start work until the signal and must stop work at a signal, etc. If there are any *special* instructions, such as a choice of questions to be answered, make sure that you note this instruction carefully.

2) When you are ready to start work on the examination, that is as soon as the signal has been given, read the instructions to each question booklet, underline any key words or phrases, such as *least, best, outline, describe* and the like. In this way you will tend to answer as requested rather than discover on reviewing your paper that you *listed without describing*, that you selected the *worst* choice rather than the *best* choice, etc.

3) If the examination is of the objective or multiple-choice type – that is, each question will also give a series of possible answers: A, B, C or D, and you are called upon to select the best answer and write the letter next to that answer on your answer paper – it is advisable to start answering each question in turn. There may be anywhere from 50 to 100 such questions in the three or four hours allotted and you can see how much time would be taken if you read through all the questions before beginning to answer any. Furthermore, if you come across a question or group of questions which you know would be difficult to answer, it would undoubtedly affect your handling of all the other questions.

4) If the examination is of the essay type and contains but a few questions, it is a moot point as to whether you should read all the questions before starting to answer any one. Of course, if you are given a choice – say five out of seven and the like – then it is essential to read all the questions so you can eliminate the two that are most difficult. If, however, you are asked to answer all the questions, there may be danger in trying to answer the easiest one first because you may find that you will spend too much time on it. The best technique is to answer the first question, then proceed to the second, etc.

5) Time your answers. Before the exam begins, write down the time it started, then add the time allowed for the examination and write down the time it must be completed, then divide the time available somewhat as follows:
    - If 3-1/2 hours are allowed, that would be 210 minutes. If you have 80 objective-type questions, that would be an average of 2-1/2 minutes per question. Allow yourself no more than 2 minutes per question, or a total of 160 minutes, which will permit about 50 minutes to review.
    - If for the time allotment of 210 minutes there are 7 essay questions to answer, that would average about 30 minutes a question. Give yourself only 25 minutes per question so that you have about 35 minutes to review.

6) The most important instruction is to *read each question* and make sure you know what is wanted. The second most important instruction is to *time yourself properly* so that you answer every question. The third most important instruction is to *answer every question*. Guess if you have to but include something for each question. Remember that you will receive no credit for a blank and will probably receive some credit if you write something in answer to an essay question. If you guess a letter – say "B" for a multiple-choice question – you may have guessed right. If you leave a blank as an answer to a multiple-choice question, the examiners may respect your feelings but it will not add a point to your score. Some exams may penalize you for wrong answers, so in such cases *only*, you may not want to guess unless you have some basis for your answer.

7) Suggestions
    a. Objective-type questions
        1. Examine the question booklet for proper sequence of pages and questions
        2. Read all instructions carefully
        3. Skip any question which seems too difficult; return to it after all other questions have been answered
        4. Apportion your time properly; do not spend too much time on any single question or group of questions

5. Note and underline key words – *all, most, fewest, least, best, worst, same, opposite*, etc.
6. Pay particular attention to negatives
7. Note unusual option, e.g., unduly long, short, complex, different or similar in content to the body of the question
8. Observe the use of "hedging" words – *probably, may, most likely*, etc.
9. Make sure that your answer is put next to the same number as the question
10. Do not second-guess unless you have good reason to believe the second answer is definitely more correct
11. Cross out original answer if you decide another answer is more accurate; do not erase until you are ready to hand your paper in
12. Answer all questions; guess unless instructed otherwise
13. Leave time for review

b. Essay questions
  1. Read each question carefully
  2. Determine exactly what is wanted. Underline key words or phrases.
  3. Decide on outline or paragraph answer
  4. Include many different points and elements unless asked to develop any one or two points or elements
  5. Show impartiality by giving pros and cons unless directed to select one side only
  6. Make and write down any assumptions you find necessary to answer the questions
  7. Watch your English, grammar, punctuation and choice of words
  8. Time your answers; don't crowd material

8) Answering the essay question

Most essay questions can be answered by framing the specific response around several key words or ideas. Here are a few such key words or ideas:

M's: manpower, materials, methods, money, management
P's: purpose, program, policy, plan, procedure, practice, problems, pitfalls, personnel, public relations
  a. Six basic steps in handling problems:
    1. Preliminary plan and background development
    2. Collect information, data and facts
    3. Analyze and interpret information, data and facts
    4. Analyze and develop solutions as well as make recommendations
    5. Prepare report and sell recommendations
    6. Install recommendations and follow up effectiveness

  b. Pitfalls to avoid
    1. *Taking things for granted* – A statement of the situation does not necessarily imply that each of the elements is necessarily true; for example, a complaint may be invalid and biased so that all that can be taken for granted is that a complaint has been registered

2. *Considering only one side of a situation* – Wherever possible, indicate several alternatives and then point out the reasons you selected the best one
3. *Failing to indicate follow up* – Whenever your answer indicates action on your part, make certain that you will take proper follow-up action to see how successful your recommendations, procedures or actions turn out to be
4. *Taking too long in answering any single question* – Remember to time your answers properly

IX. AFTER THE TEST

Scoring procedures differ in detail among civil service jurisdictions although the general principles are the same. Whether the papers are hand-scored or graded by machine we have described, they are nearly always graded by number. That is, the person who marks the paper knows only the number – never the name – of the applicant. Not until all the papers have been graded will they be matched with names. If other tests, such as training and experience or oral interview ratings have been given, scores will be combined. Different parts of the examination usually have different weights. For example, the written test might count 60 percent of the final grade, and a rating of training and experience 40 percent. In many jurisdictions, veterans will have a certain number of points added to their grades.

After the final grade has been determined, the names are placed in grade order and an eligible list is established. There are various methods for resolving ties between those who get the same final grade – probably the most common is to place first the name of the person whose application was received first. Job offers are made from the eligible list in the order the names appear on it. You will be notified of your grade and your rank as soon as all these computations have been made. This will be done as rapidly as possible.

People who are found to meet the requirements in the announcement are called "eligibles." Their names are put on a list of eligible candidates. An eligible's chances of getting a job depend on how high he stands on this list and how fast agencies are filling jobs from the list.

When a job is to be filled from a list of eligibles, the agency asks for the names of people on the list of eligibles for that job. When the civil service commission receives this request, it sends to the agency the names of the three people highest on this list. Or, if the job to be filled has specialized requirements, the office sends the agency the names of the top three persons who meet these requirements from the general list.

The appointing officer makes a choice from among the three people whose names were sent to him. If the selected person accepts the appointment, the names of the others are put back on the list to be considered for future openings.

That is the rule in hiring from all kinds of eligible lists, whether they are for typist, carpenter, chemist, or something else. For every vacancy, the appointing officer has his choice of any one of the top three eligibles on the list. This explains why the person whose name is on top of the list sometimes does not get an appointment when some of the persons lower on the list do. If the appointing officer chooses the second or third eligible, the No. 1 eligible does not get a job at once, but stays on the list until he is appointed or the list is terminated.

X. HOW TO PASS THE INTERVIEW TEST

The examination for which you applied requires an oral interview test. You have already taken the written test and you are now being called for the interview test – the final part of the formal examination.

You may think that it is not possible to prepare for an interview test and that there are no procedures to follow during an interview. Our purpose is to point out some things you can do in advance that will help you and some good rules to follow and pitfalls to avoid while you are being interviewed.

What is an interview supposed to test?

The written examination is designed to test the technical knowledge and competence of the candidate; the oral is designed to evaluate intangible qualities, not readily measured otherwise, and to establish a list showing the relative fitness of each candidate – as measured against his competitors – for the position sought. Scoring is not on the basis of "right" and "wrong," but on a sliding scale of values ranging from "not passable" to "outstanding." As a matter of fact, it is possible to achieve a relatively low score without a single "incorrect" answer because of evident weakness in the qualities being measured.

Occasionally, an examination may consist entirely of an oral test – either an individual or a group oral. In such cases, information is sought concerning the technical knowledges and abilities of the candidate, since there has been no written examination for this purpose. More commonly, however, an oral test is used to supplement a written examination.

Who conducts interviews?

The composition of oral boards varies among different jurisdictions. In nearly all, a representative of the personnel department serves as chairman. One of the members of the board may be a representative of the department in which the candidate would work. In some cases, "outside experts" are used, and, frequently, a businessman or some other representative of the general public is asked to serve. Labor and management or other special groups may be represented. The aim is to secure the services of experts in the appropriate field.

However the board is composed, it is a good idea (and not at all improper or unethical) to ascertain in advance of the interview who the members are and what groups they represent. When you are introduced to them, you will have some idea of their backgrounds and interests, and at least you will not stutter and stammer over their names.

What should be done before the interview?

While knowledge about the board members is useful and takes some of the surprise element out of the interview, there is other preparation which is more substantive. It *is* possible to prepare for an oral interview – in several ways:

1) Keep a copy of your application and review it carefully before the interview

This may be the only document before the oral board, and the starting point of the interview. Know what education and experience you have listed there, and the sequence and dates of all of it. Sometimes the board will ask you to review the highlights of your experience for them; you should not have to hem and haw doing it.

2) Study the class specification and the examination announcement

Usually, the oral board has one or both of these to guide them. The qualities, characteristics or knowledges required by the position sought are stated in these documents. They offer valuable clues as to the nature of the oral interview. For example, if the job involves supervisory responsibilities, the announcement will usually indicate that knowledge of modern supervisory methods and the qualifications of the candidate as a supervisor will be tested. If so, you can expect such questions, frequently in the form of a hypothetical situation which you are expected to solve. NEVER go into an oral without knowledge of the duties and responsibilities of the job you seek.

3) Think through each qualification required

Try to visualize the kind of questions you would ask if you were a board member. How well could you answer them? Try especially to appraise your own knowledge and background in each area, *measured against the job sought*, and identify any areas in which you are weak. Be critical and realistic – do not flatter yourself.

4) Do some general reading in areas in which you feel you may be weak

For example, if the job involves supervision and your past experience has NOT, some general reading in supervisory methods and practices, particularly in the field of human relations, might be useful. Do NOT study agency procedures or detailed manuals. The oral board will be testing your understanding and capacity, not your memory.

5) Get a good night's sleep and watch your general health and mental attitude

You will want a clear head at the interview. Take care of a cold or any other minor ailment, and of course, no hangovers.

What should be done on the day of the interview?

Now comes the day of the interview itself. Give yourself plenty of time to get there. Plan to arrive somewhat ahead of the scheduled time, particularly if your appointment is in the fore part of the day. If a previous candidate fails to appear, the board might be ready for you a bit early. By early afternoon an oral board is almost invariably behind schedule if there are many candidates, and you may have to wait. Take along a book or magazine to read, or your application to review, but leave any extraneous material in the waiting room when you go in for your interview. In any event, relax and compose yourself.

The matter of dress is important. The board is forming impressions about you – from your experience, your manners, your attitude, and your appearance. Give your personal appearance careful attention. Dress your best, but not your flashiest. Choose conservative, appropriate clothing, and be sure it is immaculate. This is a business interview, and your appearance should indicate that you regard it as such. Besides, being well groomed and properly dressed will help boost your confidence.

Sooner or later, someone will call your name and escort you into the interview room. *This is it.* From here on you are on your own. It is too late for any more preparation. But remember, you asked for this opportunity to prove your fitness, and you are here because your request was granted.

What happens when you go in?

The usual sequence of events will be as follows: The clerk (who is often the board stenographer) will introduce you to the chairman of the oral board, who will introduce you to the other members of the board. Acknowledge the introductions before you sit down. Do not be surprised if you find a microphone facing you or a stenotypist sitting by. Oral interviews are usually recorded in the event of an appeal or other review.

Usually the chairman of the board will open the interview by reviewing the highlights of your education and work experience from your application – primarily for the benefit of the other members of the board, as well as to get the material into the record. Do not interrupt or comment unless there is an error or significant misinterpretation; if that is the case, do not hesitate. But do not quibble about insignificant matters. Also, he will usually ask you some question about your education, experience or your present job – partly to get you to start talking and to establish the interviewing "rapport." He may start the actual questioning, or turn it over to one of the other members. Frequently, each member undertakes the questioning on a particular area, one in which he is perhaps most competent, so you can expect each member to participate in the examination. Because time is limited, you may also expect some rather abrupt switches in the direction the questioning takes, so do not be upset by it. Normally, a board member will not pursue a single line of questioning unless he discovers a particular strength or weakness.

After each member has participated, the chairman will usually ask whether any member has any further questions, then will ask you if you have anything you wish to add. Unless you are expecting this question, it may floor you. Worse, it may start you off on an extended, extemporaneous speech. The board is not usually seeking more information. The question is principally to offer you a last opportunity to present further qualifications or to indicate that you have nothing to add. So, if you feel that a significant qualification or characteristic has been overlooked, it is proper to point it out in a sentence or so. Do not compliment the board on the thoroughness of their examination – they have been sketchy, and you know it. If you wish, merely say, "No thank you, I have nothing further to add." This is a point where you can "talk yourself out" of a good impression or fail to present an important bit of information. Remember, *you close the interview yourself*.

The chairman will then say, "That is all, Mr. _____, thank you." Do not be startled; the interview is over, and quicker than you think. Thank him, gather your belongings and take your leave. Save your sigh of relief for the other side of the door.

How to put your best foot forward

Throughout this entire process, you may feel that the board individually and collectively is trying to pierce your defenses, seek out your hidden weaknesses and embarrass and confuse you. Actually, this is not true. They are obliged to make an appraisal of your qualifications for the job you are seeking, and they want to see you in your best light. Remember, they must interview all candidates and a non-cooperative candidate may become a failure in spite of their best efforts to bring out his qualifications. Here are 15 suggestions that will help you:

1) Be natural – Keep your attitude confident, not cocky

If you are not confident that you can do the job, do not expect the board to be. Do not apologize for your weaknesses, try to bring out your strong points. The board is interested in a positive, not negative, presentation. Cockiness will antagonize any board member and make him wonder if you are covering up a weakness by a false show of strength.

2) Get comfortable, but don't lounge or sprawl

Sit erectly but not stiffly. A careless posture may lead the board to conclude that you are careless in other things, or at least that you are not impressed by the importance of the occasion. Either conclusion is natural, even if incorrect. Do not fuss with your clothing, a pencil or an ashtray. Your hands may occasionally be useful to emphasize a point; do not let them become a point of distraction.

3) Do not wisecrack or make small talk

This is a serious situation, and your attitude should show that you consider it as such. Further, the time of the board is limited – they do not want to waste it, and neither should you.

4) Do not exaggerate your experience or abilities
In the first place, from information in the application or other interviews and sources, the board may know more about you than you think. Secondly, you probably will not get away with it. An experienced board is rather adept at spotting such a situation, so do not take the chance.

5) If you know a board member, do not make a point of it, yet do not hide it
Certainly you are not fooling him, and probably not the other members of the board. Do not try to take advantage of your acquaintanceship – it will probably do you little good.

6) Do not dominate the interview
Let the board do that. They will give you the clues – do not assume that you have to do all the talking. Realize that the board has a number of questions to ask you, and do not try to take up all the interview time by showing off your extensive knowledge of the answer to the first one.

7) Be attentive
You only have 20 minutes or so, and you should keep your attention at its sharpest throughout. When a member is addressing a problem or question to you, give him your undivided attention. Address your reply principally to him, but do not exclude the other board members.

8) Do not interrupt
A board member may be stating a problem for you to analyze. He will ask you a question when the time comes. Let him state the problem, and wait for the question.

9) Make sure you understand the question
Do not try to answer until you are sure what the question is. If it is not clear, restate it in your own words or ask the board member to clarify it for you. However, do not haggle about minor elements.

10) Reply promptly but not hastily
A common entry on oral board rating sheets is "candidate responded readily," or "candidate hesitated in replies." Respond as promptly and quickly as you can, but do not jump to a hasty, ill-considered answer.

11) Do not be peremptory in your answers
A brief answer is proper – but do not fire your answer back. That is a losing game from your point of view. The board member can probably ask questions much faster than you can answer them.

12) Do not try to create the answer you think the board member wants
He is interested in what kind of mind you have and how it works – not in playing games. Furthermore, he can usually spot this practice and will actually grade you down on it.

13) Do not switch sides in your reply merely to agree with a board member
Frequently, a member will take a contrary position merely to draw you out and to see if you are willing and able to defend your point of view. Do not start a debate, yet do not surrender a good position. If a position is worth taking, it is worth defending.

14) Do not be afraid to admit an error in judgment if you are shown to be wrong

The board knows that you are forced to reply without any opportunity for careful consideration. Your answer may be demonstrably wrong. If so, admit it and get on with the interview.

15) Do not dwell at length on your present job

The opening question may relate to your present assignment. Answer the question but do not go into an extended discussion. You are being examined for a *new* job, not your present one. As a matter of fact, try to phrase ALL your answers in terms of the job for which you are being examined.

Basis of Rating

Probably you will forget most of these "do's" and "don'ts" when you walk into the oral interview room. Even remembering them all will not ensure you a passing grade. Perhaps you did not have the qualifications in the first place. But remembering them will help you to put your best foot forward, without treading on the toes of the board members.

Rumor and popular opinion to the contrary notwithstanding, an oral board wants you to make the best appearance possible. They know you are under pressure – but they also want to see how you respond to it as a guide to what your reaction would be under the pressures of the job you seek. They will be influenced by the degree of poise you display, the personal traits you show and the manner in which you respond.

ABOUT THIS BOOK

This book contains tests divided into Examination Sections. Go through each test, answering every question in the margin. We have also attached a sample answer sheet at the back of the book that can be removed and used. At the end of each test look at the answer key and check your answers. On the ones you got wrong, look at the right answer choice and learn. Do not fill in the answers first. Do not memorize the questions and answers, but understand the answer and principles involved. On your test, the questions will likely be different from the samples. Questions are changed and new ones added. If you understand these past questions you should have success with any changes that arise. Tests may consist of several types of questions. We have additional books on each subject should more study be advisable or necessary for you. Finally, the more you study, the better prepared you will be. This book is intended to be the last thing you study before you walk into the examination room. Prior study of relevant texts is also recommended. NLC publishes some of these in our Fundamental Series. Knowledge and good sense are important factors in passing your exam. Good luck also helps. So now study this Passbook, absorb the material contained within and take that knowledge into the examination. Then do your best to pass that exam.

EXAMINATION SECTION

EXAMINATION SECTION
TEST 1

DIRECTIONS: Each question or incomplete statement is followed by several suggested answers or completions. Select the one that BEST answers the question or completes the statement. *PRINT THE LETTER OF THE CORRECT ANSWER IN THE SPACE AT THE RIGHT.*

1. Which of the following is the translucent portion of the nail that extends from the nail root to the free edge and is sometimes referred to as the nail body?
   A. Hyponychium   B. Nail plate   C. Nail bed   D. Cuticle

   1.____

2. Which of the following is the part of the nail plate that extends beyond the fingertip?
   A. Hyponychium   B. Nail plate   C. Nail bed   D. Free edge

   2.____

3. Which of the following is the skin between the free edge and the fingertip of the natural nail?
   A. Hyponychium   B. Nail plate   C. Nail bed   D. Cuticle

   3.____

4. The _____ is the portion of the skin that the nail rests upon as it grows.
   A. free edge   B. hyponychium   C. nail bed   D. cuticle

   4.____

5. The whitish half-moon shape at the base of the nail is referred to as the
   A. lunula
   B. matrix
   C. cuticle
   D. bed epithelium

   5.____

6. Which of the following refers to the living skin at the base of the nail plate that partially overlaps the lunula?
   A. Hyponychium
   B. Eponychium
   C. Perionychium
   D. Leukonychium

   6.____

7. Which of the following refers to the additional or excessive skin that overlaps onto the sides of the nail plate?
   A. Hyponychium
   B. Eponychium
   C. Perionychium
   D. Leukonychium

   7.____

8. Which of the following is the general term for any nail disease or deformity?
   A. Cytosis   B. Trichosis   C. Onychosis   D. Ketosis

   8.____

9. Which of the following, as illustrated in the image shown at the right, is inflammation of the nail matrix?
   A. Onychia
   B. Paronychia
   C. Onycholysis
   D. Onychomycosis

   9.____

10. Which of the following, as illustrated in the image shown at the right, refers to a bacterial inflammation of the skin surrounding the nail plate?
    A. Onychia
    B. Paronychia
    C. Onycholysis
    D. Onychomycosis

10.____

11. _____ is the scientific term for an ingrown nail.
    A. Melanonychia
    B. Onychophagy
    C. Onychorrhexis
    D. Onychocryptosis

11.____

12. A noticeably thin white nail plate that is more flexible than normal is referred to as a(n)
    A. agnail
    B. bruised nail
    C. eggshell nail
    D. leukonychia

12.____

13. Which of the following, as illustrated in the image shown at the right, refers to whitish discoloration of the nails caused by injury?
    A. Leukonychia
    B. Melanonychia
    C. Nail psoriasis
    D. Nail pterygium

13.____

14. As illustrated in the image shown at the right, darkening of the nails caused by excess melanin is referred to as
    A. leukonychia
    B. melanonychia
    C. nail psoriasis
    D. nail pterygium

14.____

15. _____, another term for a hangnail, is the split cuticle around the nail.
    A. Agnail
    B. Bruised nail
    C. Eggshell nail
    D. Leukonychia

15.____

16. Which condition, illustrated in the image shown at the right, is associated with the nails turning green, yellow, or brown in color and chalky white material gathering beneath the nail?
    A. Leukonychia
    B. Melanonychia
    C. Nail psoriasis
    D. Nail pterygium

16.____

17. As illustrated in the image shown at the right, the forward growth of living skin that adheres to the surface of the nail plate is referred to as
    A. onychorrhexis
    B. onychocryptosis
    C. nail psoriasis
    D. nail pterygium

17.____

18. Which of the following is the scientific name for nail biting?
    A. Onychophora
    B. Onychophagy
    C. Onychorrhexis
    D. Onychocryptosis

18.____

19. Abnormal brittleness of the nail plate is referred to as
    A. onychophora
    B. onychophagy
    C. onychorrhexis
    D. onychocryptosis

19.____

20. The _____ is a glassy, graying structure at the point where the nail plate meets the hyponychium.
    A. cuticle
    B. mantle
    C. lunula
    D. onychodermal band

20.____

21. The pocket-like structure that holds the nail root and the matrix is referred to as
    A. cuticle
    B. mantle
    C. lunula
    D. onychodermal band

21.____

22. Which of the following refers to the thin, sticky layer of the epidermis that attaches the nail plate to the nail bed?
    A. Eponychium
    B. Hyponychium
    C. Perionychium
    D. Bed epithelium

22.____

23. What condition, as illustrated in the image shown at the right, is characterized by nails with a concave shape and is commonly referred to as "spoon nails"?
    A. Leukonychia
    B. Melanonychia
    C. Koilonychia
    D. Perionychia

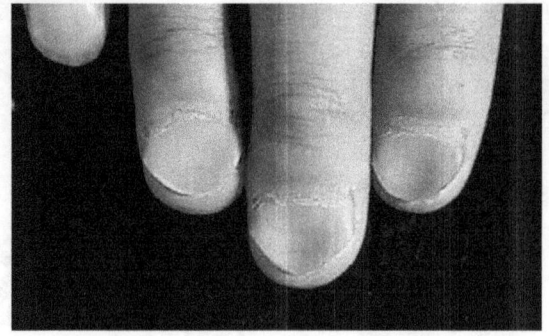

24. Indented vertical lines down the nail plate are referred to as which of the following?
    A. Furrows   B. Burrows
    C. Corrugations   D. Emaciations

25. Horizontal wavy ridges across the nail are referred to as which of the following?
    A. Furrows   B. Burrows
    C. Corrugations   D. Emaciations

KEY (CORRECT ANSWERS)

1.	B	11.	D
2.	D	12.	C
3.	A	13.	A
4.	C	14.	B
5.	A	15.	A
6.	B	16.	C
7.	C	17.	D
8.	C	18.	B
9.	A	19.	C
10.	B	20.	D

21. B
22. D
23. C
24. A
25. C

TEST 2

DIRECTIONS: Each question or incomplete statement is followed by several suggested answers or completions. Select the one that BEST answers the question or completes the statement. *PRINT THE LETTER OF THE CORRECT ANSWER IN THE SPACE AT THE RIGHT.*

1. As illustrated in the image shown at the right, what condition is characterized by the loss of the nail plate as a result of separation occurring at the nail matrix?
    A. Onychophora
    B. Onychophagy
    C. Onychomadesis
    D. Onychoatrophia

    1.____

    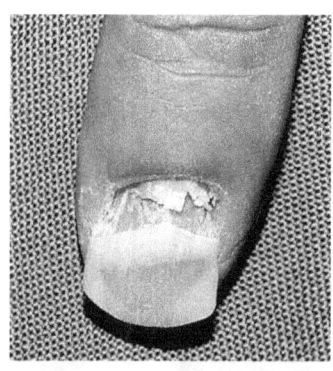

2. As illustrated in the image shown at the right, what condition is characterized by wasting away of the nail?
    A. Onychophora
    B. Onychophagy
    C. Onychomadesis
    D. Onychoatrophia

    2.____

    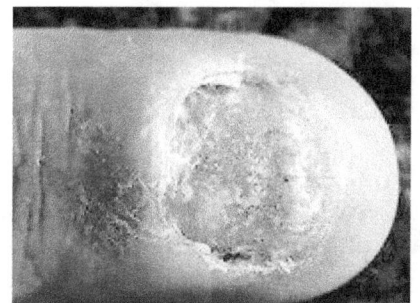

3. As illustrated in the image shown at the right, _____ is characterized by the nails shedding or falling off.
    A. Onychoptosis
    B. Onychophagy
    C. Onychomadesis
    D. Onychoatrophia

    3.____

    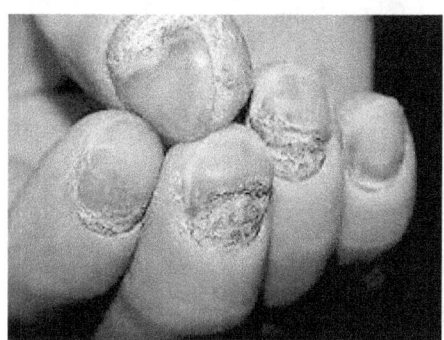

4. A thickening of the nail plate or an abnormal outgrowth of the nail or nail plate is referred to as
    A. onychoptosis
    B. onychauxis
    C. onychomadesis
    D. onychoatrophia

    4.____

    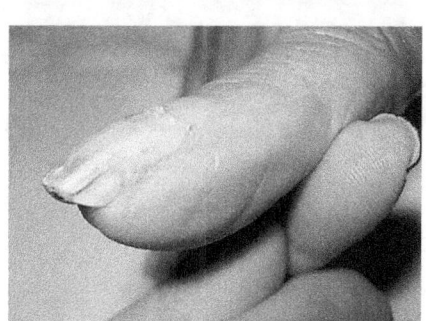

5

5. The condition of onychogryphosis is characterized by which of the following?
   A. Brittle nails
   B. Claw nails
   C. Trumpet nails
   D. Ingrown nails

6. The condition of onychomycosis is characterized by _____ of the nail.
   A. psoriasis   B. ringworm   C. bleeding   D. splitting

7. What type of nails, as illustrated in the image shown at the right, have a nail plate that appears to narrow toward the free edge as corners fold inward at the tip of the finger or toe?
   A. Claw nails
   B. Trumpet nails
   C. Plicatured nails
   D. Ingrown nails

8. What type of nails, as illustrated in the image shown at the right, have a highly curved nail plate often caused by injury to the matrix but also can be due to heredity?
   A. Claw nails
   B. Trumpet nails
   C. Plicatured nails
   D. Ingrown nails

9. A healthy nail appears to be slightly _____ in color.
   A. pink   B. white   C. yellow   D. gray

10. The nail bed and the matrix bed are attached to the underlying bone by which of the following?
    A. Skin   B. Muscles   C. Ligaments   D. Tendons

11. Adult nails grow at what rate?
    _____ inch/month
    A. 1/8   B. 1/4   C. 3/8   D. 1/2

12. Blue nails, as illustrated in the image shown at the right, can be indicative of
    A. poor diet
    B. poor blood circulation
    C. elevated blood glucose
    D. hand trauma

    12.____

13. The condition of onychogryphosis is MOST commonly seen on which of the following?
    A. Thumbs
    B. Index fingers
    C. Great toes
    D. Ring fingers

    13.____

14. Which of the following is the medical term for athlete's foot?
    A. Tinea pedis
    B. Tinea unguium
    C. Tinea corporis
    D. Tinea versicolor

    14.____

15. The human nails have a water content of
    A. 15-30%   B. 30-50%   C. 50-65%   D. 65-80%

    15.____

16. Generally, a replacement of a natural toenail takes approximately what time period?
    A. 6-12 weeks   C. 3-6 months   C. 6-9 months   D. 9-12 months

    16.____

17. The water content of the nail directly affects what feature of the nail?
    A. Growth   B. Color   C. Shape   D. Flexibility

    17.____

18. The nail plate is constructed of how many layers of nail cells?
    A. 25   B. 50   C. 75   D. 100

    18.____

19. Generally, a replacement of a natural toenail takes approximately what time period?
    A. 2-4 weeks   B. 4-8 weeks   C. 8-12 weeks   D. 3-6 months

    19.____

20. For what reason are toenails thicker than fingernails?
    A. The matrix is shorter.
    B. The matrix is longer.
    C. The nail bed is shorter.
    D. The nail bed is longer.

    20.____

21. As illustrated in the image shown at the right, which of the following are visible depressions running across the width of the natural nail plate that is usually the result of a major illness or injury that has traumatized the body?
    A. Eggshell nails
    B. Bruised nails
    C. Beau's lines
    D. Hangnails

21._____

22. The nail of which finger grows the FASTEST?
    A. Thumb
    B. Index finger
    C. Middle finger
    D. Ring finger

22._____

23. During which season do the nails grow the FASTEST?
    A. Spring   B. Summer   C. Fall   D. Winter

23._____

24. The nail of which finger grows the SLOWEST?
    A. Thumb
    B. Index finger
    C. Middle finger
    D. Ring finger

24._____

25. The nails are primarily composed of what protein?
    A. Collagen   B. Keratin   C. Paraffin   D. Melanin

25._____

KEY (CORRECT ANSWERS)

1.	C	11.	A
2.	D	12.	B
3.	A	13.	C
4.	B	14.	A
5.	B	15.	A
6.	B	16.	D
7.	B	17.	D
8.	C	18.	D
9.	A	19.	B
10.	C	20.	B

21. C
22. C
23. B
24. A
25. B

TEST 3

DIRECTIONS: Each question or incomplete statement is followed by several suggested answers or completions. Select the one that BEST answers the question or completes the statement. *PRINT THE LETTER OF THE CORRECT ANSWER IN THE SPACE AT THE RIGHT.*

1. All of the following affect the growth of nails EXCEPT
   A. health B. disease C. gender D. nutrition

   1._____

2. After an injury, infection, or disease, the natural nail will return to its healthy growth as long as which of the following is healthy and undamaged?
   A. Nail bed B. Matrix C. Lunula D. Cuticle

   2._____

3. Which of the following represents the technical term for the nail?
   A. Onyx B. Oryx C. Calyx D. Epicalyx

   3._____

4. Which of the following is the purpose of the free edge of the nail? Protect the
   A. nail bed
   B. nail matrix
   C. cuticle
   D. tip of the finger

   4._____

5. What part of the nail acts as a barrier against microbial infection?
   Hyponychium B. Nail plate C. Nail bed D. Cuticle

   5._____

6. After a trauma, growth of the nail plate stops for what period of time?
   A. 24-48 hours B. 5-7 days C. 10-14 days D. 3 weeks

   6._____

7. The hard keratin of the nails contains a high level of _____ compared to keratins of the skin.
   A. carbon B. oxygen C. sulfur D. iodine

   7._____

8. Small bone growth beneath the nail is referred to as which of the following?
   A. Hapalonychia B. Chromonychia
   C. Subungal exostosis D. Subungal osteogenesis

   8._____

9. The toenails grow at what percentage of the rate than that of fingernails?
   A. 10-20% B. 20-33% C. 33-50% D. 50-65%

   9._____

10. Which of the following statements is TRUE regarding a normal healthy nail? A normal healthy nail is firm and flexible and should be _____ and unspotted.
    A. long B. short C. uneven D. smooth

    10._____

11. A typical bacterial infection on the nail plate can be identified in the early stages as a _____ spot that becomes darker in its advanced stages.
    A. white-gray B. blue-green
    C. yellow-green D. orange-red

    11._____

12. Splinter hemorrhages are caused by physical trauma or injury to what part of the nail?
    A. Lunula   B. Nail bed   C. Nail plate   D. Free edge

13. As illustrated in the image shown at the right, which of the following is a condition in which a blood clot forms under the nail plate causing a dark purple spot?
    A. Blue nails
    B. Bruised nails
    C. Eggshell nails
    D. Plicatured nails

14. The condition of "spoon nails" can be indicative of a deficiency in which of the following?
    A. Iron   B. Calcium   C. Vitamin C   D. Vitamin B12

15. As illustrated in the image shown at the right, a red lunula can be indicative of what medical condition?
    A. Liver disease
    B. Heart disease
    C. Rheumatoid arthritis
    D. Psoriatic arthritis

16. As illustrated in the image shown at the right, double transvers white lines (Muehrcke's lines) that move out as the nail grows can be indicative of what medical condition?
    A. Liver disease
    B. Heart disease
    C. Rheumatoid arthritis
    D. Psoriatic arthritis

17. Curving of the nail with thickening of the fingertip, commonly referred to as clubbing, is indicative of what medical condition?
    A. Liver disease
    B. Heart disease
    C. Lung disease
    D. Renal disease

18. In what nail should the lunula be BEST visualized?
    A. Dominant middle finger
    B. Non-dominant middle finger
    C. Dominant hand thumb
    D. Non-dominant hand thumb

19. As illustrated in the image shown at the right, Plummer's nail can be indicative of what medical condition?
    A. Hypertension
    B. Diabetes mellitus
    C. Hypothyroidism
    D. Hyperthyroidism

20. Yellow nail syndrome is commonly associated with _____ diseases.
    A. urinary   B. cardiac   C. pulmonary   D. endocrine

21. Which of the following can cause discoloration of all 20 digits?
    A. Open heart surgery
    B. Sickle cell anemia
    C. Corticosteroid therapy for multiple sclerosis
    D. Chemotherapy for Hodgkin's lymphoma

22. _____ is defined as pain in the nail unit.
    A. Otalgia   B. Onychalgia   C. Myalgia   D. Neuralgia

23. As illustrated in the image shown at the right, Mee's lines can be apparent due to what type of poisoning?
    A. Lead
    B. Mercury
    C. Arsenic
    D. Cyanide

24. What condition may result if hangnails become infected?
    A. Paronychia
    B. Onycholysis
    C. Onychoptosis
    D. Onychomycosis

25. All of the following are conditions that can be responsible for slow nail growth EXCEPT
    A. sunlight exposure
    B. aging
    C. winter season
    D. poor nutrition

KEY (CORRECT ANSWERS)

1. C
2. B
3. A
4. D
5. A

6. D
7. C
8. D
9. C
10. D

11. C
12. B
13. B
14. A
15. C

16. A
17. C
18. C
19. D
20. C

21. D
22. B
23. C
24. A
25. A

TEST 4

DIRECTIONS: Each question or incomplete statement is followed by several suggested answers or completions. Select the one that BEST answers the question or completes the statement. *PRINT THE LETTER OF THE CORRECT ANSWER IN THE SPACE AT THE RIGHT.*

1. Which of the following statements is TRUE regarding the lunula? 1.____
   A. A red discoloration of the lunula is a normal finding.
   B. A blue lunula is indicative of pulmonary disease.
   C. A lunula can be pyramidal in shape in response to trauma.
   D. An absent lunula can be indicative of a serious medical condition.

2. A pale-blue colored lunula can be indicative of what medical condition? 2.____
   A. Hypertension   B. Diabetes mellitus
   C. Hypothyroidism   D. Hyperthyroidism

3. As illustrated in the image shown at the right, Lindsay half-and-half nails are indicative of what medical condition? 3.____
   A. Liver disease
   B. Heart disease
   C. Lung disease
   D. Renal disease

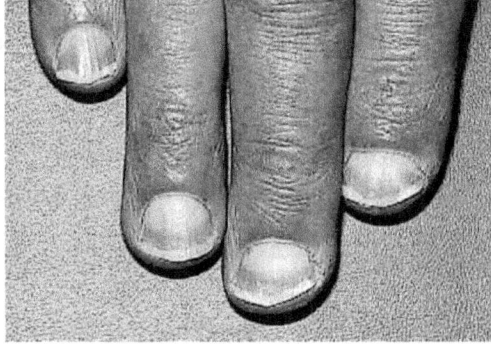

4. About 50% of nail dystrophies result from which of the following? 4.____
   A. Bacterial infection   B. Fungal infection
   C. Viral infection   D. Protozoan infection

5. As illustrated in the image shown at the right, green nail syndrome is MOST commonly associated by infection by which of the following? 5.____
   A. Pseudomonas
   B. Cryptosporidium
   C. Salmonella
   D. Escherichia coil

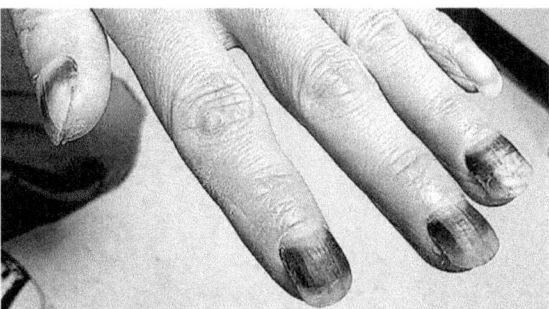

6. The nail plate is rich in _____, which exists in a concentration of 0.1% by weight which is 10 times greater than in hair but does not significantly contribute to the hardness of the nail. 6.____
   A. carbon   B. oxygen   C. sulfur   D. calcium

7. Which of the following bodies are important in maintaining acral circulation under cold conditions?
   A. Lewy   B. Glomus   C. Pick   D. Basal

8. In early childhood, the nail plate is thin and may show temporary
   A. leukonychia
   B. melanonychia
   C. koilonychias
   D. perionychia

9. In a normal finger, the distal phalangeal depth is smaller than the interphalangeal depth. In what condition is this relationship reversed?
   A. Clubbing
   B. Koilonychia
   C. Dolichonychia
   D. Brachyonychia

10. As illustrated in the image shown at the right, which of the following conditions is characterized by the length of the nail, is much greater than the width, and is common in individuals with hypopituritarism?
    A. Paronychia
    B. Koilonychia
    C. Dolichonychia
    D. Brachyonychia

11. Which of the following conditions is characterized by the width of the nail plate being greater than the length?
    A. Paronychia
    B. Koilonychia
    C. Dolichonychia
    D. Brachyonychia

12. _____ fingernails usually imply severe scratching or rubbing of the skin.
    A. Shiny   B. Pitted   C. Ridged   D. Discolored

13. _____ result from chronic rubbing of the nails against a hard surface and typically affect the middle three fingers of the dominant hand.
    A. Darier's disease
    B. Bidet nails
    C. Bifid lunula
    D. Macronychia

14. Which of the following represents the normal thickness of fingernails?
    A. 0.3 mm   B. 0.5 mm   C. 0.8 mm   D. 1.0 mm

15. Which of the following is the bacteria MOST commonly associated with acute paronychia?
    A. Pseudomonas
    B. Cryptosporidium
    C. Staphylococci
    D. Escherichia coli

16. Thickened, hyperkeratotic, irregular cuticles are MOST commonly seen with what medical condition?
    A. Dermatomyositis
    B. Dermatophytosis
    C. Dermatitis herpetiformis
    D. Seborrheic dermatitis

17. Subungal warts initially affect the _____, growing slowly toward the nail bed and finally elevating the nail plate.
    A. hyponychium   B. nail plate   C. nail bed   D. cuticle

18. Which of the following is the term used for a cryptogenic soft nail, one in which there is no primary specific local nail disease to explain the change?
    A. Paronychia   B. Hapalonychia
    C. Dolichonychia   D. Brachyonychia

19. Which of the following indicates an abnormality in color of the substance of the nail plate and/or subungual tissues?
    A. Paronychia   B. Hapalonychia
    C. Chromonychia   D. Brachyonychia

20. In what manner should the fingernails be examined? With the fingers
    A. pressed together   B. spread apart
    C. pressed against a surface   D. completely relaxed

21. What term is used when fungal infection involves the nail plate, such as superficial white onychomycoses, or when nail varnish produces keratin granulation?
    A. True leukonychia   B. Pseudoleukonychia
    C. Apparent leukonychia   D. Striate leukonychia

22. Hematomas involving more than what percentage of the visible nail is a warning sign of severe nail bed injury and possible underlying phalangeal fracture?
    A. 10%   B. 25%   C. 50%   D. 75%

23. Which of the following pathological factors is associated with rapid rate of linear nail growth?
    A. Fever   B. Psoriasis
    C. Hypothyroidism D. Beau's lines

24. Which of the following pathological factors is associated with slower rate of linear nail growth?
    A. Hyperthyroidism   B. Hypothyroidism
    C. Arteriovenous shunts   D. Pityriasis rubra pilaris

25. As illustrated in the image shown at the right, small, superficial, and regular pits are typical in clients with what medical condition?
    A. Eczema
    B. Psoriasis
    C. Tinea pedis
    D. Alopecia areata

KEY (CORRECT ANSWERS)

1.	D	11.	D
2.	B	12.	A
3.	D	13.	B
4.	B	14.	B
5.	A	15.	C
6.	D	16.	A
7.	B	17.	A
8.	C	18.	B
9.	A	19.	C
10.	C	20.	D

21. B
22. B
23. B
24. B
25. D

EXAMINATION SECTION
TEST 1

DIRECTIONS: Each question or incomplete statement is followed by several suggested answers or completions. Select the one that BEST answers the question or completes the statement. *PRINT THE LETTER OF THE CORRECT ANSWER IN THE SPACE AT THE RIGHT.*

1. Cocci are round-shaped
    A. viruses   B. fungi   C. bacteria   D. prions

2. Which of the following represents bacteria that can grow in pairs and cause pneumonia?
    A. Monococci   B. Diplococci   C. Gonococci   D. Streptococci

3. Failing to properly disinfect which of the following may cause a patient to break out due to the presence of Mycobacterium fortuitum?
    A. Styling chairs
    B. Shampoo stations
    C. Sharp instruments
    D. Whirlpool foot spas

4. Bacteria consists of an outer wall containing a liquid known as which of the following?
    A. Nucleic acid   B. Amino acid   C. Cytoplasm   D. Protoplasm

5. Which of the following refers to the process in which bacteria grow, reproduce, and divide into two new cells?
    A. Osmosis
    B. Meiosis
    C. Binary fission
    D. Binary fusion

6. A bacterial infection is characterized by the presence of which of the following?
    A. Pus   B. Mucous   C. Blood   D. Swelling

7. What type of infection would be characterized by a lesion containing pus and is confined to a particular part of the body?
    A. Local   B. Systemic   C. Primary   D. Secondary

8. Disinfectants used in salons must carry a registration number from what federal agency?
    A. Occupational Safety and Health Association
    B. Environmental Protection Agency
    C. Food and Drug Administration
    D. Department of Health and Human Services

9. What form of hepatitis is the MOST difficult to kill on a surface?
    A. A   B. B   C. C   D. D

10. Which of the following is defined as a submicroscopic particle that infects and resides in cells of biological organisms and is capable of replication only through taking over the reproductive functions of the host cell?
    A. Virus B. Fungi C. Prions D. Bacteria

11. Sterilization is the only form of decontamination that kills
    A. viruses B. spores C. fungi D. bacteria

12. Which of the following is a type of pathogenic bacteria?
    A. Flagella B. Prions C. Saprophytes D. Parasites

13. A _____ is a type of bacteria that lives on dead matter.
    A. parasite B. macrophage C. saprophyte D. lymphocyte

14. Syphilis and Lyme disease are caused by what agent?
    A. Cocci B. Bacilli C. Prions D. Spirilla

15. Bacilli are bacteria in what shape?
    A. Round B. Oval C. Rod D. Corkscrew

16. Spirilla are bacteria in what shape?
    A. Round B. Oval C. Rod D. Corkscrew

17. Which of the following are defined as slender, hair-like extensions in which certain bacteria about?
    A. Axons B. Flagella C. Fomites D. Dendrites

18. Which of the following is a difference between viruses and bacteria? Bacteria
    A. can penetrate cells
    B. can become part of cells
    C. are resistant to antibiotics
    D. can live on their own

19. Molds, mildew, and yeasts are all examples of which of the following?
    A. Fungi B. Spores C. Prions D. Bacteria

20. Removing pathogens and other substances from tools or surfaces is referred to as
    A. disinfection
    B. decontamination
    C. sterilization
    D. chemisorption

21. Which of the following should be associated with every product used in a cosmetology school or salon?
    A. MSSDS sheet
    B. FDA registration number
    C. Warning labels
    D. Identification labels

22. Which of the following statements is TRUE regarding any item that is used on a client?
 The item must be
 A. cleaned and sterilized
 B. either disinfected or discarded
 C. decontaminated and sterilized
 D. sanitized and disinfected

22.____

23. The majority of quaternary ammonium compounds are able to disinfect instruments in _____ minutes.
 A. 5-10
 B. 10-15
 C. 20-30
 D. 30-45

23.____

24. Phenolic disinfectants in 5% solution are primarily used for which of the following?
 A. Blood spills
 B. Rubber and plastic instruments
 C. Metal instruments
 D. Porous surfaces

24.____

25. States requiring hospital disinfection do not allow the use of which of the following for disinfection of instruments?
 A. Quaternary ammonium compounds
 B. Alcohol
 C. Phenols
 D. Antimicrobials

25.____

KEY (CORRECT ANSWERS)

1.	C		11.	B
2.	B		12.	D
3.	D		13.	C
4.	D		14.	D
5.	C		15.	C
6.	A		16.	D
7.	A		17.	B
8.	B		18.	D
9.	B		19.	A
10.	A		20.	B

21. A
22. B
23. B
24. C
25. B

TEST 2

DIRECTIONS: Each question or incomplete statement is followed by several suggested answers or completions. Select the one that BEST answers the question or completes the statement. *PRINT THE LETTER OF THE CORRECT ANSWER IN THE SPACE AT THE RIGHT.*

1. Which of the following represents the chemical name for bleach? Sodium 1._____
   A. hydroxide B. oxalate C. hypochlorite D. carbonate

2. Which of the following products is considered unsafe for use in a salon because it can cause numerous health issues? 2._____
   A. Bleach B. Alcohol C. Formalin D. Antiseptics

3. How often should the solution used in a wet sanitizer be changed and replaced? 3._____
   A. Hourly B. Daily C. Weekly D. Monthly

4. In which of the following circumstances would an ultraviolet (UV) sanitizer be useful? 4._____
   A. Sterilizing instruments
   B. Disinfecting instruments
   C. Storing contaminated instruments
   D. Storing disinfected instruments

5. Linens, capes, and drapes should be used once and then laundered with which of the following agents? 5._____
   A. Bleach B. Ammonia C. Phenols D. Antiseptics

6. Which of the following statements is TRUE regarding instruments, such as hair clippers, that cannot be immersed in solutions? The instrument 6._____
   A. cannot be disinfected
   B. should be disinfected
   C. should be wiped with a wet cloth after use
   D. should be rinsed immediately after use

7. How often should foot spas be disinfected with an EPA-registered disinfectant with bactericidal, fungicidal, virucidal, and tuberculocidal properties? 7._____
   A. Daily
   B. Weekly
   C. Bi-weekly
   D. After each client

8. Bi-weekly (every 2 weeks), foot spas should be filled with what substance that should be left to sit overnight? 8._____
   A. Warm, soapy water
   B. Solution containing 5% bleach
   C. Solution containing 5% quaternary ammonium compound
   D. An EPA-registered disinfectant

9. Washing your hands after each client is an example of which of the following?
   A. Sanitation   B. Disinfection   C. Sterilization   D. Contamination

10. Which of the following statements is TRUE regarding antiseptics? Antiseptics
    A. do not kill bacteria
    B. can be safely applied to the skin
    C. are classified as disinfectants
    D. are stronger than disinfectants

11. _____ is defined as the spread of infection from one person to another or from an object to a person.
    A. Direct transmission
    B. Airborne transmission
    C. Droplet transmission
    D. Cross-contamination

12. Which of the following are MOST resistant to cleansing agents?
    A. Viruses   B. Bacteria   C. Fungi   D. Prions

13. In order to be effective, the strength of ethyl alcohol must be no less than
    A. 50%   B. 60%   C. 70%   D. 80%

14. In order to meet salon requirements for use against bacteria, fungi, and viruses, a disinfectant should have the proper
    A. label
    B. efficacy
    C. concentration
    D. registration

15. What type of bacteria rarely exhibits any active motility?
    A. Cocci   B. Bacilli   C. Spirilla   D. Spores

16. The FIRST step in the decontamination process is referred to as
    A. rinsing   B. sanitation   C. disinfection   D. sterilization

17. Adherence to the bloodborne pathogen standard is regulated by what federal agency?
    A. Food and Drug Administration
    B. Centers for Disease Control and Prevention
    C. Environmental Protection Agency
    D. Occupational Safety and Health Administration

18. Which of the following refers to detergents that break down stubborn films and remove the residue of pedicure products such as scrubs, salts, and masks?
    A. Chelating agents
    B. Antifungal agents
    C. Antiseptic agents
    D. Virucidal agents

19. Which of the following is a corrosive, poisonous, acidic compound that is used as a disinfectant?
    A. Bleach   B. Ammonia   C. Phenols   D. Antiseptics

20. In what manner should you treat a salon instrument that comes into contact with blood or bodily fluids?
   The instrument should be cleaned and
   A. completely immersed in an EPA-registered disinfectant
   B. rinsed in an EPA-registered tuberculocidal antiseptic
   C. placed in an EPA-registered antiseptic that kills HIV and HepB
   D. briefly dipped in an EPA-registered solution that kills HIV

21. For which of the following would the use of an antiseptic be effective?
   A. Sterilizing equipment
   B. Disinfecting equipment
   C. Decontaminating instruments
   D. Eliminating germs on the skin

22. With regards to handwashing, for what time period should you apply soap, lather, and scrub your hands and under the free edges of the nail with a nail brush?
   A. 10 seconds   B. 20 seconds   C. 45 seconds   D. 60 seconds

23. Which of the following is a recently approved form of disinfectant that only needs to be changed every 14 days?
   A. Formalin
   B. Glutaraldehyde
   C. Accelerated hydrogen peroxide
   D. Ethanol

24. What type of disinfectants could potentially damage salon tools and equipment?
   A. Virucidal   B. Fungicidal   C. Bactericidal   D. Tuberculocidal

25. Fungal infections are much more common on what area of the body than on the hands?
   A. Face   B. Scalp   C. Feet   D. Back

KEY (CORRECT ANSWERS)

1.	C	11.	D
2.	C	12.	D
3.	B	13.	C
4.	D	14.	B
5.	A	15.	A
6.	B	16.	B
7.	D	17.	D
8.	B	18.	A
9.	A	19.	C
10.	C	20.	A

21. D
22. D
23. C
24. D
25. C

TEST 3

DIRECTIONS: Each question or incomplete statement is followed by several suggested answers or completions. Select the one that BEST answers the question or completes the statement. *PRINT THE LETTER OF THE CORRECT ANSWER IN THE SPACE AT THE RIGHT.*

1. If a disinfectant product includes the word _____ on the label, it must be diluted prior to use.   1.____
   A. solution   B. concentrate   C. catalyst   D. hydrolyze

2. Which of the following are various poisonous substances that are produced by some microorganisms?   2.____
   A. Prions   B. Toxins   C. Pathogens   D. Carcinogens

3. Which of the following repercussions can occur to a salon for not having MSDS sheets available for review during regular business hours?   3.____
   The salon
   A. can be fined
   B. can be closed
   C. can lose its license
   D. manager can be arrested

4. What type of bacteria, as illustrated in the image shown at the right, grow in clusters similar to a bunch of grapes?   4.____
   A. Gonococci
   B. Streptococci
   C. Staphylococci
   D. Diplococci

5. Which of the following statements is TRUE regarding bacteria during the spore-forming stage?   5.____
   Bacteria _____ during the spore-forming stage.
   A. grow in size
   B. perform mitosis
   C. are vulnerable to disinfectants
   D. coat themselves with wax outer shells

6. Which of the following statements is TRUE regarding phenolic disinfectants?   6.____
   Phenolic disinfectants have a
   A. mildly alkaline pH   B. neutral pH
   C. very low pH   D. very high pH

7. Regarding handwashing, what is the recommended method for brushing your nails?
   A. Diagonally
   B. Horizontally and vertically
   C. Vertically and diagonally
   D. Horizontally and diagonally

8. Which of the following is defined as the absence of disease-producing microorganisms?
   A. Sepsis   B. Asepsis   C. Immunity   D. Sterilization

9. Which of the following is defined as complete absence of all microorganisms?
   A. Sepsis   B. Asepsis   C. Immunity   D. Sterilization

10. A(n) _____ is defined as a microorganism capable of causing disease in humans.
    A. antigen   B. mutagen   C. pathogen   D. carcinogen

11. _____ is defined as the heightened ability of an organism to produce infection in its host.
    A. Persistence   B. Purulence   C. Virulence   D. Resistance

12. Which of the following is an additional term that refers to a germ or bacteria?
    A. Parasite   B. Microbe   C. Fomite   D. Dendrite

13. Which of the following refers to bacterial cells that are harmless and can even be beneficial to humans?
    A. Resistant bacteria
    B. Purulent bacteria
    C. Pathogenic bacteria
    D. Non-pathogenic bacteria

14. Nail fungus is a type of
    A. systemic infection
    B. external parasite
    C. pathogenic bacteria
    D. non-pathogenic bacteria

15. Which of the following is defined as the ability to destroy infectious agents that enter the body?
    A. Immunity
    B. Decontamination
    C. Disinfection
    D. Sterilization

16. Infection control can be divided into which of the following three categories?
    A. Bacteriology, ecology, virology
    B. Contamination, disinfection, sterilization
    C. Sanitation, disinfection, sterilization
    D. Bacteriology, virology, epidemiology

17. During a disinfection procedure, what should be done immediately following removing all hair from a brush?
The brush should be
    A. thoroughly dried
    B. washed with soap and water
    C. stored in a dry, covered container
    D. immersed in a disinfecting solution

18. Which of the following services would normally require a sterilization procedure when completed?
    A. Perming   B. Sculpting   C. Electrolysis   D. Shampooing

19. When performing first aid for a bleeding wound, what should be the NEXT step once the bleeding has stopped?
    A. Apply pressure
    B. Apply bandage
    C. Apply tourniquet
    D. Elevate affected limb

20. Bacteria grow BEST under what type of conditions?
    A. Cool, dry   B. Cool, damp   C. Warm, dry   D. Warm, damp

21. What is the FIRST thing to do when applying first aid to a chemical burn?
    A. Rinse away all traces of chemicals
    B. Apply cream or ointment to the burn
    C. Cover burn with a clean, dry cloth
    D. Immediately refer client to medical personnel

22. What is the FIRST thing to do when dealing with a heat burn and the skin is not broken?
    A. Apply ointment or cream to the burn
    B. Immerse burn in cool water or gently apply cool compresses
    C. Break the blister if one has formed
    D. Cover the burn with a clean, dry cloth

23. What is the FIRST thing to do if a client gets a salon chemical in their eyes?
    A. Flush eyes with cold water for 15-30 minutes
    B. Flush eyes with lukewarm water for 15-30 minutes
    C. Flush eyes with hot water for 15-30 minutes
    D. Place cloth over both eyes and secure with a bandage

24. Which of the following should be worn whenever there is a possibility of coming in contact with blood or other potentially infectious materials?
    A. Gloves   B. Gowns   C. Face masks   D. Goggles

25. What percentage of all bacteria are non-pathogenic?
    A. 30%   B. 50%   C. 70%   D. 90%

KEY (CORRECT ANSWERS)

1.	B		11.	C
2.	B		12.	B
3.	A		13.	D
4.	C		14.	C
5.	D		15.	A
6.	D		16.	C
7.	B		17.	B
8.	B		18.	C
9.	D		19.	B
10.	C		20.	D

21.	A
22.	B
23.	D
24.	A
25.	D

TEST 4

DIRECTIONS: Each question or incomplete statement is followed by several suggested answers or completions. Select the one that BEST answers the question or completes the statement. *PRINT THE LETTER OF THE CORRECT ANSWER IN THE SPACE AT THE RIGHT.*

1. What type of immunity occurs when the body produces white blood cells and antitoxins to fight disease? 1.____
   A. Passive   B. Acquired   C. Natural   D. Herd

2. What should be the FIRST thing you do if a client sustains a burn severe enough to break the skin? 2.____
   A. Apply ointment or cream to the burn
   B. Immerse burn in cool water or gently apply cool compresses
   C. Notify medical personnel (call 911)
   D. Cover the burn with a clean, dry cloth

3. What is the FIRST thing you should do if a client suffers a cut, scratch, or embedded object in the eye? 3.____
   A. Attempt to remove the embedded object
   B. Immediately contact an eye specialist or emergency room
   C. Flush eyes with hot water for 15-30 minutes
   D. Place cloth over both eyes and secure with a bandage

4. Which of the following is a symptom of a first degree burn? 4.____
   A. Redness   B. Blisters   C. Skin rash   D. Skin charring

5. What tissue layer(s) are involved with a first degree burn? 5.____
   A. Epidermis only
   B. Dermis and epidermis
   C. Dermis and subcutaneous tissue
   D. Epidermis, dermis, and subcutaneous tissue

6. What is the FIRST thing you should do if you feel a client may be choking? 6.____
   A. Wrap arms around client
   B. Perform upward thrusts to client's abdomen
   C. Notify medical personnel (call 911)
   D. Determine if the client can talk

7. Infection can invade the body through all of the following EXCEPT 7.____
   A. nose   B. mouth   C. healthy skin   D. broken skin

8. As bacteria absorb food, each cell grows in size and divides, resulting in how many new cells? 8.____
   A. 2   B. 4   C. 6   D. 8

2 (#4)

9. Which of the following is NOT effective in eliminating all organisms, is technically a sanitizer, and can also be used as a holding space for disinfected implements?
   A. UV light sterilizer
   B. Autoclave
   C. Chemiclave
   D. Gas sterilizer

9.____

10. Which of the following is a pressurized, steam-heated vessel that sterilizes with high pressure, heat, or pressurized steam preventing microorganisms from surviving?
    A. UV light sterilizer
    B. Autoclave
    C. Chemiclave
    D. Gas sterilizer

10.____

11. Which of the following uses high pressure, high temperature water, alcohol, and formaldehyde vapors for sterilization?
    A. UV light sterilizer
    B. Autoclave
    C. Chemiclave
    D. Gas sterilizer

11.____

12. What percentage of hydrogen peroxide can be used as an antiseptic?
    A. 1-3%   B. 3-5%   C. 5-10%   D. 10-15%

12.____

13. Which of the following uses high-frequency sound waves to create a cleansing action that cleans areas on implements or tools that are difficult to reach with a brush?
    A. Autoclave
    B. Chemiclave
    C. UV light sterilizer
    D. Ultrasonic cleaners

13.____

14. At what point would the process referred to as "double bagging" be performed?
    A. When antiseptic is used
    B. When sharp objects are involved
    C. When a blood spill occurs
    D. When instruments cannot be decontaminated

14.____

15. A non-disposable needle used to puncture the skin requires what level of infection control?
    A. Sanitation
    B. Disinfection
    C. Decontamination
    D. Sterilization

15.____

16. Which of the following is the component of household bleach that kills viruses?
    A. Sodium   B. Chlorine   C. Fluorine   D. Calcium

16.____

17. The active stage of bacteria is also known as the _____ stage.
    A. dormant   B. reproductive   C. vegetative   D. duplicative

17.____

18. For effective disinfection, which of the following represents the MINIMUM strength of a quaternary ammonium compound solution to sanitize instruments?
    A. 1:100   B. 1:250   C. 1:500   D. 1:1000

18.____

19. Which of the following represents the MOST likely manner of HIV transmission in the salon or barbershop?
    A. Air B. Droplet C. Blood D. Skin-to-skin

20. All of the following are contagious diseases that will prevent a cosmetologist or barber from servicing a client EXCEPT
    A. ringworm
    B. common cold
    C. tuberculosis
    D. HIV/AIDS

21. Due to production of potential harmful formaldehyde gas, which of the following should no longer be used in salons or barbershops?
    A. Sterilants
    B. Fumigants
    C. Disinfectants
    D. Decontaminants

22. Which of the following represents the body's first layer of defense against transmission of disease?
    A. Skin B. Hair C. Nails D. Tears

23. It is recommended that a cosmetologist washes his/her hands with which of the following prior to servicing the client?
    A. Bar soap B. Liquid soap C. Antiseptic D. Disinfectant

24. Which of the following can be spread easily in a salon or barbershop through the use of unsanitary styling implements or from dirty hands or fingernails?
    A. Viruses
    B. Fungi
    C. Parasites
    D. Pathogenic bacteria

25. What is the FIRST thing you should do if a client faints during treatment?
    A. Lay client on their back and allow plenty of fresh air
    B. Reassure client and apply cold compresses to face
    C. Roll client onto their side and keep their windpipe clear
    D. Call emergency personnel

KEY (CORRECT ANSWERS)

1.	C		11.	C
2.	C		12.	B
3.	B		13.	D
4.	A		14.	C
5.	A		15.	D
6.	D		16.	B
7.	C		17.	C
8.	A		18.	D
9.	A		19.	C
10.	B		20.	D

21. B
22. A
23. B
24. D
25. A

EXAMINATION SECTION
TEST 1

DIRECTIONS: Each question or incomplete statement is followed by several suggested answers or completions. Select the one that BEST answers the question or completes the statement. *PRINT THE LETTER OF THE CORRECT ANSWER IN THE SPACE AT THE RIGHT.*

1. What is the technical term for the nails?

    A. Mantle   B. Matrix   C. Lunula   D. Onyx

2. Which implement should be used to remove polish from a patron's cuticle?

    A. Cuticle pusher
    B. Cotton-tipped orangewood stick
    C. Scraper
    D. Cotton swab

3. Which nail shape is MOST often used to complement women's hands?

    A. Pointed   B. Square   C. Oval   D. Round

4. What are the bones of the fingers called?

    A. Digits   B. Metacarpals
    C. Tarsals   D. Phalanges

5. During a manicure, what cosmetic substance is applied underneath the free edge of the nail?

    A. Base coat   B. Nail white
    C. Top coat   D. Nail enamel

6. What is the term for the channel on either side of the nail?

    A. Groove   B. Mantle   C. Bed   D. Wall

7. On which finger is the process of nail polish removal typically begun?

    A. Little   B. Index   C. Middle   D. Thumb

8. MOST nails grow at an approximate rate of _____ inch per month.

    A. 1/16   B. 1/8   C. 1/4   D. 1/2

9. Typically, how many strokes are used to apply nail polish to each single nail?

    A. 2   B. 3   C. 4   D. 5

10. Which of the following substances should be used to sanitize a manicure table?

    A. 5% formalin solution   B. 70% alcohol solution
    C. Ammonia solution   D. Quaternary compounds

11. When performing a basic manicure, which of the following procedures would be performed FIRST?

    A. Clean under free edges
    B. Soak hand in finger bowl
    C. Apply polish
    D. Clean nails with nail brush

12. The nail is made up of a protein substance called

    A. melanin   B. keratin   C. onyx   D. albumin

13. What is another term for bacteria?

    A. Pathogens   B. Flagella   C. Microbes   D. Allergens

14. Which of the body's glands is responsible for the control of body metabolism?

    A. Pancreas   B. Pituitary   C. Adrenal   D. Thyroid

15. How often should manicuring implements be sanitized?

    A. After each use
    B. Daily
    C. Every other day
    D. Weekly

16. Artificial nail tips should be trimmed to extend _____ inch beyond the free edge of the natural nail.

    A. 1/8   B. 1/4   C. 1/3   D. 1/2

17. What is the term for the lightly colored, half-moon shaped portion at the base of the nail?

    A. Paronychia
    B. Matrix
    C. Lanugo
    D. Lunula

18. What color of nail polish would be BEST suited to complement *cool-colored* clothing?

    A. Peach   B. Mauve   C. Red   D. Coral

19. Men's nails are USUALLY filed into a(n) _____ shape.

    A. oval or round
    B. square or round
    C. oval or square
    D. pointed or round

20. What type of artificial nails are made by mixing a powder with a liquid?

    A. Sculptured
    B. Gel
    C. Acrylic
    D. Epoxy

21. What formation is USUALLY adopted by staphylococci bacteria?

    A. Cluster   B. Pair   C. Triplet   D. Chain

22. When using a nail buffer, it should be lifted between strokes to avoid

    A. scratching
    B. contamination
    C. staining
    D. heating

23. Which pf the following tissues contains nerves and blood vessels? 23._____

    A. Nail lunula   B. Eponychium
    C. Nail bed   D. Nail plate

24. What color of polish is used for a French manicure? 24._____

    A. White   B. Beige   C. Pink   D. Coral

25. What type of infection is confined to a small area of the body? 25._____

    A. Local   B. General   C. Systemic   D. Holistic

KEY (CORRECT ANSWERS)

1.	D		11.	B
2.	B		12.	B
3.	C		13.	C
4.	D		14.	D
5.	B		15.	A
6.	A		16.	A
7.	A		17.	D
8.	B		18.	B
9.	B		19.	B
10.	B		20.	A

21. A
22. D
23. C
24. B
25. A

TEST 2

DIRECTIONS: Each question or incomplete statement is followed by several suggested answers or completions. Select the one that BEST answers the question or completes the statement. *PRINT THE LETTER OF THE CORRECT ANSWER IN THE SPACE AT THE RIGHT.*

1. Where is the thinnest skin located? 1.____
   - A. Palms
   - B. Fingertips
   - C. Eyelids
   - D. Ears

2. Which of the following procedures for applying acrylic nails would be performed LAST? 2.____
   - A. Apply nail primer
   - B. File nail tip
   - C. Apply polish
   - D. Remove nail forms

3. What is the technical term for ingrown nails? 3.____
   - A. Paronychia
   - B. Onychoptosis
   - C. Onychocryptosis
   - D. Onychomycosis

4. To which of the following surfaces should disinfectants NOT be applied? 4.____
   - A. Work stations
   - B. Manicuring implements
   - C. Hair
   - D. Skin

5. When cleaning the nails with a nail brush, in which direction should the strokes be directed? 5.____
   - A. In a circular motion
   - B. Sideways
   - C. Downward
   - D. Upward

6. Each of the following is a wrist bone EXCEPT 6.____
   - A. hamate
   - B. radius
   - C. capitate
   - D. pisiform

7. Which of the following parts of the nail, if injured, would MOST likely cause irregular growth? 7.____
   - A. Wall
   - B. Hyponychium
   - C. Matrix
   - D. Free edge

8. What is the term for the large muscle covering the shoulder that aids in lifting and bending the arm? 8.____
   - A. Trapezius
   - B. Deltoid
   - C. Extensor
   - D. Biceps brachii

9. How many layers make up the epidermis? 9.____
   - A. 2
   - B. 3
   - C. 5
   - D. 7

10. What type of artificial nails are produced by mixing a powder with a liquid in a mold? 10.____
    - A. Sculptured
    - B. Brush-on
    - C. Acrylic
    - D. Press-on

11. The bones of the hand are termed the

    A. metatarsals
    B. carpals
    C. phalanges
    D. metacarpals

12. Which of the following terms is GENERALLY used to denote any nail disease?

    A. Paronychia
    B. Tinea
    C. Onychia
    D. Onychosis

13. The liquid for acrylic nail applications is typically held in a(n)

    A. finger bowl
    B. dappen dish
    C. electric heater
    D. wet sanitizer

14. Rheumatic fever and blood poisoning are examples of a(n) _____ infection.

    A. viral
    B. general
    C. epidemic
    D. local

15. What substance in the skin is responsible for waterproofing and protecting the body from bacteria?

    A. Subcutaneous tissue
    B. Melanin
    C. Serotonin
    D. Keratin

16. The nail root is located

    A. at the base of the nail
    B. under the free edge
    C. under the nail plate
    D. under the matrix

17. What type of substance is a quaternary ammonium compound?

    A. Antiseptic
    B. Disinfectant
    C. Dry sanitizer
    D. Wet sanitizer

18. In addition to the nail plate, the top coat should be applied

    A. in the nail groove
    B. over the cuticle
    C. to the nail bed
    D. under the free edge

19. Typically, how long should a patron's foot remain in a disinfectant bath?

    A. 30-60 seconds
    B. 1-2 minutes
    C. 3-5 minutes
    D. 5-10 minutes

20. On which finger do nails generally grow MOST quickly?

    A. Thumb
    B. Ring finger
    C. Middle finger
    D. Index finger

21. Which type of bacteria is a common cause of pneumonia?

    A. Streptococci
    B. Spirilla
    C. Staphylococci
    D. Diplococci

22. Which of the following procedures is typically the LAST step of a hand and arm massage?

    A. Massaging palm
    B. Stroking arm
    C. Massaging elbow
    D. Loosening fingers

23. An inflammation of the nail matrix is known as

   A. anychia
   B. paronychia
   C. onychorrhexis
   D. onychomycosis

24. Which of the following procedures for applying lamp-cured gel nails would be performed FIRST?

   A. Buff nail plate to remove ridge seam
   B. Apply bonding agent gel to inside lip of nail
   C. Buff nail plate to remove oils
   D. Apply nail builder

25. Which of the following conditions is treatable by a manicurist?

   A. Leukonychia
   B. Onychorrhexis
   C. Paronychia
   D. Onychatrophia

KEY (CORRECT ANSWERS)

1. C
2. C
3. C
4. D
5. C

6. B
7. C
8. B
9. C
10. A

11. D
12. D
13. B
14. B
15. D

16. A
17. B
18. D
19. C
20. C

21. D
22. B
23. A
24. C
25. B

TEST 3

DIRECTIONS: Each question or incomplete statement is followed by several suggested answers or completions. Select the one that BEST answers the question or completes the statement. *PRINT THE LETTER OF THE CORRECT ANSWER IN THE SPACE AT THE RIGHT.*

1. What is the term for the study of the minute structures of the body? 1._____

   A. Histology
   B. Microbiology
   C. Physiology
   D. Myology

2. To clean under the free edge of the nail, a manicurist should use an orangewood stick dipped in 2._____

   A. alcohol
   B. astringent
   C. polish remover
   D. soapy water

3. What color would NOT generally be considered to be complementary on a person whose skin is ivory, peach, or golden brown? 3._____

   A. Rust   B. Peach   C. Violet   D. Orange

4. What is the technical term for the skin that lies directly beneath the free edge of the nail? 4._____

   A. Perionychium
   B. Eponychium
   C. Pterygium
   D. Hyponychium

5. Which of the following cosmetics is used to soften the skin around the nail? 5._____

   A. Nail bleach
   B. Sealant
   C. Solvent
   D. Cuticle oil

6. When performing a basic pedicure, which of the following procedures would be performed FIRST? 6._____

   A. Apply polish
   B. Apply cuticle softener
   C. Apply astringent to the foot
   D. Trim cuticle

7. If a hot oil manicure is to be given, to what level should the electric heater's cup be filled with oil? 7._____

   A. 1/8   B. 1/5   C. 1/3   D. 1/2

8. Which muscle turns the palm upward? 8._____

   A. Flexor
   B. Supinator
   C. Pronator
   D. Biceps brachii

9. If a client's nail is covered with white spots, what condition is indicated? 9._____

   A. Paronychia
   B. Onychorrhexis
   C. Onychosis
   D. Leukonychia

10. What type of artificial nail is NOT damaged by acetone polish remover? 10._____

    A. Keratin   B. Nylon   C. Plastic   D. Gel

41

11. The soft fatty substance contained within the hollow cavity in the center of bones is called

    A. cancellous B. marrow
    C. compaction D. periosteum

12. What substance should be used to sanitize manicuring equipment?

    A. Bleach solution B. Quaternary compounds
    C. Alcohol solution D. Ammonia

13. Which artery is the MAIN source of blood supply to the arm and hand?

    A. Carotid B. Brachial C. Femoral D. Pulmonary

14. All of the following should be avoided by diabetics whose feet are being treated EXCEPT

    A. corn pads B. polish remover
    C. peroxide D. epsom salts

15. What is the commonly-used term for ringworm of the feet?

    A. Trench foot B. Tinea unguium
    C. Onychomycosis D. Athlete's foot

16. What substance is used to remove stains from the fingertips and under the free edge?

    A. Nail primer B. Nail white
    C. Cuticle oil D. Nail bleach

17. What physical agent for destroying bacteria is MOST commonly used in manicuring schools and salons?

    A. Dry heat B. Ultraviolet light
    C. Fumigant D. Moist heat

18. When applying an artificial nail tip, which of the following procedures would be performed LAST?

    A. Smooth mending tissues over nail
    B. Soak mending tissue in mending liquid
    C. Trim mending tissue to desired length
    D. Fold mending tissue over nail edge

19. When shaping the nails with a file, the filing strokes should be directed

    A. from the center to the corner
    B. from the corner to the center
    C. in a straight line, from corner to corner
    D. in one rounded stroke, from corner to corner

20. The layer of the epidermis that is constantly being shed and replaced is called the stratum

    A. lucidum B. corneum
    C. spinosum D. hyponychium

21. Which of the following is a *warm* color?

    A. Burgundy B. Lavender C. Taupe D. Green

22. An inflammation of the tissue around the nail is termed   22.____

    A. paronychia   B. onycholysis
    C. anychia   D. leukonychia

23. An enlargement of the joint at the base of the big toe is called a(n)   23.____

    A. callus   B. corn   C. ulcer   D. bunion

24. The nerves of the little finger are supplied by the _____ nerve.   24.____

    A. radial   B. ulnar   C. median   D. parietal

25. For which of the following conditions would an oil manicure be recommended?   25.____

    A. Hangnails   B. Eggshell nails
    C. Split or brittle nails   D. Yellow nails

KEY (CORRECT ANSWERS)

1.	A	11.	B
2.	D	12.	C
3.	C	13.	B
4.	D	14.	B
5.	D	15.	D
6.	B	16.	D
7.	C	17.	B
8.	B	18.	D
9.	D	19.	B
10.	B	20.	B

21. D
22. A
23. D
24. B
25. C

TEST 4

DIRECTIONS: Each question or incomplete statement is followed by several suggested answers or completions. Select the one that BEST answers the question or completes the statement. *PRINT THE LETTER OF THE CORRECT ANSWER IN THE SPACE AT THE RIGHT.*

1. A foot massage should typically begin 1.____
   - A. with the toes
   - B. at the heel
   - C. at the ball of the foot
   - D. at the top of the instep

2. Which nail shape has the GREATEST tendency to draw attention to the hands? 2.____
   - A. Pointed
   - B. Square
   - C. Oval
   - D. Round

3. Which of the following is NOT used during the repair of nail splits or tears? 3.____
   - A. Emery board
   - B. Mending tissue
   - C. Polish remover
   - D. Metal pusher

4. An area that is free of all bacteria is termed 4.____
   - A. sanitized
   - B. barren
   - C. aseptic
   - D. immune

5. Which manicurist tool should be used for the final shaping of the nails? 5.____
   - A. Scissors
   - B. Nippers
   - C. Emery board
   - D. Nail file

6. The nervous system controls 6.____
   - A. skin growth
   - B. oil glands
   - C. skin respiration
   - D. sweat glands

7. Which of the following solutions or cosmetics contains a mild detergent solution? 7.____
   - A. Finger bath
   - B. Polish remover
   - C. Cuticle cream
   - D. Top coat

8. Which of the following procedures for applying lamp-cured gel nails would be performed LAST? 8.____
   - A. Buff nail plate to remove ridge seam
   - B. Apply bonding agent gel to inside lip of nail
   - C. Buff nail plate to remove oils
   - D. Apply nail builder

9. What is the technical term for nail-biting? 9.____
   - A. Paronychia
   - B. Onycholysis
   - C. Perionychium
   - D. Onychophagy

10. What is the term for the body's ability to fight disease? 10.____
    - A. Contagion
    - B. Protraction
    - C. Sepsis
    - D. Immunity

11. Acetone nail polish remover should NOT be used more than once every   11.____

    A. two days   B. five days   C. week   D. month

12. Which part of the nail produces cells?   12.____

    A. Matrix   B. Onyx   C. Mantle   D. Root

13. The indiscriminate use of topical vitamin E on the nails can cause   13.____

    A. allergic reactions
    B. deformity of the nail
    C. ingrown nails
    D. separation of nail from nail bed

14. Which type of bacteria is the cause of syphilis and cholera?   14.____

    A. Diplococci   B. Verruca
    C. Staphylococci   D. Spirilla

15. When applying an artificial nail with an acrylic overlay, how much of the tip's length should extend beyond the free edge of the natural nail?   15.____

    A. 1/8   B. 1/4   C. 1/3   D. 1/2

16. Which of the following is another term for fatty tissue?   16.____

    A. Subcutaneous   B. Reticular
    C. Papillary   D. Corticoid

17. Which of the following conditions would MOST likely be caused by vitamin D toxicity?   17.____

    A. Split or brittle nails
    B. Allergic reactions
    C. Separation of nail from nail bed
    D. Overly thick nails

18. What structures are responsible for destroying bacteria that enter the body?   18.____

    A. Red blood cells   B. Platelets
    C. White blood cells   D. Erythrocytes

19. Which of the following terms describes a loosening of the nail without shedding?   19.____

    A. Paronychia   B. Perionychium
    C. Pterygium   D. Onycholysis

20. Which nerves supply the fingers?   20.____

    A. Carpal   B. Digital   C. Median   D. Radial

21. Which layer of the skin contains a vast network of capillaries?   21.____

    A. Epidermal   B. Papillary   C. Ancillary   D. Corneal

22. Which of the following procedures for applying silk or linen nail wraps would be performed LAST?

    A. Apply nail adhesive to entire nail plate
    B. File off excess fabric
    C. Buff nail surface
    D. Smooth fabric over nail

23. What is the term that describes the lubricating fluid in joints?

    A. Periostial
    B. Carpal
    C. Sphenoid
    D. Synovial

24. If a client's nail appears to be gradually wasting away, what condition is indicated?

    A. Onychorrhexis
    B. Onychatrophia
    C. Anychia
    D. Onychophagy

25. Which of the following is a recommended remedy for yellow nails?

    A. Rub with topical vitamin E
    B. Soak in astringent bath
    C. Cure in ultraviolet light
    D. Rub with lemon juice

KEY (CORRECT ANSWERS)

1. D		11. B	
2. A		12. A	
3. D		13. A	
4. C		14. D	
5. C		15. D	
6. D		16. A	
7. A		17. D	
8. A		18. C	
9. D		19. D	
10. D		20. B	

21. B
22. C
23. D
24. B
25. D

EXAMINATION SECTION
TEST 1

DIRECTIONS: Each question or incomplete statement is followed by several suggested answers or completions. Select the one that BEST answers the question or completes the statement. *PRINT THE LETTER OF THE CORRECT ANSWER IN THE SPACE AT THE RIGHT.*

1. A top coat is USUALLY applied   1._____

   A. before the base coat
   B. before the colored polish
   C. after the colored polish
   D. before the nail white

2. Which type of nerves are responsible for body movements?   2._____

   A. Afferent   B. Sensory   C. Autonomic   D. Efferent

3. What type of bacteria are USUALLY contained within a local infection?   3._____

   A. Flagella   B. Diplococci
   C. Staphylococci   D. Saprophytic

4. What is the term for forward growth of the cuticle at the base of the nail?   4._____

   A. Paronychia   B. Onycholysis
   C. Pterygium   D. Lunula

5. A manicure brush should be placed in a sanitizer after it has been cleaned with   5._____

   A. formalin solution   B. hot soapy water
   C. alcohol solution   D. hydrogen peroxide solution

6. Which of the following procedures is typically the FIRST step of a hand and arm massage?   6._____

   A. Massaging palm   B. Loosening wrist
   C. Massaging elbow   D. Loosening fingers

7. Which of the following may be created by means of bacteria?   7._____

   A. Antibiotics   B. Heat
   C. Disinfectant   D. Light

8. Which division of the central nervous system controls voluntary bodily functions?   8._____

   A. Autonomic   B. Central
   C. Peripheral   D. Sympathetic

9. To roughen the nail plate in preparation for the application of a powder nail overlay, a manicurist should use   9._____

   A. chamois buffer   B. nail file
   C. buffing disc   D. fine side of emery board

10. Which type of bacteria require control in a manicurist's setting?

    A. Pathogenic
    B. Microbial
    C. Parthenogenic
    D. Saprophytic

11. People with very pale or very dark skin would typically be complemented by each of the following polish colors EXCEPT

    A. deep pink
    B. brown
    C. icy pink
    D. red

12. The _____ lies directly beneath the nail.

    A. nail bed
    B. nail plate
    C. nail body
    D. cuticle

13. Where are sebaceous glands PRIMARILY found?

    A. Hands and feet
    B. Underarms
    C. Scalp and face
    D. Palms

14. Before being bonded to the natural nail, gel tips should be cured for about

    A. ten seconds
    B. thirty seconds
    C. one minute
    D. ten minutes

15. What type of solution should be used with a wet sanitizer?

    A. Antiseptic
    B. Astringent
    C. Alcohol
    D. Detergent

16. Which of the following is a *cool* color?

    A. Rust
    B. Periwinkle
    C. Orange
    D. Brown

17. Which bone is located between the shoulder and the elbow?

    A. Ulna
    B. Scapula
    C. Humerus
    D. Radius

18. Which of the following conditions may be caused by a chronic illness or systemic disorder?

    A. Hangnails
    B. Anychia
    C. Eggshell nails
    D. Onychorrhexis

19. The nerves of the index finger are supplied by the _____ nerve.

    A. radial
    B. ulnar
    C. median
    D. parietal

20. Which of the following cosmetics contains the same basic ingredients as a top coat?

    A. Base coat
    B. Nail white
    C. Liquid polish
    D. Nail bleach

21. Typically, a basic pedicure would begin with filing and shaping the

    A. little toe
    B. long toe
    C. big toe
    D. heel

22. Which of the following conditions is caused by filing too deeply in the corners of the nails?

    A. Paronychia
    B. Ingrown nails
    C. Split nails
    D. Hangnails

23. What is the term for a chemical that may kill or slow the growth of bacteria?

    A. Antiseptic
    B. Germicide
    C. Disinfectant
    D. Antibiotic

24. Separation of the nail from the nail bed can be caused by each of the following EXCEPT

    A. use of bonded or sculpted nails
    B. psoriasis
    C. heavy doses of vitamin D
    D. formalin-based solvents or base coats

25. What is the term for the curved fold of skin on either side of the nail?

    A. Wall   B. Groove   C. Mantle   D. Bed

KEY (CORRECT ANSWERS)

1.	C	11.	B
2.	D	12.	A
3.	C	13.	C
4.	C	14.	A
5.	B	15.	C
6.	D	16.	B
7.	A	17.	C
8.	B	18.	C
9.	C	19.	C
10.	A	20.	A

21. A
22. B
23. A
24. C
25. A

TEST 2

DIRECTIONS: Each question or incomplete statement is followed by several suggested answers or completions. Select the one that BEST answers the question or completes the statement. *PRINT THE LETTER OF THE CORRECT ANSWER IN THE SPACE AT THE RIGHT.*

1. Improper hygiene can cause a _____ discoloration of the nail. 1.___
   - A. blue-black
   - B. yellow
   - C. green
   - D. streaked

2. Influenza, the common cold, and smallpox are caused by 2.___
   - A. viruses
   - B. cocci
   - C. spirilla
   - D. bacilli

3. The MOST commonly used cuticle nippers have jaws that are _____ inch across. 3.___
   - A. 1/16-1/8
   - B. 1/8-1/4
   - C. 1/4-1/3
   - D. 1/4-1/2

4. What type of nerve fiber endings supply the body with the sense of touch? 4.___
   - A. Tactile corpuscles
   - B. Somatic nerves
   - C. Subcutaneous dendrites
   - D. Arrector pili

5. To prevent nail layers from peeling, a manicurist should apply _____ to the nail surface. 5.___
   - A. nail primer
   - B. lanolin
   - C. cuticle softener
   - D. nail bleach

6. Which of the following tissues completely surrounds the entire nail? 6.___
   - A. Hyponychium
   - B. Perionychium
   - C. Eponychium
   - D. Lunula

7. What is the term for the three-headed muscle of the upper arm that is responsible for bending the arm at the elbow? 7.___
   - A. Triceps brachii
   - B. Deltoid
   - C. Pectoralis
   - D. Biceps brachii

8. After they have been sanitized, where should manicuring implements be stored? 8.___
   - A. Wet sanitizer
   - B. Dry sanitizer
   - C. Alcohol solution
   - D. Peroxide solution

9. What is the term for the process of using up or storing food energy? 9.___
   - A. Peristalsis
   - B. Metabolism
   - C. Digestion
   - D. Phoresis

10. Which of the following is used to smooth and polish nails? 10.___
    - A. Nail file
    - B. Emery paper
    - C. Nail brush
    - D. Buffer

11. What type of bacteria aid in the decomposition of vegetation? 11.___
    - A. Spores
    - B. Pathogens
    - C. Saprophytes
    - D. Epiphytes

12. What is the MOST likely cause of *club nails*?

    A. Calcium deficiency
    B. Chemical contact
    C. Prolonged oxygen deficiency
    D. Formalin-based solvents

13. Which of the following would be MOST likely to cause onychorrhexis?

    A. Loose acrylic tip   B. Fungal parasites
    C. Improper filing   D. Dry or chapped skin

14. Which of the following is NOT one of the vitamins that is most useful to the nails?

    A. A   B. B   C. D   D. E

15. Which of the following is typically the LAST step in a foot massage?

    A. Rotating ankle   B. Rotating toes
    C. Massaging toes   D. Massaging instep

16. Which of the following is an example of a vegetable parasite?

    A. Mite   B. Ringworm
    C. Pediculosis   D. Scabies

17. Yellow nails can be caused by all of the following EXCEPT

    A. fungus   B. tetracycline use
    C. trauma   D. nicotine exposure

18. Which of the following is used to repair split nails?

    A. Emery paper   B. Mend paper
    C. Nail white   D. Nail glue

19. What is the term for the coloring pigment of the skin?

    A. Albumin   B. Keratin   C. Ketone   D. Melanin

20. When performing a basic pedicure, which of the following procedures would be performed LAST?

    A. Use fabric to separate toes
    B. Apply cuticle softener
    C. Apply astringent to foot
    D. Place feet in disinfectant bath

21. What is the basic structural unit of the nervous system?

    A. Axon   B. Neuron   C. Dendrite   D. Arc

22. The deep fold of skin at the base of the nail is called the nail

    A. onyx   B. groove   C. matrix   D. mantle

23. Which muscle bends the wrist and draws the hand upward?

    A. Flexor   B. Supinator   C. Pronator   D. Extensor

24. Which of the following substances is used to stop minor bleeding from a cut?   24.___

    A. Styptic powder
    B. Alcohol solution
    C. Iodine
    D. Antiseptic

25. Which of the following terms describes the shedding of a nail?   25.___

    A. Eponychium
    B. Onychophagy
    C. Leukonychia
    D. Onychoptosis

KEY (CORRECT ANSWERS)

1. C		11. C	
2. A		12. C	
3. D		13. C	
4. A		14. B	
5. B		15. B	
6. B		16. B	
7. A		17. C	
8. B		18. B	
9. B		19. D	
10. D		20. A	

    21. B
    22. D
    23. A
    24. A
    25. D

TEST 3

DIRECTIONS: Each question or incomplete statement is followed by several suggested answers or completions. Select the one that BEST answers the question or completes the statement. *PRINT THE LETTER OF THE CORRECT ANSWER IN THE SPACE AT THE RIGHT.*

1. Most disinfectants are 1._____

   A. toxic
   B. septic
   C. pathogenic
   D. sterile

2. What implement should be used for buffing nails that are to be filled? 2._____

   A. Chamois buffer
   B. Nail file
   C. Buffing disc
   D. Fine side of emery board

3. Which of the following conditions is also known as a *felon*? 3._____

   A. Onychogryposis
   B. Onychorrhexis
   C. Paronychia
   D. Onychauxis

4. Before press-on nails are applied, they should be soaked in 4._____

   A. acetone
   B. alcohol
   C. disinfectant
   D. warm water

5. When using a metal pusher, a manicurist should take care to avoid pressure 5._____

   A. at the base of the nail
   B. along the nail groove
   C. under the free edge
   D. along the nail wall

6. If an electric nail shaper is used, it should be held at a _____° angle to the nail. 6._____

   A. 15   B. 45   C. 60   D. 90

7. Which of the following procedures is used to correct corrugations in the surface of the nail? 7._____

   A. Clipping
   B. Buffing
   C. Softening
   D. Filing

8. Which of the following procedures for applying acrylic nails would be performed FIRST? 8._____

   A. Apply nail primer
   B. File nail tip
   C. Apply polish
   D. Remove nail forms

9. How are cocci bacteria shaped? 9._____

   A. Round   B. Spiral   C. Oblong   D. Rod

10. After gel nails have been applied and cured, any dust residue should be removed with a 10._____

    A. nail brush
    B. cotton-tipped orangewood stick
    C. sable brush
    D. chamois buffer

53

11. What is the term for a person who transmits a disease without being affected?

    A. Transmitter
    B. Epiphyte
    C. Median
    D. Carrier

12. What is the term for the process of strengthening fragile nail tips?

    A. Taping
    B. Wrapping
    C. Tipping
    D. Capping

13. Prolonged stress can lead to _____ nails.

    A. yellow
    B. brown
    C. white-flecked
    D. gray

14. Each of the following conditions may be present in a nail that is treated and handled by a manicurist EXCEPT

    A. tinea
    B. onychorrhexis
    C. leukonychia
    D. corrugation

15. What implement should be used to apply nail whitener?

    A. Nail brush
    B. Buffer
    C. Cotton swab
    D. Cotton-tipped orangewood stick

16. Which of the following procedures is used to keep nails from splitting?

    A. Sealing
    B. Sanitizing
    C. Beveling
    D. Filing

17. When performing a basic manicure, which of the following procedures would be performed LAST?

    A. Apply nail white
    B. Apply base coat
    C. File nails
    D. Trim cuticles

18. What is the term for the hard outer covering that protects certain bacteria?

    A. Amitosis
    B. Spore
    C. Verruca
    D. Coat

19. When applying acrylic nails, a manicurist should be careful to keep the acrylic away from the

    A. cuticle
    B. groove
    C. tip
    D. lunula

20. What colorless liquid is applied to the nail before the layer of liquid nail polish?

    A. Nail white
    B. Base coat
    C. Nail enamel
    D. Top coat

21. What type of tissue is found on the ends of long bones and the insides of flat bones?

    A. Epithelial
    B. Periosteum
    C. Synovial
    D. Cancellous

22. What is the term for the outermost layer of skin? 22.____

    A. Epidermis   B. Subcutaneum
    C. Corium   D. Dermis

23. Dark streaks on the nail are MOST likely to be caused by 23.____

    A. calcium deposits
    B. adrenal gland deficiency
    C. trauma to nail surface
    D. prolonged oxygen deficiency

24. What is another term for a disinfectant? 24.____

    A. Bactericide   B. Antiseptic
    C. Vaccine   D. Fumigant

25. Which color of polish would generally be considered unsuitable for a person whose skin 25.____
    has rosy beige or brown undertones?

    A. Burgundy   B. Coral brown
    C. Mauve   D. Olive

KEY (CORRECT ANSWERS)

1.	A	11.	D
2.	D	12.	D
3.	C	13.	D
4.	D	14.	A
5.	A	15.	D
6.	B	16.	C
7.	B	17.	B
8.	A	18.	B
9.	A	19.	A
10.	C	20.	B

21. D
22. A
23. B
24. A
25. D

TEST 4

DIRECTIONS: Each question or incomplete statement is followed by several suggested answers or completions. Select the one that BEST answers the question or completes the statement. *PRINT THE LETTER OF THE CORRECT ANSWER IN THE SPACE AT THE RIGHT.*

1. Which muscle aligns the wrist and hand in a straight line? 1.___
   A. Extensor B. Supinator C. Pronator D. Flexor

2. What are the wrist bones called? 2.___
   A. Tarsals
   C. Carpals
   B. Metacarpals
   D. Hamates

3. Which of the following procedures for applying silk or linen nail wraps would be performed FIRST? 3.___
   A. Apply nail adhesive to entire nail plate
   B. File off excess fabric
   C. Buff nail surface
   D. Cut material to shape of nail

4. What is another term for the dermis? 4.___
   A. Corneal layer
   C. Subdural layer
   B. Cuticle
   D. Corium

5. What type of tissue are bone, cartilage, tendons, and ligaments? 5.___
   A. Muscular
   C. Nervous
   B. Connective
   D. Epithelial

6. What substance is used to cleanse the nail of body oils? 6.___
   A. Nail primer
   C. Nail white
   B. Nail bleach
   D. Powder polish

7. Where is 1/2-2/3 of the body's blood supply located? 7.___
   A. Intestines
   C. Skin
   B. Lungs
   D. Brain

8. What is the solvent used to soften and remove MOST artificial nails? 8.___
   A. Alcohol B. Benzene C. Acetone D. Turpentine

9. Which nerve supplies the muscles on the cell side of the forearm? 9.___
   A. Median B. Radial C. Digital D. Ulnar

10. To smooth mending tissue, a manicurist should use an orangewood stick dipped in 10.___
    A. alcohol
    C. polish remover
    B. astringent
    D. soapy water

11. A *hairline tip* would be found at the

    A. base of the nail
    B. free edge
    C. nail groove
    D. nape area

12. During a pedicure, the nails should be shaped by

    A. filing them straight across
    B. tapering them, using the nippers
    C. filing the corners into a rounded shape
    D. clipping them in a rounded shape

13. What is the term for the process of making an object free of bacteria?

    A. Disinfection
    B. Immunization
    C. Sterilization
    D. Sanitation

14. Acrylic gel is hardened by means of

    A. a chemical epoxy
    B. ultraviolet light
    C. dry heat
    D. a blower

15. What is the term for the oil secreted by the body that keeps skin soft and supple?

    A. Sebum   B. Mucosum   C. Keratin   D. Lanolin

16. Which glands help regulate body temperature?

    A. Adrenal
    B. Sebaceous
    C. Cortical
    D. Sudoriferous

17. Typically, the application of base coat will begin with the

    A. thumb of the left hand
    B. index finger of the left hand
    C. little finger of the right hand
    D. thumb of the right hand

18. What type of container is used to hold a disinfectant solution?

    A. Wet sanitizer
    B. Dry sanitizer
    C. Fumigant
    D. Cabinet sanitizer

19. When applying an artificial nail tip, which of the following procedures would be performed FIRST?

    A. Smooth mending tissue over nail
    B. Soak mending tissue in mending liquid
    C. Trim mending tissue to desired length
    D. Fold mending tissue over nail edge

20. What color of nail polish would be BEST suited to complement *warm-colored* clothing?

    A. Berry
    B. Blue-red
    C. Coral
    D. Bright pink

21. What type of solution should be used to sanitize metal manicuring implements?

    A. Quaternary ammonium
    B. Hydrogen peroxide
    C. Witch-hazel
    D. Alcohol

22. Which of the following is NOT a likely cause of a bluish discoloration of the nails?

    A. Chemical contact
    B. Trauma
    C. Vitamin A toxicity
    D. Insufficient circulation

23. How many systems are in the human body?

    A. 3   B. 6   C. 9   D. 12

24. To make pits or ridges more noticeable on the nail plate surface, apply

    A. ridge filler
    B. antiseptic
    C. warm water
    D. polish remover

25. To what organ system does the skin belong?

    A. Endocrine
    B. Respiratory
    C. Nervous
    D. Excretory

KEY (CORRECT ANSWERS)

1.	A	11.	B
2.	C	12.	A
3.	D	13.	C
4.	D	14.	B
5.	B	15.	A
6.	A	16.	D
7.	C	17.	A
8.	C	18.	A
9.	B	19.	C
10.	C	20.	C

21.	B
22.	C
23.	C
24.	B
25.	D

EXAMINATION SECTION
TEST 1

DIRECTIONS: Each question or incomplete statement is followed by several suggested answers or completions. Select the one that BEST answers the question or completes the statement. *PRINT THE LETTER OF THE CORRECT ANSWER IN THE SPACE AT THE RIGHT.*

1. Skin is the largest organ of what bodily system? 1._____

   A. Circulatory
   B. Endocrine
   C. Integumentary
   D. Respiratory

2. The outermost layer of the skin is called the 2._____

   A. endodermis
   B. epidermis
   C. hypodermis
   D. dermis

3. Which of the following does the *dermis* contain? 3._____

   A. hair follicles
   B. sebaceous glands
   C. blood vessels
   D. all of the above

4. The adjective *cutaneous* means 4._____

   A. of the skin
   B. of the hair
   C. of the glands
   D. for cutting

5. All of the following are disorders of the skin EXCEPT 5._____

   A. psoriasis
   B. serosis
   C. acne
   D. vitiligo

6. Which of the following is NOT true of scar tissue? 6._____

   A. It is often discolored
   B. It is an area of fibrous tissue that replaces normal skin
   C. It is a natural result of the healing process
   D. It can be completely removed

59

7. All of the following are functions of the skin EXCEPT

A. protecting against pathogens
B. insulation
C. digestion
D. sensation

8. All of the following cause aging of the skin EXCEPT

A. the sun
B. gravity
C. smoking
D. face makeup

9. The signs of intrinsic aging include all of the following EXCEPT

A. thin and transparent skin
B. hollowed cheeks
C. ridges on fingernails
D. oily skin

10. A disease that rapidly accelerates the aging process, causing subjects to appear elderly in their mid-30s, is called

A. Werner's syndrome
B. anorexia nervosa
C. Alzheimer's
D. Graves' disease

11. Which of the following is NOT a temporary hair removal technique?

A. Tweezing
B. Waxing
C. Laser
D. Depilatories

12. Which of the following is NOT a technique used in a facial massage?

A. Effleurage
B. Petrissage
C. Shiatsu
D. Tapotement

13. All of the following are tools used in facial treatments EXCEPT

A. astringent
B. soap
C. moisturizers
D. sponges

14. All of the following are types of facial treatments EXCEPT   14._____

   A. vibrations
   B. masks
   C. extractions
   D. exfoliations

15. Which of the following is considered a *cool* color?   15._____

   A. Red
   B. Blue
   C. Orange
   D. Gold

16. Which of the following is considered a *warm* color?   16._____

   A. Blue
   B. Violet
   C. Red
   D. Green

17. For a softer more natural look on light skin use _____-colored makeup.   17._____

   A. light
   B. medium
   C. dark
   D. bold

18. When applying makeup, if you choose a color that is lighter than your skin it may appear   18._____

   A. greasy
   B. chalky
   C. shiny
   D. uneven

19. If your eyes are wide apart, the best way to make them look closer is to highlight the _____ portion of the _____ side of the eyelid.   19._____

   A. upper; inner
   B. lower; inner
   C. upper; outer
   D. lower; outer

20. If eyes are sunken, apply shadow 20._____

A. beyond the length of the eye
B. on the outer edges of the eyes and highlight the inner corners of the eyes
C. only in the middle of the eyelid
D. below the eye

21. If you wish to make the nose appear shorter, 21._____

A. apply a dark shadow right below the nose and over the tip of the nose
B. use a highlighter just below the nose and under the tip of the nose
C. use a highlight along the two sides of the nose
D. apply a shadow along the two sides of the nose and use a highlighter down the center of the nose

22. To make lips appear thicker, one should do all of the following EXCEPT 22._____

A. apply lip liner just outside the curve of the lips
B. use a rich color lipstick
C. highlight the center of the upper and lower lip with lip gloss
D. apply a lip liner, matching a light colored lipstick, just outside the curve of the lips with one coat of gloss

23. To create the illusion of a striking jawline with high cheekbones when the face is round, you should 23._____

A. apply shadow under the cheekbones
B. apply a dark shadow over and under the jawline
C. use a highlighter on and below the jawbone
D. apply shadow on the chin

24. Which of the following is NOT a safety precaution that should be used when applying makeup? 24._____

A. Insert contact lenses before applying makeup
B. Stop using any product that causes an allergic reaction
C. Always apply eyeliner inside the lash line
D. Do not share makeup

25. Disinfection includes all of the following EXCEPT _____ standards. 25._____

A. wet disinfection
B. dry disinfection
C. storage
D. use

KEY (CORRECT ANSWERS)

1. C	6. D	11. C	16. C	21. A
2. B	7. C	12. C	17. A	22. D
3. D	8. D	13. B	18. B	23. A
4. A	9. D	14. A	19. A	24. C
5. B	10. A	15. B	20. C	25. D

TEST 2

DIRECTIONS: Each question or incomplete statement is followed by several suggested answers or completions. Select the one that BEST answers the question or completes the statement. *PRINT THE LETTER OF THE CORRECT ANSWER IN THE SPACE AT THE RIGHT.*

1. All of the following are parts of the hard surface of the nail EXCEPT the   1._____

   A. root
   B. body
   C. cuticle
   D. free edge

2. The tissue upon which the nail rests is called the   2._____

   A. cuticle
   B. matrix
   C. nail sinus
   D. nail root

3. The lunula (little moon) is largest in the _____ and often absent in the _____.   3._____

   A. thumb; little finger
   B. little finger; thumb
   C. nail bed; matrix
   D. nail plate; matrix

4. Fingernails grow about ____ mm per week.   4._____

   A. 0.5
   B. 1
   C. 1.5
   D. 2

5. The nail plate is made of translucent   5._____

   A. carbohydrates
   B. fats
   C. proteins
   D. alcohols

6. Nails are a form of   6._____

   A. hair
   B. skin
   C. fat
   D. muscle

7. Fingernails require _____ to regrow completely. 7._____

A. 2 to 4 weeks
B. 1 to 2 months
C. 3 to 6 months
D. 12 to 18 months

8. Toenails require _____ months to regrow completely. 8._____

A. 1 to 2
B. 6 to 8
C. 12 to 18
D. 18 to 24

9. All of the following are diseases of the nail EXCEPT 9._____

A. oogenesis
B. onychia
C. onychocryptosis
D. onychogryposis

10. Dark nails are associated with Vitamin ____ deficiency. 10._____

A. A
B. B_{12}
C. C
D. D

11. Small white patches are known as 11._____

A. leukonychia punctata
B. leukoplakia
C. Mees' lines
D. melanonychia

12. Redness of the nail bed is associated with 12._____

A. chronic bronchitis
B. diabetes
C. heart conditions
D. liver disorders

13. Smoking is associated with 13._____

A. stains of the nail plate
B. white lines
C. white patches
D. yellowing of the nail bed

14. An infection caused by improper removal of a hangnail is called   14._____

A. melanonychia
B. paronychia
C. erythronychia
D. onychomatricoma

15. All of the following are common manicure tools EXCEPT   15._____

A. bowl of warm water
B. nail clippers
C. knife
D. cuticle pusher

16. All of the following are common manicure supplies EXCEPT   16._____

A. hand cream
B. nail polish
C. cotton balls/pads
D. rubbing alcohol

17. Paraffin wax   17._____

A. can be used to soften and moisturize
B. can make nails harder
C. does not contain any oils
D. is first cooled before applying to the hands

18. All of the following can be used in a hot oil manicure EXCEPT   18._____

A. mineral oil
B. olive oil
C. commercial preparation in an electric heater
D. vegetable oil

19. Specialty pedicures may include use of all of the following EXCEPT   19._____

A. chocolate-scented lotion
B. lime salt scrubs
C. sugar scrub
D. grape seed scrub

20. All of the following are essential for healthy nails EXCEPT   20._____

A. proper water intake
B. sufficient protein intake
C. fresh fruits and vegetables
D. a vitamin supplement

21. Which of the following is NOT a common type of artificial nail?

A. Acrylic.
B. Gel.
C. Silk.
D. Paper.

22. All of the following are synonymous with a fungal infection of the toenail EXCEPT

A. onychomycosis
B. ringworm of the nail
C. melanonychia
D. tinea unguium

23. Which of the following is NOT true of athlete's foot?

A. It is a communicable disease
B. It is typically transmitted in dry environments
C. It can also cause fungal infections on other parts of the body
D. It causes itching

24. All of the following statements are true of ingrown toenails EXCEPT

A. They are more common in children than adults
B. If left untreated, they can lead to an abscess
C. Any toenail can become ingrown
D. All of the above

25. Which of the following is NOT a method of infection control?

A. Sanitation
B. Liquification
C. Sterilization
D. Disinfection

KEY (CORRECT ANSWERS)

1. C	6. A	11. A	16. D	21. D
2. B	7. C	12. C	17. A	22. C
3. A	8. C	13. A	18. D	23. B
4. A	9. A	14. B	19. C	24. A
5. C	10. B	15. C	20. D	25. B

FACIALS AND MANICURING

EXAMINATION SECTION
TEST 1

DIRECTIONS: Each question consists of a statement. You are to indicate whether the statement is TRUE (T) or FALSE (F). *PRINT THE LETTER OF THE CORRECT ANSWER IN THE SPACE AT THE RIGHT.*

1. Correct massage is given by stretching the skin in an upward and downward direction. 1.____
2. The loss of elasticity of the muscles will cause wrinkles. 2.____
3. Tapotement is the slapping movement. 3.____
4. Large pores in the skin are caused by the use of good astringents. 4.____
5. Skin bleaching lubricates the skin. 5.____
6. Heat causes the skin to contract. 6.____
7. Facials may be given once a week if necessary. 7.____
8. Vanishing creams are non-absorbent and serve as a powder base. 8.____
9. Fine skin requires less cleansing treatments than coarse skin. 9.____
10. Astringent lotion lubricates the underlying tissues. 10.____
11. Makeup of all kinds should correspond to the natural coloring of the individual. 11.____
12. Cleansing creams are absorbed by the skin. 12.____
13. Tissue cream is used to nourish the skin. 13.____
14. A double chin is due to a lack of adipose tissue. 14.____
15. All eyebrows should be arched the same way. 15.____
16. Petrissage is a kneading movement. 16.____
17. A clay pack tends to expand the skin tissue. 17.____
18. A sudden loss of weight may be responsible for wrinkles. 18.____
19. Lanolin is a beneficial ingredient in tissue creams. 19.____
20. The eyes should be covered with pads when exposing the face to therapeutic lights. 20.____
21. The matrix is the reproductive organ of the nail. 21.____
22. The nail receives its nourishment from the matrix during growth. 22.____
23. The nail bed is composed of the same layers as the corium of the skin. 23.____

24. The shape of the nail is determined by the shape of the finger. 24.___
25. The nail should be filed from the center to the corners. 25.___
26. Hangnails are a splitting of the epidermis at the side of the finger. 26.___
27. Liquid polish is injurious to the nail. 27.___
28. Onychophagy should be treated as a disease. 28.___
29. Nails filed long and given oil manicures will aid in keeping them from splitting. 29.___
30. Onychia is inflammation of the nail matrix. 30.___
31. If a nail is torn, cut or injured, a new one will always grow. 31.___
32. A styptic pencil is used to stop bleeding from a minor cut or abrasion. 32.___
33. The nails contain numerous cells joined together to form epithelial tissue. 33.___
34. The matrix extends beneath the nail root. 34.___
35. Onychosis is ringworm of the nail. 35.___
36. Leuconychia is white spots in the nail. 36.___
37. A hand and arm massage can be given both for thin and fat hands. 37.___
38. Paronychia is a non-infectious disease of the nails. 38.___
39. Chapped hands are caused by frequent washing and exposure to the cold. 39.___
40. The cuticle of the nail is the same as the outside of the hair. 40.___
41. The nail is very thick in the region of the root. 41.___
42. Hot oil manicures are beneficial for ridged and brittle nails. 42.___
43. Nail infections are caused by sterilized instruments. 43.___
44. A sharp instrument should never be used to push back the cuticle. 44.___
45. Digital nerves are not branches of the radial and ulnar nerves. 45.___
46. Buffing is always a part of the manicure when a liquid polish is not to be used. 46.___
47. Abrasions are less likely to result with an orangewood stick than with a metal cleaner. 47.___
48. The color of a healthy nail is white. 48.___
49. Corns should be removed when giving a pedicure. 49.___
50. Alcohol is a good remedy for perspiring hands. 50.___

KEY (CORRECT ANSWERS)

1. F	11. T	21. T	31. F	41. F
2. T	12. F	22. T	32. F	42. T
3. T	13. T	23. T	33. F	43. F
4. F	14. F	24. T	34. T	44. T
5. F	15. F	25. F	35. F	45. F
6. F	16. T	26. T	36. T	46. T
7. T	17. F	27. F	37. T	47. T
8. T	18. T	28. F	38. F	48. F
9. F	19. T	29. T	39. T	49. F
10. F	20. T	30. T	40. F	50. T

TEST 2

Questions 1-4.

DIRECTIONS: Each question consists of a statement. You are to indicate whether the statement is TRUE (T) or FALSE (F). *PRINT THE LETTER OF THE CORRECT ANSWER IN THE SPACE AT THE RIGHT.*

1. Hydrogen peroxide solution is used as a germicide in manicuring. 1.____

2. The nail blade has a vascular supply while the matrix has none. 2.____

3. Muscle toning treatments are recommended for oily skin. 3.____

4. Massage helps to eliminate the waste products of metabolism. 4.____

Questions 5-14.

DIRECTIONS: Fill in the blanks with the MOST appropriate word from the set of words at the beginning of each section. Each answer may be used only once.

file	sterilized	convex	free edge
new	arranged	old	centers
dry	infections	long	nail bed
short	sanitary	brittle	blemishes

5. Manicuring beautifies the nails and keeps them in a _____ condition. 5.____

6. An efficient manicurist keeps her instruments properly _____ and conveniently _____ so that they are readily accessible. 6.____

7. As applied to the shape of nails, concave is the opposite of _____. 7.____

8. Before giving a manicure, the operator should examine the hands for _____ and _____. 8.____

9. If the shape of the nail conforms to the type of finger, then a long, oval-shaped nail should be selected for a _____ stumpy finger. 9.____

10. A manicure starts with the removal of _____ nail polish and ends with the application of a _____ film of nail polish. 10.____

11. Nails are filed from either corner to their _____. 11.____

12. Nail whitening is applied under the _____ of the nail. 12.____

13. The emery board is used in the same manner as the nail 13.____

14. An oil manicure is beneficial for ridged and _____ nails and _____ cuticles. 14.____

Questions 15-35.

DIRECTIONS: In each set of questions, match the items in Column I with the appropriate item in Column I. *PRINT THE LETTER OF THE CORRECT ANSWER IN THE SPACE AT THE RIGHT.*

COLUMN I

Questions 15-19.

15. Leuconychia
16. Atrophy
17. Onychia
18. Onychoptosis
19. Onychophyma

COLUMN II

A. Inflammation of the nail matrix with pus formation
B. Swelling of the nails
C. White spots on the nails
D. Periodical shedding of the nails
E. Wasting away of the nail

15._____
16._____
17._____
18._____
19._____

Questions 20-24.

20. Nail body
21. Nail bed
22. Nail root
23. Matrix
24. Cuticle

A. Base of nail imbedded underneath the skin
B. Part of nail bed extending beneath nail root
C. Overlapping skin around the nail
D. Skin on which nail body rests
E. Nail extending from root to fingertips

20._____
21._____
22._____
23._____
24._____

Questions 25-30.

25. Humerus
26. Carpus
27. Radial blood vessel
28. Radius
29. Phalanges
30. Ulna

A. Large bone of the forearm
B. Small bone of the forearm
C. Bones of the wrist
D. Bone of the upper arm
E. Supplies outer side of arm and back of hand
F. Bones of fingers and toes

25._____
26._____
27._____
28._____
29._____
30._____

Questions 31-35.

COLUMN I	COLUMN II	
31. Vibroid	A. Kneading movement	31.___
32. Friction	B. Tapping movement	32.___
33. Petrissage	C. Vibratory movement	33.___
34. Effleurage	D. Deep rubbing movement	34.___
35. Tapotement	E. Stroking movement	35.___

KEY (CORRECT ANSWERS)

1. F	11. centers	21. D	31. C
2. F	12. free edge	22. A	32. D
3. F	13. file	23. B	33. A
4. T	14. brittle, dry	24. C	34. E
5. sanitary	15. C	25. D	35. B
6. sterilized, arranged	16. E	26. C	
7. convex	17. A	27. E	
8. blemishes, infections	18. D	28. B	
9. short	19. B	29. F	
10. old, new	20. E	30. A	

EXAMINATION SECTION
TEST 1

DIRECTIONS: Each question or incomplete statement is followed by several suggested answers or completions. Select the one that *BEST* answers the question or completes the statement. *PRINT THE LETTER OF THE CORRECT ANSWER IN THE SPACE AT THE RIGHT.*

1. A substance having the ability to check the growth and multiplication of bacteria without destroying them, is called a(n)   1.____

    A. germicide   B. deodorant   C. antiseptic   D. disinfectant

2. A disinfectant can be applied with safety to   2.____

    A. the body
    C. clothing
    B. instruments
    D. an opening in the skin

3. Pathogenic bacteria are   3.____

    A. beneficial
    C. harmless
    B. harmful
    D. not disease producing

4. Asteatosis is an   4.____

    A. abundance of the sebaceous secretions
    B. absence of the sebaceous secretions
    C. abundance of the sudoriferous secretions
    D. absence of the sudoriferous secretions

5. A vinegar rinse is a(n) _____ rinse.   5.____

    A. alkaline
    C. acid
    B. neutral
    D. coloring

6. A dry shampoo is given with   6.____

    A. liquid soap
    C. powdered soap
    B. powdered orris root
    D. an antiseptic

7. The study of the nervous system and its disorders is called   7.____

    A. myology   B. dermatology   C. histology   D. neurology

8. The dead cells of the stratum corneum   8.____

    A. never shed
    C. shed according to season
    B. constantly flake off
    D. are difficult to remove

9. The skin is an absorbing organ to   9.____

    A. a limited extent
    C. no extent
    B. a great extent
    D. liquids only

10. Inflammation of the skin is known as

    A. dermatology
    B. dermatosis
    C. dermatologist
    D. dermatitis

11. Astringent tonics or ointments are most effective on

    A. normal skin
    B. dry skin
    C. oily skin
    D. sunburned skin

12. The use of strong soaps should be avoided on _____ skin.

    A. oily
    B. normal
    C. freckled
    D. dry

13. Face powders are intended to improve the _____ of the skin.

    A. texture
    B. appearance
    C. color
    D. function

14. Dry, brittle nails are aggravated by

    A. hot oil treatments
    B. tissue cream
    C. alkaline soaps
    D. cuticle cream

15. A group of similar cells performing the same function is called a(n)

    A. organ   B. tissue   C. gland   D. system

16. In cleaning the free edge of the nail, abrasions are less likely to occur if the operator uses a(n)

    A. metal cleaner
    B. small brush
    C. orangewood stick
    D. bone instrument

17. The harmless types of hair colorings are the

    A. metallic dyes
    B. vegetable dyes
    C. aniline dyes
    D. compound hennas

18. The medical term for gray hair is

    A. albinism   B. canities   C. leucoderma   D. lentigo

19. The addition of a few drops of a 28% solution of ammonia to peroxide will

    A. hasten its bleaching action
    B. stop its bleaching action
    C. lessen its bleaching action
    D. make the bleach more lasting

20. The treatment for trichoptilosis is

    A. thinning   B. shingling   C. clipping   D. bobbing

21. Located at the back and lower part of the cranium is the

    A. frontal bone
    B. occipital bone
    C. parietal bone
    D. temporal bone

22. In machine permanent waving, coarse hair requires

    A. the same steaming time as fine hair
    B. less steaming time than fine hair
    C. more steaming time than fine hair
    D. double the steaming time for fine hair

23. The technical name for baldness is

    A. alopecia   B. pityriasis   C. dermatitis   D. albinism

24. Scalp treatments are NOT intended to

    A. preserve the health of the hair
    B. correct dandruff or loss of hair
    C. stimulate glandular activity
    D. cure infectious diseases of the scalp and hair

25. Processing in cold waving should be determined by

    A. the amount of hair   B. test curl
    C. texture of hair   D. previous waving time

KEY (CORRECT ANSWERS)

1. C   11. C
2. B   12. D
3. B   13. B
4. B   14. C
5. C   15. B

6. B   16. C
7. D   17. B
8. B   18. B
9. A   19. A
10. D   20. C

21. B
22. B
23. A
24. D
25. C

TEST 2

DIRECTIONS: Each question or incomplete statement is followed by several suggested answers or completions. Select the one that *BEST* answers the question or completes the statement. *PRINT THE LETTER OF THE CORRECT ANSWER IN THE SPACE AT THE RIGHT.*

1. It is advisable to brush hair before giving a shampoo because it   1.____
   A. saves combing after shampoo
   B. stimulates the scalp
   C. helps the operator to give the shampoo more rapidly
   D. saves one soaping

2. When bacteria get into the body, they are usually destroyed by   2.____
   A. white blood cells   B. red blood cells
   C. lymph   D. plasma

3. Nails are composed of keratin, which is also found in the   3.____
   A. muscles   B. hair shaft   C. glands   D. bones

4. Eyelashes should NOT be tinted with hair dye because   4.____
   A. it may cause injury to the eyes
   B. it may not match the hair
   C. it may be too strong and make them too dark
   D. the operator may not be experienced in using it

5. Overbleached hair is difficult to permanent-wave because it has lost its   5.____
   A. melanin   B. elasticity   C. medulla   D. cortex

6. A spiral flat wave is   6.____
   A. twisted   B. half-twisted
   C. wound from ends to roots   D. wound from roots to ends

7. Excessive perspiration may be caused by   7.____
   A. cold   B. mental excitement
   C. lack of exercise   D. relaxation

8. A condition in which the cuticle splits around the nail is known as   8.____
   A. felon   B. onychia   C. hangnail   D. infection

9. A comedone extractor is a small instrument for removing   9.____
   A. scars   B. pimples   C. milia   D. blackheads

10. Nails are composed of a horny protein substance called   10.____
    A. cortex   B. keratin   C. allergens   D. cicatrix

11. The amount of melanin in the hair determines the   11.____
    A. texture   B. strength   C. elasticity   D. color

78

12. A disinfectant can also be used as an antiseptic if it is   12._____

    A. diluted
    B. concentrated
    C. applied full strength in smaller quantity
    D. mixed with a germicide

13. Hair is more resistant to dye   13._____

    A. behind the ears   B. at the back of the head
    C. at the crown   D. at the forehead and temples

14. A license which entitles an operator to work in a city beauty shop is issued by the   14._____

    A. department of health   B. department of state
    C. department of labor   D. city bureau of licenses

15. If, during the manicure, the skin is cut, the operator should apply   15._____

    A. powdered alum   B. formalin
    C. styptic pencil   D. herpicide

16. Pediculosis is treated by the application of   16._____

    A. tincture of larkspur   B. oil of wintergreen
    C. lanolin   D. vinegar

17. To disentangle oversteamed hair, one should use a(n)   17._____

    A. alkaline rinse   B. peroxide rinse
    C. neutral rinse   D. acid rinse

18. Of the following, the harmless types of hair colorings are the   18._____

    A. aniline dyes   B. compound henna
    C. metallic dyes   D. vegetable dyes

19. Which of these statements about bone is untrue?   19._____

    A. The technical term for bone is os.
    B. Bone is composed of animal and mineral matter.
    C. Bone is pink externally and white internally.
    D. The two types of bone tissue are dense and cancellous.

20. Which of these statements is untrue?   20._____

    A. Boiling water destroys all bacteria except spores.
    B. Spore-forming bacteria can be destroyed by exposure to steam at 15 pounds pressure.
    C. Dry heat is often used in the beauty shop.
    D. A disinfectant solution can be changed to an antiseptic by dilution.

21. Chemicals should be stored in   21._____

    A. open containers in a dark, dry and cool place
    B. closed containers in a dark, dry and cool place
    C. closed containers in a light, damp and cool place
    D. closed containers in a dark, damp and warm place

22. How should coarse hair and fine hair be wound for cold-waving?

    A. Coarse hair should be wound in smaller curls than fine hair.
    B. Coarse hair should be wound in larger curls than fine hair.
    C. Coarse hair cannot be cold-waved as easily as fine hair.
    D. Coarse hair takes a shorter time than fine hair for cold-waving.

23. Which of these statements is untrue? The

    A. ends of the bones are covered with cartilage
    B. occipital bone is located at the crown
    C. cranium consists of 10 bones
    D. mandible bone is bone of the lower jaw

24. Ringworm on the skin is caused by a

    A. bacterium   B. fungus   C. protozoan   D. worm

25. Cold applications tend to

    A. decrease the supply of blood in the area to which they are applied
    B. dilate the blood vessels
    C. bring a greater supply of blood to the area to which they are applied
    D. increase the pressure on the nerve endings

KEY (CORRECT ANSWERS)

1. B
2. A
3. B
4. A
5. B

6. D
7. B
8. C
9. D
10. B

11. D
12. A
13. C
14. B
15. A

16. A
17. D
18. D
19. C
20. C

21. B
22. A
23. B
24. B
25. A

EXAMINATION SECTION
TEST 1

DIRECTIONS: Each question or incomplete statement is followed by several suggested answers or completions. Select the one that BEST answers the question or completes the statement. *PRINT THE LETTER OF THE CORRECT ANSWER IN THE SPACE AT THE RIGHT.*

1. Which of the following statements are CORRECT?
    I. The skin is the same thickness over the entire body.
    II. Hair is an appendage of the nails.
    III. Keratin is the horny substance of which hair is made.
    IV. The amount of pigment contained in the cortex determines the color of hair.
    The CORRECT answer is:

    A. I, II   B. I, III   C. III, IV   D. II, IV

2. Which of the following statements is (are) CORRECT?
    I. Keratosis is a form of skin disease characterized by thinning epidermis.
    II. An acute disease is one of long duration.
    III. Canities is caused by fever, shock, nervousness, or senility.
    IV. Eczema is a contagious, parasitic disease of the skin, with crust formations, emitting a mousy odor.
    The CORRECT answer is:

    A. III only   B. I only   C. II, III   D. III, IV

3. Which of the following statements is (are) INCORRECT?
    I. Lanolin is a beneficial ingredient in tissue creams.
    II. The eyes should be covered with pads when exposing the face to therapeutic lights.
    III. Muscle toning treatments are recommended for oily skin.
    IV. Massage helps to eliminate the waste products of metabolism.
    The CORRECT answer is:

    A. III only   B. IV only   C. I, II   D. III, IV

4. Which of the following statements is (are) INCORRECT?
    I. A dry shampoo cleanses the hair by absorbing the dirt and oil.
    II. Cocoanut oil is a desirable ingredient in shampoos because it helps to form a thick lather.
    III. A gasoline shampoo is dangerous because it is inflammable.
    IV. Vinegar and lemon rinses help to neutralize the alkaline soap residue on the hair and scalp.
    The CORRECT answer is:

    A. I only   B. I, II, III
    C. I, II, III, IV   D. None of the above

5. Which of the following statements is (are) CORRECT?
   I. The most hygienic way to stimulate the circulation of the scalp is by scratching it.
   II. In the treatment for alopecia, the high-frequency current is applied with a glass rake electrode but without sparks.
   III. The cosmetologist is most concerned with the treatment of scalp diseases.
   IV. A shampoo rarely accompanies a scalp treatment.
   The CORRECT answer is:

   A. I only   B. II only   C. I, III, IV   D. II, III

6. Which of the following statements is (are) INCORRECT?
   I. Ordinary household ammonia can be used to mix with peroxide for bleaching purposes.
   II. The newer growth near the scalp is most resistant to a hair dye.
   III. It is better to be lavish than sparing in the use of hair tint.
   IV. A synthetic hair dye is progressive in action; whereas a hair color restorer acts instantaneously.
   The CORRECT answer is:

   A. II only   B. I, II, III   C. II, III, IV   D. I, III, IV

7. Which of the following statements is (are) INCORRECT?
   I. Pointed neck lines are suggested for long, slender necks.
   II. The principal difference between a shingle bob and a feather-edge is the height at which the hair is cut.
   III. The thumb is uppermost on the scissors when shingling or feather-edging.
   IV. In singeing the hair, the lighted taper is passed over loose hair.
   The CORRECT answer is:

   A. II only   B. I, II, III   C. II, III, IV   D. I, III, IV

8. Which of the following statements are CORRECT?
   I. It is better to oversteam than to understeam the hair.
   II. It is always advisable to make a test curl.
   III. Hair of a porous nature is the most difficult to wave.
   IV. A vinegar rinse will help to remove snarls occasioned by oversteamed or kinky hair.
   The CORRECT answer is:

   A. I, II   B. I, III   C. III, IV   D. II, IV

9. Which of the following statements are INCORRECT?
   I. Recommend beauty treatments which offer the greatest profits, without considering the benefits to the patron.
   II. A spiral permanent wave can be substituted for a croquignole permanent wave.
   III. Trade practices and secrets can be revealed to the public.
   IV. An operator is justified in condemning her competitors.
   The CORRECT answer is:

   A. I, II, III, IV   B. I, II, III
   C. II, III, IV   D. I, III, IV

10. Which of the following statements are CORRECT?
    I. The skin is the organ of protection, absorption, elimination, heat regulation, respiration, and sensation.
    II. Age has no effect on the elasticity of the skin.
    III. The skin is the seat of the organ of touch.
    IV. The sebaceous glands secrete an oily substance called sebum.

    The CORRECT answer is:

    A. I, II, III
    B. II, III, IV
    C. I, III, IV
    D. I, II, IV

KEY (CORRECT ANSWERS)

1. C
2. A
3. A
4. D
5. B
6. D
7. D
8. D
9. A
10. C

TEST 2

DIRECTIONS: Each question or incomplete statement is followed by several suggested answers or completions. Select the one that BEST answers the question or completes the statement. PRINT THE LETTER OF THE CORRECT ANSWER IN THE SPACE AT THE RIGHT.

1. Which of the following statements is (are) CORRECT?
   I. Keloid is a wartlike growth commonly located in the eyelids.
   II. A communicable disease is one that can be transmitted from person to person.
   III. Alopecia areata is baldness at time of birth.
   IV. Pityriasis is the term applied to an excessively oily condition of the scalp.
   The CORRECT answer is:

   A. I, II, III   B. II, III, IV   C. III, IV   D. II only

2. Which of the following statements is (are) CORRECT?
   I. Fine skin requires less cleansing treatments than coarse skin.
   II. Astringent lotion lubricates the underlying tissues.
   III. Makeup of all kinds should correspond to the natural coloring of the individual.
   IV. Cleansing creams are absorbed by the skin.
   The CORRECT answer is:

   A. III only   B. II, III   C. I, III   D. IV only

3. Which of the following statements is (are) INCORRECT?
   I. Corns should be removed when giving a pedicure.
   II. Alcohol is a good remedy for perspiring hands.
   III. Hydrogen peroxide solution is used as a germicide in manicuring.
   IV. The nail blade has a vascular supply while the matrix has none.
   The CORRECT answer is:

   A. II only   B. I, II, III   C. II, III, IV   D. I, III, IV

4. Which of the following statements is (are) INCORRECT?
   I. A peroxide rinse is used to give the hair a reddish tint.
   II. Henna rinse and henna compound have the same base.
   III. Tar shampoos are advised for light hair only.
   IV. Egg shampoos are advised for bleached, dry and brittle hair.
   The CORRECT answer is:

   A. I, II   B. I only   C. III, IV   D. I, III

5. Which of the following statements is (are) CORRECT?
   I. Synthetic organic dyes are penetrating dyes.
   II. Metallic dyes only coat the hair shaft.
   III. Any person can receive a hair dye with perfect safety.
   IV. A predisposition test is only applied if a lesion or an inflammation of the scalp is present.
   The CORRECT answer is:

   A. I, II, III   B. II, III, IV   C. I only   D. I, II

6. Which of the following statements is (are) INCORRECT?
    I. A correct haircut will emphasize the attractive features and minimize the defects.
    II. Alcohol may be used for sterilizing clippers and shears.
    III. Bangs are best suited to a face with a high forehead.
    IV. The hair should be thinned before a marcel wave.
   The CORRECT answer is:

   A. I, II   B. II, III   C. I, II, IV   D. III only

7. Which of the following statements are CORRECT?
    I. Medium warm irons are employed for croquignole marcel waving.
    II. Start a croquignole marcel wave at the back of the head.
    III. In marcelling, the hair should be picked up with a comb, not with an iron.
    IV. Brushing and combing injure marcel waves.
   The CORRECT answer is:

   A. I, II   B. II, III   C. III, IV   D. I, IV

8. Which of the following statements is (are) INCORRECT?
    I. All systems of heat permanents are dependent upon moisture, alkali, contraction and expansion of the hair.
    II. Average healthy hair can be stretched about twenty percent of its own length.
    III. The hydroscopic quality of hair means its ability to absorb liquids.
    IV. When hair becomes too kinky from a permanent wave, hot oil treatments will help.
   The CORRECT answer is:

   A. I, II, III, IV   B. I, II, III
   C. II, III   D. None of the above

9. Which of the following statements is (are) CORRECT?
    I. An operator can discuss controversial issues in a beauty shop.
    II. The borrowing and lending of supplies and instruments are to be encouraged.
    III. Do not represent a marcel wave to be the same as a finger wave.
    IV. Inferior supplies can be substituted for standard goods.
   The CORRECT answer is:

   A. I, II, IV   B. I, II   C. III only   D. II, III, IV

10. Which of the following statements are INCORRECT?
    I. The appendages of the skin are the nails, hair, sebaceous and sudoriferous glands.
    II. Skin absorbs water readily.
    III. Health, age, and occupation have no influence on the texture of the skin.
    IV. Elimination is an important function of the skin.
   The CORRECT answer is:

   A. I, II   B. II, III   C. III, IV   D. I, IV

KEY (CORRECT ANSWERS)

1. D
2. A
3. D
4. D
5. D
6. D
7. B
8. D
9. C
10. B

SKIN & HAIR

EXAMINATION SECTION
TEST 1

DIRECTIONS: Each question consists of a statement. You are to indicate whether the statement is TRUE (T) or FALSE (F). *PRINT THE LETTER OF THE CORRECT ANSWER IN THE SPACE AT THE RIGHT.*

1. Heat contracts and cold dilates the skin. 1.____
2. The subcutaneous layer of the skin lies directly beneath the corium. 2.____
3. Corium, derma, and true skin are the same. 3.____
4. The skin is an external non-flexible covering of the body. 4.____
5. Dermatology is the study of the hair. 5.____
6. The skin is an organ of elimination. 6.____
7. The appendages of the skin are the nails, hair, sebaceous and sudoriferous glands. 7.____
8. Skin absorbs water readily. 8.____
9. Health, age, and occupation have no influence on the texture of the skin. 9.____
10. Elimination is an important function of the skin. 10.____
11. The skin is the organ of protection, absorption, elimination, heat regulation, respiration, and sensation. 11.____
12. Age has no effect on the elasticity of the skin. 12.____
13. The skin is the seat of the organ of touch. 13.____
14. The sebaceous glands secrete an oily substance called sebum. 14.____
15. The skin is the same thickness over the entire body. 15.____
16. Hair is an appendage of the nails. 16.____
17. Keratin is the horny substance of which hair is made. 17.____
18. The amount of pigment contained in the cortex determines the color of hair. 18.____
19. The blood vessels which nourish the hair are located in the hair papillae. 19.____
20. When the blood supply is cut off, the growth of hair is stopped. 20.____
21. Under normal conditions, hair grows about one-half inch a month. 21.____
22. Hair does not act as a protection. 22.____

23. Hair will grow again even though the papilla has been destroyed. 23____
24. The life of an eyelash is from four to five months. 24____
25. There are more hairs than follicles. 25____
26. After a hair has fallen out, a new hair will appear in about ten days. 26____
27. Hair has no blood vessels. 27____
28. The average life of a hair is from six to eight years. 28____
29. Canities can be cured by scalp treatments. 29____
30. The health of the hair depends on the health of the body. 30____

KEY (CORRECT ANSWERS)

1.	F	11.	T	21.	T
2.	T	12.	F	22.	F
3.	T	13.	T	23.	F
4.	F	14.	T	24.	T
5.	F	15.	F	25.	F
6.	T	16.	F	26.	F
7.	T	17.	T	27.	T
8.	F	18.	T	28.	F
9.	F	19.	T	29.	F
10.	T	20.	T	30.	T

TEST 2

DIRECTIONS: Each question consists of a statement. You are to indicate whether the statement is TRUE (T) or FALSE (F). *PRINT THE LETTER OF THE CORRECT ANSWER IN THE SPACE AT THE RIGHT.*

1. Acne is the most common skin disorder encountered in beauty shops.   1_____
2. Trichophytosis is the term applied to ringworm of the scalp.   2_____
3. Carbuncles are caused by a germ.   3_____
4. Anthrax may be treated by a beautician.   4_____
5. Regular alopecia treatments alternated with hot oil treatments will correct canities.   5_____
6. Scabies refers to head lice.   6_____
7. Tinea tonsurans is ringworm of the scalp.   7_____
8. Keloid is a wartlike growth commonly located in the eyelids.   8_____
9. A communicable disease is one that can be transmitted from person to person.   9_____
10. Alopecia areata is baldness at time of birth.   10_____
11. Pityriasis is the term applied to an excessively oily condition of the scalp.   11_____
12. Keratosis is a form of skin disease characterized by thinning epidermis.   12_____
13. An acute disease is one of long duration.   13_____
14. Canities is caused by fever, shock, nervousness, or senility.   14_____
15. Eczema is a contagious, parasitic disease of the skin, with crust formations, emitting a mousy odor.   15_____
16. Scalp hair is known as hypertrichosis.   16_____
17. Dermatitis venenata is the technical name for dye poisoning.   17_____
18. Trichorrhexis nodosa is the technical name for matted hair and can be treated with oil and vinegar.   18_____
19. Scars, ulcers, and fissures are known as secondary lesions.   19_____
20. Favus is not a disease of the hair, but of the hair follicle, and can be recognized by being gray in color, cup-like in shape, and having a mousy odor.   20_____
21. Symptoms of alopecia areata and alopecia senilis are the same.   21_____
22. Brushing is avoided in treatments for an oily scalp.   22_____
23. Pediculosis capitis is a scaly condition of the scalp.   23_____
24. Hair has no blood vessels.   24_____

25. A tight scalp is favorable to the growth of hair. 25____
26. The cause of eczema is unknown. 26____
27. Water is absorbed through the skin; oils and ointments are not. 27____
28. Eczema may be either an acute or chronic inflammation. 28____
29. The skin cannot function properly if the pores are clogged with dust, creams, or sebum. 29____
30. If the skin has a tendency to be very dry, soap should be used regularly. 30____
31. Erysipelas is an acute inflammation of the skin. 31____
32. The technical name for freckle is lentigo. 32____
33. Impetigo is not contagious. 33____
34. Sebum keeps the skin lubricated and pliable. 34____
35. Favus is a form of ringworm. 35____
36. Ringworm is a non-contagious disease. 36____
37. Erythema is a blue condition of the skin. 37____
38. Pityriasis is the presence of white scales in the hair and scalp. 38____
39. Pityriasis is the technical name for dandruff. 39____
40. The symptoms of pityriasis capitis are itching scalp, dry dandruff, and a partial loss of hair. 40____
41. Certain ingredients in cosmetics may cause a dermatitis. 41____
42. Hot packs are recommended for acne rosacea treatments. 42____
43. Dandruff is considered a disease if the shedding of scales is excessive. 43____
44. An albino is a person with an abnormal deficiency of pigment in the skin, hair, and eyes. 44____
45. Oily foods tend to aggravate a dry condition of the skin. 45____
46. Objective symptoms are visible and hence can be treated by a beautician. 46____
47. Acne rosacea affects the sweat glands. 47____
48. A macule is the same as a freckle. 48____
49. Anidrosis means the same as excessive perspiration. 49____
50. Fatty foods give the skin a sheen. 50____

KEY (CORRECT ANSWERS)

1. T	11. F	21. F	31. T	41. T
2. T	12. F	22. T	32. T	42. F
3. T	13. F	23. F	33. F	43. T
4. F	14. T	24. T	34. T	44. T
5. F	15. F	25. F	35. T	45. F
6. F	16. F	26. T	36. F	46. F
7. T	17. T	27. F	37. F	47. F
8. F	18. F	28. T	38. T	48. T
9. T	19. T	29. T	39. T	49. F
10. F	20. T	30. F	40. T	50. F

TEST 3

DIRECTIONS: Fill in the blanks with the MOST appropriate word from the set of words at the beginning of each section. Each answer may be used only once.

Questions 1-10.

corneum	water	corium	98.6
pliable	face	dermis	pigment
cuticle	tactile	tubular	sacular

1. The two main divisions of the skin are the epidermis or _____ and the dermis or _____ .

2. Scale-like cells which flake off are found in the stratum

3. The elastic cells of the dermis make the skin _____.

4. Papillae containing nerve fibres are called corpuscles .

5. Subcutaneous tissue is found below the _____.

6. The sweat glands are simple _____ glands and the oil glands are of the _____ type.

7. The color of the skin depends upon its blood supply and _____ content.

8. The skin regulates the temperature of the body to about _____ degrees Fahrenheit.

9. Oil glands are most numerous upon the.

10. Perspiration consists mainly of _____.

Questions 11-20.

sebum	blood	coarse	sebaceous
20	cold	silky	medulla
lips	short	scalp	bristly
fear	cortex	white	cuticle

11. No hair is found on the palms, soles, and _____.

12. Soft, long hair grows under the armpits and on the _____.

13. The eyebrows and eyelashes have _____ or _____ hair.

14. The three layers of the hair are the medulla, _____ , and _____.

15. The source of pigment in the hair is probably derived from color-forming substances in the _____ .

16. Air spaces and a lack of pigment makes the hair appear _____.

17. The arrector pilli muscle contracts because of _____ or _____.

18. Normal hair will stretch _____ percent of its natural length.

19. The _____ glands empty an oily substance at the mouth of the hair follicle called _____.

20. The operator should be able to differentiate between fine and _____, or wiry and _____ hair texture.

Questions 21-30.

parasitic	papule	pus	epidermis
chronic	disease	birth	circulatory
pimple	vesicle	bulla	deficiency

21. A yellow-green crust present in a skin disease is indicative of dried _____.

22. A congenital disease is present at the time of _____.

23. Primary skin lesions containing a serum-like fluid are _____ and _____.

24. A scale is a separated portion of the _____.

25. The opposite of health is _____.

26. Neglect to take care of an acute disease may result in the development of a _____ disease.

27. A constitutional disease spreads all over the body by way of the _____ system.

28. A _____ disease is due to the lack of an important element in the diet.

29. Scabies and ringworm are examples of _____ diseases.

30. A skin eruption common to adolescents is called a _____.

Questions 31-40.

papules	pits	comedones	milia
blackheads	face	lesions	nose
pustules	scars	digestive	dry
seborrhea	cyst	alkalies	tumor

31. Whiteheads are called _____, and blackheads are known as _____.

32. Comedones appear most frequently on the _____ and _____.

33. The skin lesions present in acne rosacea are _____ and _____.

34. A sign of asteatosis is a _____ skin.

35. A local condition of asteatosis may be caused by _____ in soaps.

36. Steatoma is a sebaceous _____ or _____.

37. An oily and shiny condition of the scalp, nose, and forehead is an indication of _____.

38. Disturbances of the _____ system is a contributory cause of acne.

39. The healing of skin lesions in acute hypertrophica may result in the formation of conspicuous _____ and _____ .

40. Abnormal changes in skin tissue formation are known as a _____ .

KEY (CORRECT ANSWERS)

1. cuticle, corium
2. corneum
3. pliable
4. tactile
5. dermis
6. tubular, sacular
7. pigment
8. 98.6
9. face
10. water
11. lips
12. scalp
13. short, bristly
14. cortex, cuticle
15. blood
16. white
17. fear, cold
18. 20
19. sebaceous, sebum
20. coarse, silky
21. pus
22. birth
23. bulla, vesicle
24. epidermis
25. disease
26. chronic
27. circulatory
28. deficiency
29. parasitic
30. pimple
31. milia, comedones
32. face, nose
33. papules, pustules
34. dry
35. alkalies
36. cyst, tumor
37. seborrhea
38. digestive
39. pits, scars
40. lesions

TEST 4

DIRECTIONS: In each set of questions, match the descriptions in Column *II* with the appropriate item in Column I. *PRINT THE LETTER OF THE CORRECT ANSWER IN THE SPACE AT THE RIGHT.*

Questions 1-6. Skin Lesions.

COLUMN I

1. Fissure
2. Papule
3. Tumor
4. Ulcer
5. Pustule
6. Scar

COLUMN II.

A. Open skin lesion having pus 1.____
B. Healed wound or ulcer 2.____
C. Inflamed elevation of the skin having pus 3.____
D. Pimple 4.____
E. Deep crack in the skin 5.____
F. External swelling 6.____

Questions 7-11. Forms of Acne.

7. Acne papulosa
8. Acne punctata
9. Acne induBrata
10. Acne rosacea
11. Acne pustulosa

A. Deep-seated hardened lesion 7.____
B. Congestion of the skin 8.____
C. Inflamed pimples 9.____
D. Pimples containing pus 10.____
E. Red papules containing blackheads 11.____

Questions 12-17. Diseases.

12. Anidrosis
13. Hyperidrosis
14. Miliary fever
15. Bromidrosis
16. Chromidrosis
17. Miliaria rubra

A. Foul smelling perspiration 12.____
B. Prickly heat 13.____
C. Discolored perspiration 14.____
D. Lack of perspiration 15.____
E. Sweating sickness 16.____
F. Excessive perspiration 17.____

Questions 18-24. Diseases.

18. Canities
19. Dermatitis

A. Dandruff 18.____
B. Dry type of dandruff 19.____

COLUMN I	COLUMN II	
20. Urticaria	C. Oily type of dandruff	20.____
21. Pityriasis steatoides	D. Grey hair	21.____
22. Pityriasis capitis	E. Inflammation of the skin	22.____
23. Furuncle	F. Eruption of itching wheals	23.____
24. Pityriasis	G. Boil	24.____

Questions 25-31. Diseases.

25. Psoriasis	A. Large boil	25.____
26. Syphilis	B. Vesicles resting on an inflamed base	26.____
27. Eczema	C. Malignant pustule	27.____
28. Carbuncle	D. Patches of dry, white scales	28.____
29. Pityriasis pilaris	D. Dry or moist lesions	29.____
30. Herpes simplex	E. Papules, pustules, tubercles, and ulcerations	30.____
31. Anthrax	F. Papules surrounding the hair follicles	31.____

Questions 32-38. Diseases.

32. Alopecia adnata	A. Ringworm of the scalp	32.____
33. Fragilitas crinium	B. Baldness in spots	33.____
34. Monilethrix	C. Head louse	34.____
35. Alopecia areata	D. Congenital baldness	35.____
36. Trichoptilosis	E. Beaded hair	36.____
37. Trichophytosis	F. Brittle hair	37.____
38. Pediculosis capitis	G. Split hair	38.____

Questions 39-45. Diseases.

39. Hypertrophy	A. Congenital absence of pigment in the body	39.____
40. Albinism	A. Malignant skin cancer	40.____
41. Chloasma	C. Abnormal growth of an organ	41.____

42.	Epithelioma	D. Defective skin pigmentation	42.____
43.	Leucoderma	E. Increased skin pigmentation	43.____
44.	Trachoma	F. Granulated eyelids	44.____
45.	Atrophy	G. Abnormal wasting of an organ or structure	45.____

KEY (CORRECT ANSWERS)

1.	E	11.	D	21.	C	31.	C	41.	E
2.	D	12.	D	22.	B	32.	D	42.	B
3.	F	13.	F	23.	G	33.	F	43.	D
4.	A	14.	E	24.	A	34.	E	44.	F
5.	C	15.	A	25.	D	35.	B	45.	G
6.	B	16.	C	26.	F	36.	G		
7.	C	17.	B	27.	E	37.	A		
8.	E	18.	D	28.	A	38.	C		
9.	A	19.	E	29.	G	39.	C		
10.	B	20.	F	30.	B	40.	A		

BACTERIOLOGY, HYGIENE, SANITATION & STERILIZATION
EXAMINATION SECTION
TEST 1

DIRECTIONS: Each question consists of a statement. You are to indicate whether the statement is TRUE (T) or FALSE (F). *PRINT THE LETTER OF THE CORRECT ANSWER IN THE SPACE AT THE RIGHT.*

1. Bacteriology is the science that treats infection. 1.____
2. Germs are microbes. 2.____
3. Immunity means freedom from disease. 3.____
4. Bacilli are rod-shaped organisms. 4.____
5. Pathogenic organisms produce disease. 5.____
6. All bacteria are harmful. 6.____
7. Freezing will destroy bacteria. 7.____
8. Moisture is essential for the growth of bacteria. 8.____
9. Parasites are harmful bacteria. 9.____
10. Parasites and saprophytes are the same. 10.____
11. Asepsis means absence of germ life. 11.____
12. Infection refers to the entrance of bacteria into the tissues. 12.____
13. Bacteria are found everywhere. 13.____
14. Bacteria will grow more favorably in sunlight than in dark, damp places. 14.____
15. A germ, a microbe, and a bacillus are the same. 15.____
16. Sepsis means the absence of septic matter, or freedom from pathogenic disease. 16.____
17. Non-pathogenic germs are not disease-producing. 17.____
18. Strong acids and alkalies, and intense heat will destroy bacteria. 18.____
19. Bacteria are the same as protozoa. 19.____
20. Bacteria are to be found where dirt and unsanitary conditions exist. 20.____
21. A saprophytic organism derives its nourishment from living matter, whereas a parasitic organism obtains its food from dead matter. 21.____
22. Bacterial spores are more difficult to destroy because they are more resistant to heat and chemical disinfectants. 22.____

23. The staphylococci bacteria produce boils and abscesses. 23.___
24. The poisonous products produced by bacteria are known as toxins. 24.___
25. Bacteria occur in three principal shapes. 25.___
26. Prophylaxis refers to the practice of definite protective measures to prevent disease. 26.___
27. Asepsis refers to the presence of germ life. 27.___
28. Skin infections can be transferred. 28.___
29. A deodorant is used for cuts and wounds. 29.___
30. An antiseptic is an agent that prevents the growth of germs. 30.___
31. An antiseptic is a germicide. 31.___
32. A germ is any microorganism. 32.___
33. Sepsis is poisoning due to putrescent material. 33.___
34. Infection is the destroying of harmful germs in the body. 34.___
35. A deodorant may or may not be a germicide. 35.___
36. Sanitation applies to public health only. 36.___
37. Toxic means poisonous. 37.___
38. Sanitation measures and hygiene do not prevent the spread of disease. 38.___
39. Spatulas are used for removing creams from jars only because this method is more convenient. 39.___
40. The head rest on each chair need not be changed for each patron. 40.___
41. When a comb is not in use, the operator may keep it in her pocket. 41.___
42. Lump alum may be used as a styptic. 42.___
43. The hands should always be washed before and after working on each patron. 43.___
44. Open powder boxes are prohibited in beauty parlors by the Board of Health. 44.___
45. The most important factors in the beauty shop are hygiene and sanitation. 45.___

KEY (CORRECT ANSWERS)

1. F	11. T	21. F	31. F	41. F
2. T	12. T	22. T	32. T	42. F
3. T	13. T	23. T	33. T	43. T
4. T	14. F	24. T	34. F	44. T
5. T	15. T	25. T	35. F	45. T
6. F	16. F	26. T	36. F	
7. F	17. T	27. F	37. T	
8. T	18. T	28. T	38. F	
9. T	19. F	29. F	39. F	
10. F	20. T	30. T	40. F	

TEST 2

DIRECTIONS: Each question consists of a statement. You are to indicate whether the statement is TRUE (T) or FALSE (F). *PRINT THE LETTER OF THE CORRECT ANSWER IN THE SPACE AT THE RIGHT.*

1. An object that has fallen to the floor should be treated as though it had already been used. 1.____
2. Sunshine is no good for health because it is capable of producing a sunburn. 2.____
3. When the resistance is high, bacteria can produce disease. 3.____
4. It is not worth the bother to cover coughs and sneezes with a handkerchief because it does no good anyhow. 4.____
5. It is dangerous to visit a sick person if there is a quarantine card on the door. 5.____
6. Infectious diseases could be controlled if no germs were passed from the sick to the well. 6.____
7. A communicable disease is one which cannot be avoided. 7.____
8. One way in which the body fights disease-producing bacteria is by forming substances in the blood which render harmless the poison produced by the bacteria. 8.____
9. The Board of Health regulations are to be followed only in times of epidemics. 9.____
10. To be sterilized, water must be heated to 150 degrees Fahrenheit. 10.____
11. Hydrogen peroxide is used as an antiseptic. 11.____
12. Lysol is used in 2% solutions as an antiseptic; 10% solution as a disinfectant. 12.____
13. Vapors are used to keep objects sterile. 13.____
14. Any article that cannot withstand heat may be sterilized by chemicals. 14.____
15. Boric acid solution is used as a germicide. 15.____
16. Instruments that cannot be boiled may be sterilized by dipping them into 40% alcohol. 16.____
17. A disinfectant and a germicide are the same, both being agents which destroy germs. 17.____
18. Infection may be caused by improper use of the tweezers. 18.____
19. Alcohol is the best antiseptic recommended for shop use. 19.____
20. Metal instruments, glass, towels, and linens may be sterilized by boiling for five minutes. 20.____
21. Phenol is also known as carbolic acid. 21.____
22. Rubber combs and hair brushes are sterilized by boiling. 22.____
23. Electric appliances may be sterilized with alcohol used on a cotton pledget. 23.____
24. Glycerin added to formalin will prevent the rusting of instruments. 24.____

25. An object is sterile when it is free from living organisms. 25.____
26. Disinfectants may be used on the human body. 26.____
27. Formaldehyde is a germicide. 27.____
28. 60% alcohol may be used on the skin as an antiseptic. 28.____
29. Combs and brushes are sufficiently sterilized by placing them in a vapor sterilizer. 29.____
30. Adding a small quantity of baking soda to the water in which instruments are boiled will keep them bright. 30.____
31. Complete sterilization is essential in order to destroy all germs and prevent infection. 31.____
32. When using alcohol as a germicide, it should be heated. 32.____
33. To insure complete sterilization, articles must be boiled for at least twenty minutes. 33.____
34. If peroxide solution is kept in a warm place, its strength remains the same. 34.____
35. A dry sterilizer requires the use of dry steam. 35.____
36. Chemical sterilization employs heat and boiling water. 36.____
37. A dry sterilizer is intended to sterilize dirty objects. 37.____
38. Objects kept in the pocket remain sterile. 38.____
39. Formalin is a 40% solution of formaldehyde gas in water. 39.____
40. Soiled towels can be kept on the counter. 40.____

KEY (CORRECT ANSWERS)

1.	T	11.	T	21.	T	31.	T
2.	F	12.	T	22.	F	32.	F
3.	F	13.	T	23.	T	33.	T
4.	F	14.	T	24.	T	34.	F
5.	T	15.	F	25.	T	35.	F
6.	T	16.	F	26.	F	36.	F
7.	F	17.	T	27.	T	37.	F
8.	T	18.	T	28.	T	38.	F
9.	F	19.	F	29.	F	39.	T
10.	F	20.	F	30.	T	40.	F

TEST 3

DIRECTIONS: Fill in the blanks with the MOST appropriate word from the set of words at the beginning of each section. Each answer may be used only once.

Questions 1-11.

infection	dead	typhoid	general
microscope	spores	immunity	direct
beneficial	harmful	diphtheria	living
reproduce	grow	bacteria	indirect

1. Bacteria become visible to the eye when observed under a _____.
2. Pathogenic bacteria are _____, whereas non-pathogenic bacteria are _____.
3. Parasites thrive best on _____ matter as food.
4. Saprophytes can make use of _____ matter as food.
5. Without food, bacteria will not _____ and _____.
6. In the presence of unfavorable conditions, the anthrax bacilli will form _____.
7. A _____ infection involves the blood circulation from which bacteria are carried to all parts of the body.
8. A contagious disease is spread from one person to another by _____ and _____ contact.
9. First aid treatment for cuts and wounds helps to prevent _____.
10. _____ is the ability of the body to fight pathogenic bacteria.
11. A person who has had _____ or _____ may be a disease carrier.

Questions 12-20.

sepsis	asepsis	16	dark
spores	alcohol	cool	100
steam	dilution	dry	212

12. Boiling water destroys all bacteria except _____.
13. The temperature of boiling water is _____ degrees Centigrade and _____ degrees Fahrenheit.
14. Spore-forming bacteria can be destroyed by exposure to _____ at 15 lbs. pressure.
15. _____ heat is rarely used in the beauty shop.
16. A disinfectant solution can be changed to an antiseptic by _____.
17. The surface of an electrical appliance can be sterilized with cotton dampened in _____.
18. One pint contains _____ ounces.
19. The opposite of sepsis is _____
20. Chemicals should be stored in closed containers in a _____, dry and _____ place.

Questions 21-30.

infectious	towels	before	closed
sterilized	fingers	open	cabinet
sleeping	cotton	water	dry
spatula	food	cups	eating

21. The local government protects the health of the community by ensuring a wholesome _____ and _____ supply. 21._____

22. Operators or patrons with _____ diseases are a source of contagion to others. 22._____

23. The best time to have the beauty shop swept is _____ patrons arrive. 23._____

24. It is unsanitary to use a beauty shop for _____ or _____ purposes. 24._____

25. All refuse should be kept in _____ containers. 25._____

26. The washroom should be provided with soap, _____, and _____ for individual use. 26._____

27. Objects dropped on the floor should not be used again unless _____. 27._____

28. Sterilized objects should be kept in a _____ or _____ sterilizer before being used. 28._____

29. Never use the _____ to remove cosmetics from a container. 29._____

30. Only a clean _____ or sterile _____ should be used for the removal or application of cosmetics. 30._____

Questions 31-38.

DIRECTIONS: In each set of questions, match the descriptions in Column II with the appropriate item in Column I. *PRINT THE LETTER OF THE CORRECT ANSWER IN THE SPACE AT THE RIGHT.*

COLUMN I		COLUMN II	
31. Sprilla	A.	Round-shaped micro-organisms	31._____
32. Staphylococci	B.	Spore producers	32._____
33. Bacilli	C.	Disease producers	33._____
34. Streptococci	D.	Rod-shaped micro-organisms	34._____
35. Cocci	E.	Grow in cold temperatures	35._____
36. Tetanus bacilli	F.	Grows in bunches or clusters	36._____
37. Pathogenic bacteria	G.	Grows in chains	37._____
38. Psychrophilic bacteria	H.	Corkscrew-shaped micro-organisms	38._____

COLUMN I	COLUMN II	
Questions 39-45.		
39. 60% grain alcohol	A. Styptic	39.___
40. 25% formalin solution	B. In dry sterilizer	40.___
41. 5% formalin solution	C. Mild antiseptic	41.___
42. Sodium carbonate	D. Sterilize skin	42.___
43. Borax and formalin	E. Sterilize instruments	43.___
44. Boric acid solution	F. Keeps instruments bright in boiling water	44.___
45. Powdered alum		45.___
	G. Rinse hands	

KEY (CORRECT ANSWERS)

1. microscope
2. harmful, beneficial
3. living
4. dead
5. grow, reproduce

6. spores
7. general
8. direct, indirect
9. infection
10. immunity

11. typhoid, diphtheria
12. spores
13. 100, 212
14. steam
15. dry

16. dilution
17. alcohol
18. 16
19. asepsis
20. cool, dark

21. food, water
22. infectious
23. before
24. eating, sleeping
25. closed

26. towels, cups
27. sterilized
28. dry, cabinet
29. fingers
30. spatula, cotton

31. H
32. F
33. D
34. G
35. A

36. B
37. C
38. E
39. D
40. E

41. G
42. F
43. B
44. C
45. A

ANATOMY & PHYSIOLOGY
EXAMINATION SECTION
TEST 1

DIRECTIONS: Each question consists of a statement. You are to indicate whether the statement is TRUE (T) or FALSE (F). *PRINT THE LETTER OF THE CORRECT ANSWER IN THE SPACE AT THE RIGHT.*

1. A cell is a minute mass of protoplasm containing a nucleus. 1.____
2. Protoplasm is a jelly-like substance, present in all living matter. 2.____
3. Protoplasm is a lifeless matter. 3.____
4. Connective tissue serves to unite, support, and bind together other tissues. 4.____
5. Tendon is one of the varieties of connective tissue. 5.____
6. Muscle tissue is composed of cells modified to form fibers. 6.____
7. Organs are groups of systems. 7.____
8. Anabolism is the chemical change which involves the breaking down process within the cells. 8.____
9. Catabolism is the chemical change which involves the building up process within the cells. 9.____
10. Metabolism is the chemical change which involves the building up and breaking down process within the cells. 10.____
11. Nerves can be both motor and sensory. 11.____
12. Nerves can be stimulated by chemicals, massage, electricity, and heat. 12.____
13. Heat causes contraction of nerves. 13.____
14. Nervous fatigue is more prostrating than physical fatigue. 14.____
15. The cerebrum is the chief portion of the brain. 15.____
16. Nerves which carry information as to heat, cold, pressure, touch, and pain are called sensory nerves. 16.____
17. Sensory nerves and efferent nerves are the same. 17.____
18. The nervous system consists of cerebrospinal nervous system and the sympathetic nervous system. 18.____
19. The medulla oblongata is the bony structure protecting the brain. 19.____
20. Ganglia is a disease of the nervous system. 20.____

21. Nerves are a system of communication to all parts of the body. 21.___
22. Nerves have their origin in the brain. 22.___
23. Motor nerves carry impulses to the brain. 23.___
24. There are thirty-one pairs of cranial nerves. 24.___
25. There are fifteen pairs of spinal nerves. 25.___
26. The trifacial nerve is the smallest of all the cranial nerves. 26.___
27. The facial nerve is both motor and sensory. 27.___
28. The optic nerve is the nerve of the special sense of smell. 28.___
29. The mental nerve supplies lower lip and chin. 29.___
30. The temporal nerve supplies the frontalis muscle. 30.___
31. Mandibular nerve supplies the muscles of mastication. 31.___
32. The seventh pair of cranial nerves and the trifacial are the same. 32.___
33. The facial nerve supplies the muscles of expression in the face. 33.___
34. The lesser occipital nerve is a motor nerve. 34.___
35. The temporal is both sensory and motor nerve. 35.___
36. The blood vascular system controls the circulation of blood. 36.___
37. The walls of the arteries are elastic. 37.___
38. The veins lie deeper than the arteries. 38.___
39. General circulation is also known as systemic circulation. 39.___
40. Capillaries have thinner walls than arteries and veins. 40.___
41. About one-twentieth of the body weight is blood. 41.___
42. The heart is called an involuntary muscle. 42.___
43. Hemoglobin is the coloring matter of the red corpuscles. 43.___
44. Systemic circulation carries the blood from the heart to the lungs. 44.___
45. The blood carries oxygen to the cells and carbon dioxide from them. 45.___
46. Arteries carry the impure blood. 46.___
47. Study of the vascular system includes blood and lymph. 47.___
48. Red corpuscles attack germs that enter the blood. 48.___

49. Arteries, veins, and capillaries are tubular vessels.   49.____

50. A leucocyte is a red corpuscle.   50.____

51. Leucocyte is the technical term for white blood corpuscle.   51.____

52. Cardiac is the technical term for heart.   52.____

53. Circulation may be stimulated by physical and chemical means.   53.____

54. Lymph reaches parts of the body not reached by the blood.   54.____

55. The occipital artery supplies the forehead.   55.____

KEY (CORRECT ANSWERS)

1. T	11. T	21. T	31. T	41. T	51. T
2. T	12. T	22. T	32. F	42. T	52. T
3. F	13. F	23. F	33. T	43. T	53. T
4. T	14. T	24. F	34. F	44. F	54. T
5. T	15. T	25. F	35. T	45. T	55. F
6. T	16. T	26. F	36. T	46. F	
7. F	17. F	27. T	37. T	47. T	
8. F	18. T	28. F	38. F	48. F	
9. F	19. F	29. T	39. T	49. T	
10. T	20. F	30. F	40. T	50. F	

TEST 2

DIRECTIONS: Each question consists of a statement. You are to indicate whether the statement is TRUE (T) or FALSE (F). *PRINT THE LETTER OF THE CORRECT ANSWER IN THE SPACE AT THE RIGHT.*

1. The technical term for bone is os. 1.____
2. Bone is composed of animal and mineral matter. 2.____
3. Bone is pink externally and white internally. 3.____
4. The external membrane covering bone is called pericardium. 4.____
5. The shafts of long bones are solid. 5.____
6. The two types of bone tissue are dense and cancellous. 6.____
7. Dense tissue forms the interior of bone and cancellous tissue the exterior of bone. 7.____
8. The cranium is the bony case which encases the brain. 8.____
9. The skull is the technical term given the skeleton of the head. 9.____
10. The skull includes the cranial and the facial bones. 10.____
11. Red and white corpuscles are derived from red and yellow bone marrow. 11.____
12. Articulations and joints are the same. 12.____
13. Periosteum is a disease of the bone. 13.____
14. The entire skeleton consists of 106 bones. 14.____
15. The ends of bones are covered with cartilage. 15.____
16. The occipital bone is located at the crown. 16.____
17. The parietal bones are located at the forehead. 17.____
18. Maxillae are bones which form the upper jaw. 18.____
19. The cranium consists of ten bones. 19.____
20. The ethmoid is a small bone of the ear. 20.____
21. The malar bones form the prominence of the cheeks. 21.____
22. The turbinal bones form the eyesockets. 22.____
23. The mandible is the bone of the lower jaw. 23.____
24. The frontal bone forms the cheeks. 24.____
25. The temporal bones are located in the ear region. 25.____

26. Cartilage is sometimes called gristle.   26.____
27. Muscles are the active organs of locomotion.   27.____
28. The heart muscles are described as non-striated.   28.____
29. Voluntary muscles are controlled by the will.   29.____
30. The cardiac is a voluntary muscle.   30.____
31. Aponeurosis is a fibrous membrane.   31.____
32. Muscles may be stimulated by massage, heat, and electric current.   32.____
33. Striated muscles are involuntary.   33.____
34. Muscles are always connected directly to bones.   34.____
35. The muscular system relies upon the skeletal and nervous systems for its activities.   35.____
36. Contractility means able to be stretched or extended.   36.____
37. Muscles clothe and support the framework of the body.   37.____
38. The epicranius includes both the occipitalis and frontalis muscles.   38.____
39. The frontalis causes the forehead to wrinkle.   39.____
40. The occipitalis draws the scalp backward.   40.____
41. The levator palpebrae is the muscle that dilates the nostrils.   41.____
42. The orbicularis oculi is the muscle that surrounds the mouth.   42.____
43. The orbicularis oris is the muscle that surrounds the eye.   43.____
44. The trapezius muscle is a muscle of the face.   44.____
45. The temporalis is a muscle of mastication.   45.____
46. The masseter is a muscle that raises the lower jaw against the upper jaw.   46.____
47. The risorius is a muscle that retracts the angle of the mouth.   47.____
48. The sterno-cleido-mastoid muscle depresses and rotates the head.   48.____
49. The platysma is the large muscle in the back of the neck.   49.____
50. The trapezius is the muscle that raises the lower jaw.   50.____
51. The corrugator causes vertical wrinkles at the root of the nose.   51.____
52. The arrector pili is one of the largest muscles of the face.   52.____
53. The epicranius controls the movements of the scalp and wrinkles the forehead.   53.____

54. Muscles of the mouth are supplied by the facial nerve. 54.___

55. The deltoid muscle is a muscle of the lower back. 55.___

KEY (CORRECT ANSWERS)

1. T	11. T	21. T	31. T	41. F	51. T
2. T	12. T	22. F	32. T	42. F	52. F
3. F	13. F	23. T	33. F	43. F	53. T
4. F	14. F	24. F	34. F	44. F	54. T
5. F	15. T	25. T	35. T	45. T	55. F
6. T	16. F	26. T	36. F	46. T	
7. F	17. F	27. T	37. T	47. T	
8. T	18. T	28. F	38. T	48. T	
9. T	19. F	29. T	39. T	49. F	
10. T	20. F	30. F	40. T	50. F	

TEST 3

DIRECTIONS: Fill in the blanks with the MOST appropriate word from the set of words at the beginning of each section. Each answer may be used only once.

Questions 1-10.

tissues	circulatory	skeletal	growth
tendons	reproduction	muscular	nervous
cells	respiratory	organs	glandular

1. Fibrous tissues which connect muscles with bones are called _____.   1._____
2. The cytoplasm of the cell is essential for _____ and the nucleus is essential for _____.   2._____
3. Tissues are combinations of similar _____.   3._____
4. Organs are groups of two or more _____.   4._____
5. Systems are groups of _____.   5._____
6. The physical foundation of the body is the _____ system.   6._____
7. Contraction and movement are characteristic of _____ tissue.   7._____
8. The _____ system coordinates bodily functions.   8._____
9. The _____ system carries food to tissues and waste products from them.   9._____
10. The _____ system purifies the blood by the removal of carbon dioxide gas and the intake of oxygen gas.   10._____

Questions 11-20.

ligaments	flat	gristle	cancellous
mineral	dense	strength	immovable
sphenoid	shape	lacrimal	periosteum
cartilage	muscle	marrow	endosteum

11. Bone is composed of two-thirds _____ matter.   11._____
12. Bones are covered by a thin membrane known as _____.   12._____
13. The functions of the bones are to give _____ and _____ to the body.   13._____
14. The ends of bones are covered with _____.   14._____
15. The skull has _____ shaped bones and _____ joints.   15._____
16. The bone which joins all the bones of the cranium is the _____.   16._____
17. The _____ bones are the smallest and most fragile bones of the face.   17._____
18. Another name for cartilage is _____.   18._____

19. _____ are strong flexible or fibrous tissue that help to hold the bones together at the joints.

20. There are two types of bone tissue, namely _____ and _____.

Questions 21-28.

tendons	fascia	trapezius	aponeurosis
500	will	gristle	voluntary
fixed	myology	movable	mandible

21. The origin of a muscle refers to the more _____ attachment; whereas the insertion of a muscle applies to the more _____ attachment.

22. There are about _____ muscles in the body.

23. Muscles are joined to bones by means of glistening cords called _____.

24. A flat expanded tendon which serves to connect one muscle with another is called an _____.

25. A _____ is a membrane covering and separating layers of muscles.

26. The muscle which draws the head backward and sideways is the _____.

27. Voluntary muscles are put into action by the _____.

28. _____ is the study of the muscles.

Questions 29-38.

brain	cerebrospinal	digestion	blood
occipital	involuntary	maxillary	glands
muscles	sympathetic	trochlear	nerve
olfactory	mandibular	voluntary	accessory

29. Every muscle has its own _____ and _____ supply.

30. Sensory nerves carry impulses from the sense organs to the _____.

31. Motor nerves carry impulses from the brain to the _____.

32. The cerebrospinal nervous system controls the movements of _____ muscles.

33. The sympathetic nervous system controls the movements of _____ muscles.

34. The _____ nerve controls the movement of the superior oblique muscle of the eye.

35. The posterior auricular nerve supplies the _____ muscle.

36. The three main branches of the trigeminal nerve are the _____, _____, and _____.

37. The _____ system is under the control of the conscious will.   37._____

38. The _____ system controls the functions of circulation, digestion, and secretion of _____.   38._____

Questions 39-50.

superior vena cava	filtration	chest	oxygen
pulmonary veins	arteries	lungs	atrium
pulmonary arteries	ventricle	aorta	inferior
capillaries	bacteria	auricle	liquid

39. The main artery of the body is the _____.   39._____

40. _____ connect the smaller arteries with the veins.   40._____

41. The pulmonary circulation is the blood traveling to and from the heart and _____.   41._____

42. The red blood corpuscles carry _____ to the cells.   42._____

43. White blood cells destroy and devour harmful _____.   43._____

44. Plasma is the _____ portion of the blood.   44._____

45. Lymph is derived from the plasma of the blood by _____.   45._____

46. The upper chamber of the heart is called _____ or _____ and the lower chamber is known as a _____.   46._____

47. Vessels which carry blood from the extremities to the heart are called _____.   47._____

48. Vessels which carry blood from the heart to the lungs are called _____.   48._____

49. Vessels which carry blood from the lungs to the heart are called _____.   49._____

50. Vessels which carry blood from the heart to all parts of the body are called _____.   50._____

KEY (CORRECT ANSWERS)

1. tendons
2. growth, reproduction
3. cells
4. tissues
5. organs

6. skeletal
7. muscular
8. nervous
9. circulatory
10. respiratory

11. mineral
12. periosteum
13. strength, shape
14. cartilage
15. flat, immovable

16. sphenoid
17. lacrimal
18. gristle
19. ligaments
20. dense, cancellous

21. fixed, movable
22. 500
23. tendons
24. aponeurosis
25. fascia

26. trapezius
27. will
28. myology
29. nerve, blood
30. brain

31. muscles
32. voluntary
33. involuntary
34. trochlear
35. occipital

36. ophthalmic, maxillary, mandibular
37. cerebrospinal
38. sympathetic, glands
39. aorta
40. capillaries

41. lungs
42. oxygen
43. bacteria
44. liquid
45. filtration

46. atrium, auricle, ventricle
47. inferior, superior
48. pulmonary arteries
49. pulmonary veins
50. arteries

TEST 4

DIRECTIONS: In each set of questions, match the descriptions in Column II with the appropriate item in Column I. *PRINT THE LETTER OF THE CORRECT ANSWER IN THE SPACE AT THE RIGHT.*

COLUMN I	COLUMN II	

Questions 1-5. Joints.

1. Condyloid	A. Spine	1.____
2. Hinge	B. Neck	2.____
3. Gliding	C. Wrist	3.____
4. Ball and socket	D. Hips	4.____
5. Pivot	E. Elbows	5.____

Questions 6-11. Cranial Bones.

6. Frontal	A. Between the orbits	6.____
7. Sphenoid	B. Ear region	7.____
8. Occipital	C. Crown of head	8.____
9. Ethmoid	D. Forehead	9.____
10. Temporal	E. Base of skull	10.____
11. Parietal	F. Base or brain and back of orbit	11.____

Questions 12-16. Facial Bones.

12. Malar	A. Cheek	12.____
13. Mandible	B. Septum of nose	13.____
14. Nasal	C. Upper jaw	14.____
15. Maxillae	D. Bridge of nose	15.____
16. Vomer	E. Lower jaw	16.____

2 (#4)

COLUMN I	COLUMN II	
Questions 17-23. Terms.		
17. Anterior	A. On the side	17.___
18. Superior	B. Situated lower	18.___
19. Posterior	C. Situated higher	19.___
20. Inferior	D. In front of	20.___
21. Levator	E. In back of	21.___
22. Lateral	F. That which enlarges	22.___
23. Dilator	G. That which lifts	23.___
Questions 24-29. Location of Muscles.		
24. Orbicularis oris	A. Eyeball	24.___
25. Epicranius	B. Ear	25.___
26. Rectus superior	C. Neck	26.___
27. Procerus	D. Scalp	27.___
28. Superior auricular	E. Mouth	28.___
29. Platysma	F. Nose	29.___
Questions 30-37. Function of Muscles.		
30. Orbicularis oculi	A. Opens eye	30.___
31. Orbicularis oris	B. Rotates head	31.___
32. Levator palpebrae	C. Rotates eyeball	32.___
33. Rectus muscle	D. Wrinkles forehead	33.___
34. Depressor septi	E. Contracts cheeks	34.___
35. Buccinator	F. Opens and closes mouth	35.___
36. Sterno-cleido-mastoideus	G. Closes eye	36.___
37. Epicranius	H. Contracts nostrils	37.___

COLUMN I

Questions 38-44. Function of Nerves.

38. Olfactory
39. Trigeminal
40. Glossopharyngeal
41. Accessory
42. Optic
43. Oculomotor
44. Auditory

Questions 45-52. Distribution of Nerves.

45. Infraorbital
46. Mental
47. Supraorbital
48. Palpebral
49. Lingual
50. Nasociliary
51. Auriculo-temporal
52. Ciliary

Questions 53-59. Terms.

53. Atrium
54. Fibrinogen
55. Hemoglobin
56. Lymphatics
57. Ventricle
58. Veins
59. Pericardium

COLUMN II

A. Sensory nerve of sight
B. Sensory-motor nerve of face and muscles of mastication
C. Sensory nerve of hearing
D. Controls movement of eyes
E. Sensory nerve of smell
F. Sensory-motor nerve of taste
G. Controls movement of trapezius muscle

38. _____
39. _____
40. _____
41. _____
42. _____
43. _____
44. _____

A. Upper eyelid and forehead
B. Cornea and iris
C. Lower lip and chin
D. Nose
E. Nose and upper lip
F. Lower eyelids
G. Side of scalp
H. Tongue

45. _____
46. _____
47. _____
48. _____
49. _____
50. _____
51. _____
52. _____

A. A membrane enclosing the heart
B. Vessels which convey lymph
C. Upper cavity of the heart
D. Blood vessels containing valves
E. Coloring matter of red blood corpuscles
F. A substance essential for coagulation of blood
G. Lower cavity of the heart

53. _____
54. _____
55. _____
56. _____
57. _____
58. _____
59. _____

COLUMN I	COLUMN II	

Questions 60-65. Distribution of Blood Vessels.

60. Orbital	A. Back of ears and scalp	60.___
61. Septal	B. Deeper portion of face	61.___
62. Posterior auricular	C. Neck and back part of scalp	62.___
63. Superior labial	D. Nostrils	63.___
64. Occipital	E. Eye cavity	64.___
65. Internal maxillary	F. Upper lip	65.___

KEY (CORRECT ANSWERS)

1.	C	16.	B	31.	F	46.	C	61.	D
2.	E	17.	D	32.	A	47.	A	62.	A
3.	A	18.	C	33.	C	48.	F	63.	F
4.	D	19.	E	34.	H	49.	H	64.	C
5.	B	20.	B	35.	E	50.	D	65.	B
6.	D	21.	G	36.	B	51.	G		
7.	F	22.	A	37.	D	52.	B		
8.	E	23.	F	38.	E	53.	C		
9.	A	24.	E	39.	B	54.	F		
10.	B	25.	D	40.	F	55.	E		
11.	C	26.	A	41.	G	56.	B		
12.	A	27.	F	42.	A	57.	G		
13.	E	28.	B	43.	D	58.	D		
14.	D	29.	C	44.	C	59.	A		
15.	C	30.	G	45.	E	60.	E		

EXAMINATION SECTION
TEST 1

DIRECTIONS: Each question or incomplete statement is followed by several suggested answers or completions. Select the one that BEST answers the question or completes the statement. *PRINT THE LETTER OF THE CORRECT ANSWER IN THE SPACE AT THE RIGHT.*

1. The basic functional unit of life is called a

   A. nerve
   B. cell
   C. molecule
   D. tendon

   1._____

2. The study of the organization of tissues is called

   A. cytology
   B. embryology
   C. histology
   D. anatomy

   2._____

3. Which of the following organelles plays a critical role in energy production in a eukaryotic cell?

   A. mitochondria
   B. Golgi apparatus
   C. nucleus
   D. ribosome

   3._____

4. Which of the following is NOT a structure outside the cell wall?

   A. capsule
   B. flagella
   C. fimbriae
   D. endoplasmic reticulum

   4._____

5. The most conspicuous organelle in a eukaryotic cell is the

   A. mitochondria
   B. nucleus
   C. Golgi apparatus
   D. ribosome

   5._____

6. The region of the human body which contains the heart, lung, esophagus, thymus and pleura is the

A. abdomen
B. thorax
C. pelvis
D. neck

6._____

7. The thyroid is part of the _____ system.

A. circulatory
B. respiratory
C. endocrine
D. lymphatic

7._____

8. Which of the following is an autoimmune disorder whereby the body's own immune system reacts with the thyroid tissues in an attempt to destroy it?

A. postpartum thyroiditis
B. Hashimoto's disease
C. hypothyroidism
D. hyperthyroidism

8._____

9. The system of the body that contributes to balance and sense of spatial orientation is the _____ system.

A. vestibular
B. nervous
C. musculoskeletal
D. integumenary

9._____

10. An electrically excitable cell that processes and transmits information by electrical and chemical signaling is called a

A. synapse
B. tendon
C. neuron
D. tissue

10._____

11. How many bones does the hand contain?

A. 14
B. 22
C. 27
D. 31

11._____

12. Contractile tissue of animals derived from the mesodermal layer of embryonic germ cell is

A. tendon
B. muscle
C. bone
D. joint

13. The body part that forms the supporting structure of a human being is the

A. tendon
B. muscle
C. dermis
D. skeleton

14. The longest bone in the human body is the

A. patella
B. ulna
C. humerus
D. femur

15. The part of the body made up by the cervical, thoracic, and lumbar vertebrae is the

A. head
B. spine
C. arm
D. leg

16. All of the following are facial bones EXCEPT

A. phalanges
B. frontal
C. parietal
D. mandible

17. The human body is composed of approximately _____ muscles.

A. 125
B. 350
C. 640
D. 710

18. The science of the mechanical, physical, bioelectrical and biochemical functions of humans in good health, their organs and the cells of which they are composed is

A. cytology
B. anatomy
C. physiology
D. embryology

18._____

19. The organ system used for breathing and composed of the pharynx, larynx, trachea, bronchi, lungs and diaphragm is the _____ system.

A. respiratory
B. digestive
C. lymphatic
D. vestibular

19._____

20. The smallest of the body's blood vessels are the

A. veins
B. arteries
C. capillaries
D. villi

20._____

21. Arteries that carry deoxygenated blood to the heart and towards the lungs, where carbon dioxide is exchanged for oxygen are

A. pulmonary arteries
B. systemic arteries
C. arterioles
D. capillaries

21._____

22. An enclosed cable-like bundle of peripheral axons is called a

A. nucleus
B. vein
C. bone
D. nerve

22._____

23. The scientific generic name for a blood cell is a

A. erythrocyte
B. leukocyte
C. hematocyte
D. thrombocyte

23._____

24. Platelets have a lifetime of about 24._____

A. 24 hours
B. 1 day
C. 10 days
D. 1 month

25. Endocrine glands secrete 25._____

A. sweat
B. hormones
C. oils
D. enzymes

KEY (CORRECT ANSWERS)

1. B	6. B	11. C	16. A	21. A
2. C	7. C	12. B	17. C	22. D
3. A	8. B	13. D	18. C	23. C
4. D	9. A	14. D	19. A	24. C
5. B	10. C	15. B	20. C	25. B

TEST 2

DIRECTIONS: Each question or incomplete statement is followed by several suggested answers or completions. Select the one that BEST answers the question or completes the statement. *PRINT THE LETTER OF THE CORRECT ANSWER IN THE SPACE AT THE RIGHT.*

1. A group of unicellular organisms having characteristics of both plant and animals are

    A. fungi
    B. bacteria
    C. parasites
    D. mites

1._____

2. A small infectious agent that can replicate only inside the cells of living organisms is a

    A. spore
    B. dermophyte
    C. virus
    D. parasite

2._____

3. Bacteria can be found

    A. in the ocean
    B. on land
    C. in soil
    D. everywhere on Earth

3._____

4. There are approximately _____ bacteria on earth.

    A. 500 thousand
    B. 500 million
    C. 500 billion
    D. 5 nonillion

4._____

5. All of the following are diseases caused by pathogenic bacteria EXCEPT

    A. cholera
    B. syphilis
    C. influenza
    D. leprosy

5._____

6. Bacteria are now regarded as

    A. prokaryotes
    B. eukaryotes
    C. plants
    D. animals

6._____

7. The first bacteria to be discovered were 7._____

   A. round
   B. rod-shaped
   C. square
   D. triangular

8. Bacteria lack a(n) 8._____

   A. nucleus
   B. Golgi apparatus
   C. Endoplasmic reticulum
   D. all of the above

9. Rigid protein structures that are used for motility are 9._____

   A. flagella
   B. fimbriae
   C. pili
   D. macrophages

10. What kind of energy do phototrophs use? 10._____

    A. sunlight
    B. organic compounds
    C. inorganic compound
    D. oxygen

11. The first phase of bacterial growth is called the _____ phase. 11._____

    A. log
    B. lag
    C. stationary
    D. repair

12. Blood-sucking insects that transmit disease from one organism to another are known as 12._____

    A. viruses
    B. bacteriae
    C. vectors
    D. parasites

13. Generally, viruses are _____ bacteria. 13._____

    A. smaller than
    B. larger than
    C. the same size as
    D. more abundant than

14. The process by which a strand of DNA is broken and then joined to the end of a different DNA molecule is called

   A. genetic drift
   B. antigenic shift
   C. genetic recombination
   D. viral evolution

14._____

15. The process in which the viral capsid is removed is called

   A. attachment
   B. penetration
   C. uncoating
   D. replication

15._____

16. A process that kills the cell by bursting its membrane and cell wall if present is called

   A. lysis
   B. budding
   C. penetration
   D. modification

16._____

17. Replication of RNA viruses usually takes place in the

   A. nucleus
   B. cytoplasm
   C. Golgi apparatus
   D. endoplasmic reticulum

17._____

18. The _____ virus can cause cancer.

   A. herpes
   B. Epstein-Barr
   C. papilloma
   D. human immunodeficiency

18._____

19. All of the following are common human diseases caused by viruses EXCEPT

   A. influenza
   B. chicken pox
   C. cold sores
   D. strep throat

19._____

20. A biological term that describes a state of having sufficient biological defenses to avoid infection, disease or other unwanted biological invasion is called

   A. bacteriology
   B. immunity
   C. inoculation
   D. safety

20._____

21. T cells belong to a group of white blood cells called

   A. thrombocytes
   B. lymphocytes
   C. leukocytes
   D. erythrocytes

21._____

22. A substance that contains an antigen and is used to artificially acquire active immunity is known as a

   A. platelet
   B. vaccine
   C. serum
   D. venom

22._____

23. Parasitism is a type of _____ relationship between organisms of different species where one organism, the parasite, benefits at the expense of the other, the host.

   A. moral
   B. monogamous
   C. symbiotic
   D. mellifluous

23._____

24. Parasites that live on the surface of the host are called

   A. ectoparasites
   B. endoparasites
   C. epiparasites
   D. brood parasites

24._____

25. The most important measure for preventing the spread of pathogens is effective

   A. vaccination
   B. protective equipment
   C. hand washing
   D. isolation

25._____

KEY (CORRECT ANSWERS)

1. B	6. A	11. B	16. A	21. B
2. C	7. B	12. C	17. B	22. B
3. D	8. D	13. A	18. C	23. C
4. D	9. A	14. C	19. D	24. A
5. C	10. A	15. C	20. B	25. C

GLOSSARY OF COSMETOLOGY

Compiled of words used in connection with beauty culture, defined in the sense of anatomical, medical, electrical, and beauty culture relationship only. Key to pronunciation will be found at bottom of each page.

A

abdomen (ăb-dō'měn): the belly; the cavity in the body between the thorax and the pelvis.
abducens (ab-dū'sênz): drawing away from.
abducent nerve (ăb-dū'sênt nûrv): the sixth cranial nerve; a small motor nerve supplying the external rectus muscle of the eye.
abductor (ăb-dŭk't ēr): a muscle that draws a part away from the median line (opp., adductor).
ability (â-bĭl'ĭ-tē): quality or state of being able to perform.
abnormal (âb-nôr'mâl): irregular; contrary to the natural law or customary order.
abnormality (âb-nôr-măl'ĭ-tē): the state of being abnormal; a deformity or malformation.
abortion (ă-bôr'shûn): act of giving premature birth; miscarriage.
abortion, artificial (är-tĭ-fi'sh'l): induced abortion.
abortionist (ă-bôr'shŭn-ĭst): one who practices abortion.
abrade (ăb-rād'): to rub off; to remove by friction or chafing; to roughen by friction.
abrasion (ă-brā'zhûn): scraping of the skin; excoriation.
abreast (ă-brĕst'): in line with; side by side with; up to the mark.
abscess (ăb'sĕs): a circumscribed cavity containing pus.
absorb (ăb-sôrb'): to suck in; to swallow up; engulf.
absorbent (ăb-sôr'bênt): anything that absorbs.
absorption (ăb-sôrp'shûn): assimilation of one body by another; act of absorbing.
absurd (ăb-sûrd'): inconsistent with reason.
acceleration (ăk-sĕl-ēr-ā'shûn): an increase in rapidity.
accelerator (ăk-sĕl'ēr-ā-tēr): any agent which hastens or quickens action.
accessory (ăk-sĕs'ô-r ē): any person or thing which aids subordinately, or assists.
accentuate (ăk-sĕn'tū-āt): to bring out distinctly; emphasize.
accessory nerve (nûrv): spinal accessory nerve; eleventh cranial nerve; affects the sterno-cleido-mastoid and trapezius muscles of the neck.
accidental (ăk-sĭ-dĕn'tâl): happening by chance.
accretion (â-krē'shôn): an accumulation of foreign matter in any cavity.
acetic (ă-sĕt'ĭk): pertaining to vinegar; sour.
acid (ăs'ĭd): a sour substance; any chemical compound having a sour taste.
acid rinse (ăs'ĭd rĭns): a solution of water and lemon juice or vinegar.
acidosis (ăs-ĭ-dō'sĭs): a condition in which there is an excess of acid products in the blood or excreted in the urine.
acidum boricum (ăs'ĭ-dûm bôr'ĭ-kûm): boric acid.
acne (ăk'nē): inflammation of the sebaceous glands from retained secretion.
acne albida (ăl'bĭ-dă): milium; white-head.
acne artificialis (är-tĭ-físh-al'ĭs): pimples due to external irritants or drugs taken internally.
acne atrophica (ă-trŏf'ĭ-kă): acne in which the lesions leave a slight amount of scarring.
acne cachecticorum (kă-kĕk-tĭ-kôr-ŭm): pimples occurring in the subjects having anemia or some debilitating constitutional disease.

acne hypertrophica (hī-pēr-trŏf'ĭ-kă): pimples in which the lesions on healing leave conspicuous pits and scars.
acne indurata (ĭn-dū-rä'tă): deeply seated pimples with hard tubercles occurring chiefly on the back.
acne keratosa (kĕr-ă-tō'să): an eruption of papules consisting of horny plugs projecting from the hair follicles, accompanied by inflammation.
acne punctata (pŭnk-tá'tă): appear as red papules in which are usually found blackheads.
acne pustulosa (pŭs-tū-lō'să): acne in which the pustular lesions predominate.
acne rosacea (rō-zā'shē-ă): a form of acne usually occurring around the nose and cheeks, due to congestion, in which the capillaries become dilated and sometimes broken.
acne simplex (sĭm'plĕks): acne vulgaris; simple uncomplicated pimples.
acne vulgaris (vŭl-găr'ĭs): acne simplex; simple uncomplicated pimples.
acoustic (ă-koos'tĭk): auditory; eighth cranial nerve; controlling the sense of hearing.
acquire (â-kwīr'): to receive; to attain; to master.
acrolein (ă-krō'iê-ĭn): a light volatile oily liquid giving off irritant vapor.
actinic (ăk-tĭn'ĭk): relating to the chemically active rays of the spectrum.
action (ăk'shŭn): the performance of a function.
activity (ăk-tĭv'ĭ-tē): natural or normal function or operation; physical motion or exercise of force.
acute (ă-kūt'): attended with severe symptoms; having a short and relatively short course; not chronic, said of a disease.
ad (ăd): a prefix denoting to, toward, addition, intensification.
adapt (ă-dăpt): to make suitable; to alter so as to fit for a new use.
adaptable (ă-dăpt'ă-b'l): capable of or given to adapting one's self to new conditions and uses.
adductor (â-dŭk'tēr): a muscle that draws a part toward the median line.
adenoma sebaccum (â-děn-ō'mȧsē-bā'sē-ûm): small tumor of translucent appearance, originating in the sebaceous glands.
adhere (ăd-hēr'): to remain in contact; to unite.
adipose (ăd'ĭ-pōs): relating to fat.
adipose tissue (tĭsh'û): fatty tissue; areolar connective tissue containing fat cells; subcutaneous tissue.
adjust (â-jŭst'): to make exact; to fit; to bring into proper relations.
adnata, alopecia (ă-nă'tă): baldness at birth.
adolescence (ăd-ō-lěs'êns): state or process of growing from childhood to manhood or womanhood.
adrenal (ăd-rē'năl): an endocrine gland situated on the top of the kidneys.
adult (ă-dŭlt'): grown up to full age, size or strength.
adulterate (ă-dûl'tēr-āte): to falsify; to alter, make impure by combining other substances.
aeration (ā-ẽr-ā'shŭn): airing; saturating a fluid with air, carbon dioxide or other gas; the change of venous into arterial blood in the lungs.
aerobic (ā-ẽr-ō'bĭk): unable to live without oxygen.
aesthetic, esthetic (ĕs-thĕt'ĭk): relating to sensation, either mental or physical; appreciation of beauty and art.
afferent (ăf'êr-ênt): bearing or carrying toward the center, or inward.
afferent nerves (nûrvz): convey stimulus from the external organs to the brain.
affinity (â-fĭn-ĭ-tē): attraction; in chemistry, the force which impels certain atoms to unite with certain others to form compounds.
agent (ā'jĕnt): an active power which can produce a physical, chemical, or medicinal effect

fāte, câre, ăm, finâl, ärm, ȧsk, sofă; ēve, évent, ěnd, recênt, evẽr; īce, ĭll; ōld, ŏbey, ôrb, ŏdd, cônnect, sŏft, food, foot; ūse, ûrn, ŭp, circûs

agnail (ăg′nāl): hangnail.

air circulator (ăr sûr′kû-lā-tẽr): a fan circulating cold air, attached to the permanent waving machine.

al (âl): a word termination denoting belonging to, of, or pertaining to.

ala (ā′lă); pl. **alae** (-lē): a wing-like structure, as the wing of the nose.

alae nasi (ā′lē nā′zī): the wing cartilage of the nose.

albida, acne (ăl′bĭ-dă): whitehead; milium.

albinism (ăl-bĭ-nĭz′m): congenital leukoderma or absence of pigment in the skin and its appendages; it may be partial or complete.

albino (ăl-bī′nō): a subject of albinism; a person with very little or no pigment in the skin, hair, or iris.

albumen, albumin (ăl-bū′měn): white of an egg; found also in milk and vegetables.

albuminous (ăl-bū′mĭ-nûs): relating in any way to albumen.

alcohol (ăl′kŏ-hŏl): a readily evaporating colorless liquid with a pungent odor and burning taste; powerful stimulant and antiseptic.

aliment (ăl′ĭ-mênt): nourishment; food or anything which feeds or adds to a substance in natural growth.

alimentary (âl-ĭ-měn′tă-rē): nourishing; relating to food or nutrition; the alimentary canal extends from the mouth to the anus.

alkali (ăl′kă-lī): an electropositive substance; capable of making soaps from fats; used to neutralize acids.

alkaline (ăl′kă-līn): having the properties of an alkali.

allergic (â-lûr′jĭk): sensitive to; susceptible.

allure (ăl-lūr′): to attract.

almond (ä′mûnd, ăl′mûnd): the kernel or seed of the fruit.

alopecia (ăl-ō-pē′shē-ă): deficiency of hair; baldness.

alopiecia, adnate (ăd-nă′tă): baldness at birth].

alopecia areata (ā-rḗ-ă′tă): baldness in spots or patches.

alopecia cicatrisata (sĭ-kă-trĭ-sä′tă): baldness in irregular spots or patches, due to atrophy of the skin in the areas.

alopecia dynamica (dī năm′ĭ-kă): loss of hair due to destruction of the hair follicle by ulceration or some other disease process.

alopecia follicularis (fŏl-ĭk-u-lăr′ĭs): loss of hair due to inflamed hair follicles.

alopecia localis (lō-kā′lĭs): loss of hair occurring in patches on the course of a nerve at the site of an injury.

alopecia maligna (mă-lĭg′nă): a term applied to any form of alopecia that is severe and persistent.

alopecia premature (prē-mă-tū′ră): baldness beginning before middle age.

alopecia seborrheica (sěb-ôr-ē′ŭ-kă): baldness caused by diseased sebaceous glands.

alopecia senilis (sē-nĭl′ĭs): baldness occurring in old age.

alopecia syphilitica (sĭf-ĭl-it′ĭ-kă): loss of hair resulting from syphilis; usually a symptom of the second stage of the disease.

alopecia universalis (ū-nĭ-vēr-să′lĭs): a condition manifested by general falling out of the hair of the body.

alternating (ă′těr-nāt-ĭng): reversing periodically and rapidly in direction of flow, as in electricity.

alternating current, A.C. (kŭr′ânt): a current which rises and falls in strength of flow, alternating in opposite directions at regular intervals.

---

fāte, câre, ăm, finâl, ärm, ȧsk, sofȧ; ēve, évent, ěnd, recênt, evẽr; īce, ĭll; ōld, ŏ́bey, ôrb, ŏdd, cônnect, sŏft, fo͞od, fo͝ot; ūse, ûrn, ŭp, circŭs

alum, alumen (ăl'ŭm, ă-lū'mên): sulphate of potassium and aluminum; an astringent; used as a styptic.

aluminum (ă-lū'mĭ-nûm): a whitish metal with a low specific gravity; noted for its lightness and its resistance to oxidation.

alveola (ăl-vē'ō-lă); pl., **alveolae** (-lē): a small hollow; alveolae border, the portion of the jaws bearing the teeth; branch of the internal maxillary artery.

amber (ăm'bēr): the fossil resin of pine trees found in northern Europe; it becomes negatively electrified in friction; the oil is sometimes used as a stimulant.

ameliorate (ă-mēl'yô-rāt): to make better; improve.

amino acid (ăm'ĭ-nō ăs 'ĭd): an important constituent of proteins.

amitosis (ăm-ĭ-tō'sĭs): cell multiplication by direct division of the nucleus in the cell.

ammeter (ăm'mē-tĕr): an instrument for measuring the amperage of a current.

ammonia (ă-mō'nē-ă): a colorless gas with a pungent odor; very soluble in water.

amperage (ăm-pâr'âj, ăm'pĕr-âj): the strength of an electric current.

ampere (ăm-pâr'): the unit of measurement of strength of an electric current.

amyl acetate (âm'ĭl ăs'ê-tât): banana oil; a colorless, aromatic and inflammable liquid employed as a solvent in making nail polishes.

anabolism (ăn-ăb'ô-lĭz'm): constructive metabolism; the process of assimilation of nutritive mater and its conversion into living substance.

analysis (ă-năl'ĭ-sĭs): a process by which the nature of a substance is recognized and is chemical composition determined.

analyze (ăn'ă-līz): to make an analysis.

anaphoresis (ăn-ă-fôr-ē'sĭs): the process of forcing liquids into the tissues from the negative toward the positive pole.

anaplasty (ăn'ă-plăs-tē): an operation for the restoration of lost parts; grafting.

anaplerosis (ăn-ă-plē-rō'sĭs): plastic surgery; replacement of defective parts caused by injury or disease.

anatomy (ă-năt'ō-mē): the science of the organic structure of the body.

anemia, anaemia (ă-nē'mē-ă): a condition in which the blood is deficient in red corpuscles, or in hemoglobin, or both.

anesthesia, anaesthesia (ăn-ĕs-thē'sē-ă, -zhē-ă): a state of being painless.

anesthetic, anaesthetic (ăn-ēs-thĕt'ĭk): a substance administered to make the body incapable of feeling pain.

angiology (ăn-jē-ŏl'ō-jē): the science of the blood vessels and lymphatics.

angioma (ăn-jē-ō'mă): a tumor formed of blood vessels and lymphatics.

Angstrom (ăng'strôm): a unit of measurement for the wavelength of light.

angular artery (ăng'û-lăr är'tĕr-ē): supplies the lacrimal sac and the eye muscle.

angulus (ăng'û-lûs); pl., **anguli** (-lī): an angle or corner.

anidrosis, anhidrosis (ăn-ĭ-drō'sĭs): a deficiency in perspiration.

aniline (ăn'ĭ-lĭn, -lēn): a product of coal tar used in the manufacture of artificial dyes.

anion (ăn'ĭ-ôn): the ion which carries a charge of negative electricity; the element which, during electrolysis of a chemical compound, appears at the positive pole or anode.

annular finger (fĭn'gĕr): ring finger.

anode (ăn'ōd): the positive terminal of an electric source.

anomalous (ă-nŏm'ă-lûs): abnormal; unusual; irregular.

anterior (ăn-tē'rē-ĕr): situated before or in front of.

anthrax (ăn'thrăks): malignant pustule; gangrenous carbuncle-like lesion.

antibody (ăn'tĭ-bŏd-ĭ): a substance in the blood which builds resistance to disease.

antidote (ăn'tĭ-dōt): an agent preventing or counteracting the action of a poison.

fāte, câre, ăm, finâl, ärm, åsk, sofă; ēve, évent, ĕnd, recênt, evẽr; īce, ĭll; ōld, ŏ́bey, ôrb, ŏdd, cônnect, sŏft, fōod, fŏŏt; ūse, ûrn, ŭp, circûs

anti-perspirant (ăn-tĭ-pēr-spĭ′rănt): a strong astringent liquid or cream used to stop the flow of perspiration in the region of the armpits, hands, or feet.
antiseptic (ăn-tĭ-sĕp′tĭk): a chemical agent that prevents the growth of bacteria.
antitoxin (ăn-tĭ-tôk′sĭn): a substance in serum which binds and neutralizes toxin (poison).
antrum (ăn′trŭm): a cavity or hollow space, especially in a bone.
anus (ā′nŭs): the lower opening of the digestive tract, through which fecal matter is eliminated.
aorta (ā-ôr′tă): the main arterial trunk leaving the heart, and carrying blood to the various arteries throughout the body.
apex (ā′pĕks): the summit or extremity; the upper end of a lung or the heart.
aponcurosis (ăp-ó-nū-rō′sĭs): a broad, flat tendon; attachment of muscles.
apoplexy (ăp′ó-plĕk-sē): disabled by a stroke generally caused by rupture of blood vessels in the brain.
apparatus (ăp-ă-rā′tŭs): a collection of instruments or devices adapted for a special purpose.
apparent (â-pâr′ênt, â-păr′-): seeming; appearing to be like.
appendage (â-pĕn′dĕj): that which is attached to an organ, and is a part of it.
appendix (â-pĕn′dĭks): a small intestinal organ.
applicator (ăp′lĭ-kā-tĕr): an instrument for the application of remedies.
apposition (ăp-ó-zĭsh′ŭn): the act of fitting together; the state of being fitted together.
appropriate (ă-prō′prē-āt): suitable; fitting.
approximately (ă-prŏk′sĭ-māt-lē): about; nearly; closely.
aqueous (ā′kwē-ŭs): watery; pertaining to water.
araneous (â-rā′nē-ŭs): like a cobweb.
area (ā′rē-ă): an open space; a limited extent of surface.
areata, alopecia (ā-rē-ă′tă): baldness appearing in spots or patches.
areola (ă-rē′ó-lă): any small ring-like discoloration; the pigmented ring surrounding the nipple of the breast.
areolar tissue (tĭsh′ū): loose connective tissue with many interspaces.
argyria (är-jĭr′ē-ă): a form of discoloration of the skin produced by the prolonged administration of silver salts.
arnica (är′nĭ-kă): tincture; a preparation employed externally as an application to sprains and bruises.
aromatic (är-ó-mat′ĭk): pertaining to or containing aroma; fragrant.
arrector pili (â-rĕk′tôr pī′lī): plural of arrectores pilorum.
arnectores pilorum (â-rĕk-tō′rēz pĭ-lôr′ŭm): the minute involuntary muscle fibers in the skin inserted into the bases of the hair follicles.
arsenical compound (är-sĕn′ĭ-kâl kôm′-pound): a white poisonous powder, useful in the treatment of certain skin diseases; has a considerable caustic action on the skin.
art (ărt): skill; dexterity; an especial facility in performing any operation, intellectual or physical, acquired by experience or study; knack.
arterial (är-tē′rē′âl): pertaining to an artery.
arteriole (är-tē′rē-ôl): a minute artery; a terminal artery continuous with the capillary network.
arteriosclerosis (är-tē″rē-ó-sklé-rō′sĭs): abnormal hardness and dryness of the arterial coats resulting from chronic inflammation.
artery (är′tĕr-ē): a vessel that conveys blood from the heart.
articular (är-tĭk′ū-lăr): pertaining to an articulation or joint.
articulation (är-tĭk-û-lā′shŭn): joint; a connection between two or more bones, whether or not allowing any movement between them.
artificial (är-tĭ-fĭsh′âl): not natural.
artificialis, acne (är-tĭ-fĭsh-âl′ĭs): pimples due to external irritants or drugs taken internally.

fāte, câre, ăm, finâl, ärm, ȧsk, sofȧ; ēve, évent, ĕnd, recênt, evẽr; īce, ĭll; ōld, óbey, ôrb, ŏdd, cônnect, sŏft, fo͞od, fo͝ot; ūse, ûrn, ŭp, circûs

asbestos scalp pad (ăs-bĕs'tôs scălp-păd): a heat resisting scalp protector.
ascertain (ăs-ẽr-tān'): to acquire an accurate knowledge of.
asepsis (ă-sĕp'sĭs): a condition in which pathogenic bacteria are absent.
aseptic (ă-sĕp'tĭk): free from pathogenic bacteria.
assimilate (â-sĭm'ĭ-lāt): to absorb; to incorporate into the body the digested food products.
assimilation (â-sĭm-ĭ-lā'shôn): the incorporation of materials, prepared by digestion from food, into the tissues of the body.
asteotosis (ăs-tē-â-tō'sĭs): a deficiency or absence of the sebaceous secretions.
astringent (ăs-trĭn'jênt): a substance or medicine that causes contraction of the tissues, and checks secretions.
athlete's foot (ăth'lēts fōōt): a fungus foot infection; epidermophytosis.
atmosphere (ăt'môs-fẽr): the whole mass of air surrounding the earth.
atom (ăt'ûm): the part of an element incapable of further division; the smallest part capable of entering into the formation of a chemical compound, or uniting with another to form a molecule.
atrichia (ă-trĭk'ē-ă): absence of hair, congenital or acquired.
atrium (ăt'rē-ûm); pl. **atria** (-ă): the auricle of the heart.
atrophic (ă-trôf'ĭk): relating to atrophy.
atrophica, acne (ă-trôf'ĭ-kă): acne in which the lesions leave a slight amount of scarring.
atrophy (ăt'rṓ-fē): a wasting away of the tissues of a part or of the entire body from lack of nutrition.
attachment (â-tâch'mënt): that which is connected to.
attenuate (â-tĕn'û-āt): to make thin; to lessen the effect of an agent.
attolens (â-tŏl'ênz): a term applied to muscles that elevate.
attolens aurem (ô'rêm): muscle that elevates the ear.
attrahens (ăt'ră-hênz): a muscle that draws or pulls forward.
attrahens aurem (ô'rêm): a muscle which pulls the ear forward.
attune (ă-tūn'): to bring into harmony.
auditory (ô 'dĭ-tō-rē): eighth cranial nerve; controlling the sense of hearing.
auricle (ô'rĭ-k'l): the external ear; one of the upper cavities of the heart.
auriculo temporal (ô-rĭk'û-lō têm'pôr-âl): sensory nerve affecting the temple and pinna.
auricular (ô-rĭk'û-lăr): pertaining to the ear or cardiac auricle.
auto (ô't ṓ): a prefix meaning self; of itself.
autoclave (ô'tō-klāv): an apparatus used to sterilize objects with steam under pressure.
autonomic; autonomous (ô-tôn'ō-mĭ k; -mûs): independent in origin, action or function; self-governing.
autonomic nervous system (nûrv'ûs sĭs'tĕm): the sympathetic nervous system; controls the involuntary muscles.
axilla (ăk-sĭl'ă): the armpit.
axillary (ăk'sĭ-lā-rē): pertaining to the axilla, or armpit.
axon (ăk'sŏn): a long nerve fiber extending from the nerve cell.

B

bacillus (bă-sil'us); pl. **bacilli** (-ĭ): rod-like shaped bacterium.
back combing (băk kōm'ĭng): combing the short hair toward the scalp while the hair strand is held in a vertical position; also called teasing.
bacteria (băk-tē'rē-ă): microbes, or germs.
bacterial (băk-tē'rē-âl): pertaining to bacteria.

fāte, câre, ăm, finâl, ärm, åsk, sofă; ēve, ĕ́vent, ĕnd, recênt, evẽr; īce, ĭll; ōld, ṓbey, ôrb, ŏdd, cônnect, sŏft, fōōd, fŏŏt; ūse, ûrn, ŭp, circûs

bactericide (băk-tē'rĭ-sīd): an agent that destroys bacteria.
bacteriology (băk-tē-rē-ôl'ṓ-j ē): the science which deals with bacteria.
bacterium (băk-tē'rē-ûm); pl. **bacteria** (-ă): unicellular vegetable microorganism.
bakelite shield (bāk'kê-līt shēld): a strong shield made of a substance of strong chemical resistance, used as a scalp protector.
baldness (bôld'nêss): deficiency of hair; hair loss].
balsam of Peru (bôl'sâm of pê-r$\overline{oo}$): a thick, dark brown oily fluid exuded from the cut bark of Toluifera pereirae; used as an antiseptic and astringent..
bang (băng): the front hair cut so as to fall over the forehead; often used in the plural, as to wear bangs.
barber (bär'bẽr): one whose occupation it is to shave or trim the beard, and to cut and dress the hair.
barber science (sī'êns): the study of the beard and hair, and its treatment.
barber's itch (bär'bẽrz ĭch): tinea sycosis; ringworm of the beard; chronic inflammation of the hair follicles.
barium sulphide (bā'rē-ûm sŭl'fīd): a yellowish powder which decomposes in water with the liberation of hydrogen sulphide gas; used in depilatory preparations.
basal (bās'âl): foundation; pertaining to or located at the base.
basal layer (lā'er): the layer of cells at base of epidermis closest to the dermis.
base (bās): the lower part or bottom; chief substance of a compound; an electropositive element that unites with an acid to form a salt.
basilica vein (ba-sĭl'ĭk vān): the vein of the upper arm.
basis (bā'sĭs): foundation; the principal component part of a thing.
battery (băt'ĕr-ē): an apparatus containing two or more cells, for generating electricity.
bayberry plant (bā'bĕr-ē plânt): the leaves of Myrcia acris yield oil of bay which is used to make bay rum.
bay rum (bā rŭm): after-shaving lotion; used as a tonic and astringent.
beautician (blū-tĭsh'ân): one skilled in the art of beautifying the personal appearance.
beauty culture (bū'tē kŭl'tur): the study and practice of the improvement of the appearance.
belch (bĕlch): to emit gas from the stomach through the mouth.
belladonna (bĕl-ă-dŏn'ă): a poisonous European plant, used for medicinal purposes.
beneficial (bĕn-ḗ-fĭsh'âl): conferring real improvement to a desired end.
benign (bḗ-nīn): mild in character.
benzine (bĕn'zēn): an inflammable liquid derived from petroleum and used as a cleansing fluid.
benzoin (bĕn'zṓ-ĭn, -zoin): a balsamic resin used as a stimulant, and also as a perfume.
beriberi (bĕr'ē-bĕr'ē): a deficiency disease due to lack of vitamins in the diet.
Bernay tablets (bŭr'nā tăb'lĕts): a trade name; special tablets dissolved in water to be used as an antiseptic.
bevel (bĕv'êl): to slope the edge of a surface.
bi (bī): a prefix denoting two, twice, double.
bicarbonate of soda (bī-kär'bôn-ât of sō'dă): baking soda; relieves burns, itching, urticarial lesions and insect bites; is often used in bath powders as an aid to cleansing oily skin. Adding baking soda to the water in which instruments are to be boiled will keep them bright.
biceps (bī'sĕps): having two heads; a muscle producing the contour of the front and inner side of the upper arm.

fāte, câre, ăm, finâl, ärm, åsk, sofà; ēve, ḗvent, ĕnd, recênt, evẽr; īce, ĭll; ōld, ṓbey, ôrb, ŏdd, cônnect, sŏft, f$\overline{oo}$d, f$\overline{oo}$t; ūse, ûrn, ŭp, circūs

bichloride (bī-klō′rīd): a compound having two parts or equivalents of chlorine to one of the other element.
bichromate (bī-krō′māt): a compound having two parts of chromic acid to one of the base.
bicipital (bī-sĭp′ĭ-tâl): pertaining to the biceps muscle.
bile (bīl): a yellowish or greenish viscid fluid secreted by the liver; an aid to digestion.
binding posts (bīn′dĭng pōsts): small metal posts in which are fitted the metal tips of the conducting cords.
biology (bī-ôl′ō-jē): the science of life and living things.
bipolar (bī-pō′lăr): having two poles.
birthmark (bûrth′märk): any mark which is present at birth, usually lasting; a form of nevus.
biterminal (bī-tûr′mĭ-nâl): two terminals or poles of an electric current.
blackhead (blăk′hĕd): a comedone; a plug of sebaceous matter.
bladder (blăd′ĕr): a sac for the holding of urine.
bleach (blēch): to whiten or lighten.
bleached hair (blēcht hâr): hair from which the color has been wholly or partially removed by means of a bleaching solution.
bleaching solution (blēch′ĭng sō-lū-shûn): hydrogen peroxide with addition of ammonia.
bleb (blĕb): a blister of the skin filled with watery fluid.
blemish (blĕm′ĭsh): a mark, spot, or defect, marring the appearance.
blend (blĕnd): to form a uniform mixture.
blister (blĭs′têr): a vesicle; a collection of serous fluid causing a raised elevation of the skin.
blond; blonde (blond): a person of air complexion, with light hair and eyes.
blood (blŭd): the nutritive fluid circulating through the arteries and veins.
blood poison (poi′z′n): an infection which gets into the blood stream.
blood vascular system (văs′ku-lär sĭs′tĕm): comprised of structures (the heart, arteries, veins and capillaries) which distribute blood throughout the body.
blood vessel (vĕs′êl): an artery, vein or capillary.
blue light (bloō lit): a therapeutic lamp used to soothe the nerves and ease pain.
bluing rinse (bloō′ĭng rĭns): a solution used to neutralize the unbecoming yellowish tinge on gray or white hair.
blunt (blŭnt): having a thick or rounded edge or point.
B.N.A.: an abbreviation for Basle Anatomical Nomenclature; a list of anatomical terms adopted by the German Anatomical Society in 1895.
bob (bŏb): a short haircut for women and children.
boil (boil): a furuncle; a subcutaneous abscess which drains out onto the surface of the skin.
boiling point (boil′ĭng point): 212°F or 100°C., the temperature at which a liquid begins to boil.
bone (bōn): os; the hard tissue forming the framework of the body.
bookkeeping (boōk′kēp-ĭng): the practice of keeping systematic business records.
borax (bō′răks): sodium tetraborate; a white powder used as an antiseptic and cleansing agent.
boric acid (bō′rĭk ăs′ĭd): acidum boricum; used as an antiseptic dusting powder; in liquid form as an eye wash.
brachial (brā′kĭ-âl): pertaining to the arm.
brachial artery (är′tĕr-ĭ): the main artery of the upper arm.
brachioradialis (brā″kĭ-ō-rā-dĭ-ā′lĭs): a flexor muscle on the radial side of the forearm.
braid (brād): to weave, interlace, or entwine together.
brain (brān): that part of the central nervous system contained in the cranial cavity, and consisting of the cerebrum, the cerebellum, the pons, and the medulla oblongata.
brew (broō): to extract the active ingredients by boiling.

fāte, câre, ăm, finâl, ärm, ȧsk, sofă; ēve, ĕ́vent, ĕnd, recênt, evẽr; īce, ĭll; ōld, ŏ́bey, ôrb, ŏdd, cônnect, sŏft, foōd, foŏt; ūse, ûrn, ŭp, circŭs

brilliantine (brĭl-yân-tēn'): an oily composition that imparts luster to the hair.
bristle (brĭs'l): short, stiff hairs found on brushes.
brittle (brĭt"l): easily broken; fragile.
broken circuit (brō'k'n sûr'kĭt): interruption in the flow of the electric current.
bromide (brō'mīd): a compound used as sedatives to allay nervous excitement.
bromidrosis (brō-mĭ-drō'sĭs): perspiration which smells foul.
bromo-acid (brō-mō-ăs'ĭd): a soluble dye used to impart a red indelible color in lipsticks.
bronchial (brŏn'kē-âl): pertaining to the wind pipe.
bronchus (brŏn'kûs); pl., **bronchi** (-kī): The main branch of the wind pipe.
brow (brou): the forehead.
bruise (brōoz): to injure, as by a blow or collision, without laceration.
brunette (brōō-nĕt): a person having brown or olive skin, brown or black hair and eyes.
brush curl (brŭsh cûrl): to wind the hair into ringlets with the aid of a hair brush.
bucca (bŭk'ă): the hollow part of the cheek.
buccal nerve (bŭk'âl nûrv): a motor nerve affecting the buccinators and the orbicularis oris muscle.
buccinators (bŭk'sĭ-nā-têr): a thin, flat muscle of the cheek, shaped like a trumpet.
bulbous (bŭl'bûs): pertaining to, or like a bulb in shape or structure.
bulky (bŭl'kē): of great thickness or of great weight.
bulla (bōōl'ă, bŭl'ă): a large bleb or blister.
bundle (bŭn'd'l): a structure composed of a group of muscular or nerve fibers.

C

cachecticorum, acne (kă-kĕk-tĭ-kōr'-ûm): pimples occurring in patrons having anemia or some debilitating constitutional disease.
cadmium (kăd'mĭ-ŭm): a white metallic element whose compounds are sometimes used in metallic hair dyes.
calamine (kăl'ă-mīn; -mĭn): zinc carbonate; pinkish powder, employed as a dusting powder or lotion.
calamine lotion (lō'shûn): zinc carbonate in alcohol used for the treatment of dermatitis in its various forms.
calcium (kăl'sē-ûm): a brilliant silvery-white metal; enters into the composition of bone.
caliber, caliber (kăl'ĭ-bẽr): the diameter of a tube, such as the esophagus or urethra.
callous, callus (kăl'ûs): skin which has become hardened;; thick-skinned.
calory, calorie (kăl'ō-rē): a unit of heat.
chamomile (kăm'ŏ-mĭl): an herb whose flowers are brewed like tea and used as a brightening rinse for blond hair.
camphor (kăm'fẽr): a mild cutaneous stimulant; it produces redness and warmth, and has a slightly anaesthetic and cooling effect.
canaliculus (kăn-ă-lĭk'ū-lūs): a small canal or groove.
cancellous (kăn'sê-lûs): having a porous or spongy structure.
cancer (kăn'sẽr): a malignant growth, especially one attended with great pain and ulceration.
caninus (kȧn-nīn'ûs): the levator anguli oris muscle which lifts the angle of the mouth.
canitics (kă-nĭt'ĭks): the science which treats of canities.
canities (kă-nĭsh'ĭ-ēz): grayness or whiteness of the hair.
canitics, accidental (ăk-sĭ-dĕn'tȧl): grayness of hair caused by fright.
canities, congenital (kŏn-jĕn'ĭ-tăl): a type of gray hair transmitted by heredity as in albinism.

fāte, câre, ăm, finâl, ärm, ȧsk, sofă; ēve, ével, ĕnd, recênt, evẽr; īce, ĭll; ōld, ŏbey, ôrb, ŏdd, cônnect, sŏft, fōōd, fŏŏt; ūse, ûrn, ŭp, circûs

canities, premature (prē-mă-tūr): grayness of hair at an early age.
canities, senile (sē'nīl,-nĭl): grayness of hair in old age.
cantharides (kăn-thăr'ĭ-dēz): a preparation of dried blister beetles, a powerful counter-irritant.
canthus (kăn'thŭs): the corner of each side of the eye where the upper and the lower lids meet.
cape (kāp): a sleeveless garment used to protect the patron's clothing during beauty treatments.
capillary (kăp'ĭ-là-rē): any one of the minute blood vessels which connect the arteries and veins; hair-like.
capillurgy (kăp-ĭ-lôr'jē): the art of destroying superfluous hair.
capitate (kăp'ĭ-tāt): the large bone of the wrist.
capsicum (kăp'sĭ-kŭm): pungent berries or peppers; a counter-irritant which reddens the skin.
capsule (kăp'sūl): a membrane or sac-like structure enclosing a part or an organ; a small sac or case to enclose powders or drugs of disagreeable taste.
caput (kā'pŭt): poss., **capitis** (kăp'ĭ-tĭs): pertaining to the head.
carbohydrate (kär-bō-hī'drāt): a substance containing carbon, hydrogen, and oxygen, the two latter in the proportion to form water; sugars, starches and cellulose belong to the class of carbohydrates.
carbolic acid (kär-bŏl'ĭk ăs'ĭd): phenol made from coal tar; a caustic and corrosive poison; used in dilute solution as an antiseptic.
carbon (kär'bôn): coal; an elementary substance in nature which predominates in all organic compounds and occurs in three distinct forms: black lead, charcoal, and lampblack.
carbona (kär-bō'nă): a trade name; a cleaning fluid containing carbon tetrachloride which is sometimes used in giving a liquid dry shampoo.
carbon-arc lamp (kär'bônärk lămp): an instrument which produces ultraviolet rays.
carbon dioxide (di-ŏk'sīd): carbonic acid gas; product of the combustion of carbon with a free supply of air.
carbon monoxide (mŏn-ŏk'sīd): a colorless, odorless and poisonous gas; its toxic action being due to its strong affinity for hemoglobin.
carbonic acid (kär-bŏn'ĭk ăs'ĭd): an acid formed by the union of carbon dioxide and water.
carbuncle (kär'bŭn-k'l): a large circumscribed inflammation of the subcutaneous tissue, similar to a furuncle, but much more extensive.
carcinoma (kär-sĭ-nō'mă): cancer; a malignant new growth of epithelial or gland cells infiltrating the surrounding tissues.
cardiac (kär'dē-ăk): pertaining to the heart.
caries (kā'rĭ-ē z): tooth decay.
carotid (kă-rŏt'ĭd): the principal artery of the neck.
carpal (kär'păl): pertaining to the wrist or carpus.
carpus (kär'pŭs): the wrist; the eight bones of the wrist.
cartilage (kär'tĭ-làj): gristle; a non-vascular connective tissue softer than bone.
casein (kā'sḗ-ĭn): the protein in milk and the principal constituent of cheese.
castor oil (käs'tẽroil): an oil obtained from the castor bean.
castile soap (kăs'tēl sōp): a fine, hard, white soap containing olive oil and other oils; originally came from Castile, Spain.
catabolism (kă-tăb'ô-lĭz'm): chemical changes which involve the breaking down process within the cells.
cataphoresis (kă-tăf-ṓ-rē'sĭs): the process of forcing medicinal substances into the deeper tissues, using the galvanic current from the positive towards the negative pole.

fāte, câre, ăm, finâl, ärm, àsk, sofă; ēve, évent, ĕnd, recênt, evẽr; īce, ĭll; ōld, ṓbey, ôrb, ŏdd, cônnect, sŏft, fo͞od, fo͝ot; ūse, ûrn, ŭp, circŭs

catarrh (kă-tär): an inflammatory affection of the mucous membrane, especially of the nose and air passages; chronic rhinitis.
cathode (kăth'ōd): the negative pole or electrode of a constant electric current.
cation (kāt'ĭ-ŏn): an ion carrying a charge of positive electricity; the element which, during electrolysis of a chemical compound, appears at the negative pole or cathode.
caustic (kôs'tik): an agent that burns and chars tissue.
cauterize (kô'tĕr-īz): to burn or sear with a caustic.
cautery (kô'tĕr-ē): an agent used for scarring or burning the skin or tissues by means of heat or of a caustic chemical.
cava (kā'vă): a vena cava; any external cavity or hollow of the body.
cavity (kăv'ĭ-tē): a hollow space.
cell (sĕl): a minute mass of protoplasm forming the structural unit of every organized body.
cellophane retention paper (sĕ l'ṓ-fān rḗ-tĕn'shŭn pā'pĕr): material used to wrap hair in permanent waving.
cellular (sĕl'û-lăr): consisting of or pertaining to cells.
cellulose (sĕl'û-lōs): a carbohydrate, such as vegetable fiber.
centigrade (sĕn't ĭ-grād): consisting of 100 degrees; one hundredth part of a circle; of or pertaining to centigrade thermometer.
centrosome (sĕn'trṓ-sōm): a cellular body which controls the division of the cell.
cephalic vein (sḗ-făl'ĭk vān): the vein of the upper arm.
cerebellum (sĕr-ḗ-bĕl'ûm): the posterior and lower part of the brain.
cerebral (sĕr'ḗ-brâl): pertaining to the cerebrum.
cerebrospinal system (sêr-ē-brō-spī'năl sĭs'tĕm): consists of the brain, spinal cord, spinal nerves, and the cranial nerves.
cerebrum (sĕr'ḗ-brûm): the superior and larger part of the brain.
cerumen (sḗ-rōō'mĕ n): the earwax.
cervix (sûr'vĭks): the neck; any neck-like structure.
cervical (sûr'vī-kâl): pertaining to the neck.
chancre (shăn'kĕr): the primary lesion of syphilis.
characterize (kăr'âk-tē r-īz): to indicate, or describe the character of.
chafe (chāf): to rub and make warm; to excite heat by friction; to irritate.
chemical (kĕm'ĭ-kâl): relating to chemistry.
chemical dye remover (dī rē-mōōv'ĕr): a dye remover containing a chemical solvent.
chemism (kĕm'ĭz'm): chemical action or influence.
chemistry (kĕm'ĭs-trē): the science dealing with the composition of substances; the elements and their mutual reactions, and the phenomena resulting from the formation and decomposition of compounds.
chic (shēk): stylish, smart.
chignon (shē'nyôn): a knot or mass of hair.
chiropody (kī-rêp'ṓ-dĭ): the art of treating minor diseases of the hands and feet.
chloasma (klṓ-ăz'mă): large brown irregular patches on the skin, such as liver spots.
chlorazene (klō'ră-zēne): a trade term; a chemical used for preparing an antiseptic or disinfectant.
chloride (klō'rīd): a compound of chlorine with another element.
chlorine (klō'rĭn, -rēn): greenish yellow gas, with a disagreeable suffocating odor; used in combined form as a disinfectant and a bleaching agent.
chlorophyll (klō'rṓ-fĭl): the green coloring matter found in plants.

fāte, câre, ăm, finâl, ärm, ȧsk, sofă; ēve, ĕvent, ĕnd, recênt, evẽr; īce, ĭll; ōld, ṓbey, ôrb, ŏdd, cônnect, sŏft, fōod, fŏŏt; ūse, ûrn, ŭp, circûs

chlorozol (klō′rō-zōl): a trade name; a special tablet used for preparing an antiseptic or disinfectant.
cholesterin; cholesterol (kō-lĕs′tĕr-ĭn; -ōl): a waxy alcohol found in animal tissues and their secretions; it is present in lanolin, and used as an emulsifier.
choroid (kō′roid): the middle coat of the eyeball.
chromosome (krō′mô-sōm): tiny dark-stained bodies found in the nucleus of the cell; transmits hereditary characteristics in cell division.
chromatin (krō′mă-tĭn): a substance found in the nucleus of a cell.
chromidrosis (krō-mī-drō′sĭs): the excretion of colored sweat.
chronic (krŏn′ĭk): long-continued; the reverse of acute.
chrysarobin (krĭs-ă-rō′bĭn): a powerful parasiticide; used in the treatment of various forms of tinea.
chuck (chŭk): to strike vigorously; a term used in massage.
chyle (kīl): a creamy fluid taken up by the lacteals from the intestine during digestion.
chyme (kīm): food reduced to a liquid form in the process of digestion.
cicatrisata, alopecia (sĭ-kă-trĭ-sä′tă, ăl-ō-pē′shē-ă): baldness in irregular spots or patches, due to atrophy of the skin in certain áreas.
cicatrix (sī-kă′trĭks, sĭk′ă-trĭks); pl., **cicatrices** (s ĭ k-ă-tr ī ′s ē z): the skin or film which forms over a wound, later contracting to form a scar.
cilia (sĭl′ĭ-ă): the eyelashes; microscopic hair-like extensions which assist bacteria in locomotion.
circuit (sûr′kĭt): the path of an electric current.
circuit, broken (brō′kĕn): caused by anything which diverts the current from its regular circuit.
circuit, closed (klōz′d): a circuit in which a current is continually flowing.
circuit, complete (kŏm-plēt): the path of an electric current in actual operation.
circuit, ground (ground): electricity in which one pole is used to deliver current and the other pole is connected to a ground (waterpipe or radiator).
circuit, open (ō′pên): a circuit through which the flow of current is interrupted.
circuit, short (shôrt): caused by anything which diverts the current from its regular circuit.
circulation (sûr-kû-lā′shûn): the passage of blood throughout the body.
circulation, general (jĕn′êr-âl): blood circulation from the heart throughout the body and back again.
circulation, pulmonary (pŭl′mō-nā-rē): blood circulation from the heart to the lungs and back to the heart.
circumscribed (sûr-kûm-skrīb′d′): enclosed within limits.
citric acid (sĭt′rĭk ăs′ĭd): acid found in the lemon, orange, grapefruit; used for making a lemon rinse.
clasp (klăsp): a catch or hook used to hold objects together; ornamented hair clasp to hold the hair together.
clavicle (klăv′ĭ-k′l): collar bone, joining the sternum and scapula.
clay (klā): an earthy substance containing kaolin, etc. and used for facial packs.
cleido (klī′dố): prefix meaning pertaining to the clavicle.
clicking (klĭk′ĭng): small sharp sounds made by gentle blows one upon another, such as are made by rapidly opening and closing the marcel waving irons.
clipless sachet (klĭp′lĕs sásh-ā′): a special sachet which does not require a metal clip and can be folded to form a perfect steam chamber.
clipping (klĭp′ĭng): the act of cutting split hair ends with the shears or the scissors; the operation of removing the hair by the use of hair clippers.
clog (klŏg): to obstruct; to hamper.

fāte, câre, ăm, finâl, ärm, ȧsk, sofă; ēve, évent, ĕnd, recênt, evẽr; īce, ĭll; ōld, ő̄bey, ôrb, ŏdd, cônnect, sŏft, fo͞od, fo͝ot; ūse, ûrn, ŭp, circŭs

closed circuit (klōz'd sûr'kĭt): a continuous flow of the electric current.
clot (klŏt): a mass or lump of coagulated blood.
club cutting (klŭb kŭt'ĭng): cutting the hair straight off without thinning or slithering.
cluster (klŭs'tẽr): to gather in a group or groups.
coagulate (kō-ăg'ū-lāt): to clot; to convert a fluid into a soft jelly-like solid.
coalescence (kō-ă-lĕs'êns): to grow together; the union of two or more parts or things previously separate.
coccus (kŏk'ŭs); pl., **cocci** (kŏk'sī): spherical cell bacterium.
coiffeur (kwä-fûr'): a male hairdresser.
coiffeuse (kwä-fûz'): a female hairdresser.
coiffure (kwä-fūr'): an arrangement or dressing of the hair.
coil (coil): to twist or wind spirally; a spiral of wire used to produce an electric current by induction.
cold waving (kōld wāv'ĭng): a system of permanent waving involving the use of chemicals rather than heat.
cold waving solution (sṓ-lū'shŭn): a chemical solution which acts to soften the hair in cold waving.
collapse (kô-lăps'): any abnormal sinking or closing of the walls of an organ.
collodion (kô-lō'dē-ŭn): a thick liquid used to form an adhesive covering.
colloid (kŏl'oid): particles having a certain degree of fineness and possessing a sticky consistency.
color rinse (kŭl'ẽrrĭns): a rinse which gives a temporary tint to the hair.
coma (kō'mă): a state of profound unconsciousness from which one cannot be roused.
comb (kōm): an instrument used to dress, comb, and arrange the hair.
combustion (kôm-bŭs'chŭn): the rapid oxidation of any substance, accompanied by the production of heat and light.
comedo; comedone (kōm'ē-dō; -dŏn): blackhead; a worm-like mass in an obstructed sebaceous duct.
comedome extractor (ĕks'trăk'tẽr): an instrument used for the removal of blackheads.
communicable (kō-mū'nĭ-kă-b'l): able to be communicated; transferable.
commutator (kōm'ū-tā-tẽr): an instrument for automatically interrupting or reversing the flow of electricity.
compact (kôm'pĕkt): a handy container used in carrying facial makeup.
compact tissue (tĭsh'ū): a dense, hard type of bony tissue.
complete circuit (kŏm-plēlt' sûr'kĭ t): a continuous flow of current which operates the electrical device.
complexion (kôm-plĕk'shŭn): hue or general appearance of the skin, especially the face.
complexus muscle (kôm-plĕk'sŭs mŭs"l): a broad muscle of the back of the neck.
component (kôm-pō'nênt): entering into the composition of a part of the whole; a constituent part; an ingredient.
composition (kôm-pō-zĭsh'ŭn): the quality of being put together.
compound (kŏm'pound): a substance formed by a chemical union of two or more elements, and different from any of them.
compound henna (hĕn'ă): Egyptian henna to which has been added one or more metallic preparations.
compressor (kôm-prĕs'ẽr): a muscle that presses; an instrument for applying pressure on a blood vessel to prevent loss of blood.
concave (kŭn'kăv): hollow and round.
concentrated (kŏn'sên-trāt-ĕd): condensed; increasing the strength by diminishing the bulk.

fāte, câre, ăm, finâl, ärm, ȧsk, sofă; ēve, évent, ĕnd, recênt, evẽr; īce, ĭll; ōld, ṓbey, ôrb, ŏdd, cônnect, sŏft, fo͞od, fo͝ot; ūse, ûrn, ŭp, circŭs

concha (kŏn'kă): a structure comparable to a shell in shape, as the auricle or pinna of the ear or a turbinated bone in the nose.
concise (kôn-sīs'): brief and comprehensive.
condensation (kŏn-dĕn-sā'shŭn): a physical change whereby a gas is converted into a liquid.
conducting cords (kôn-dŭkt'ĭng kôrdz): insulated copper wires which convey the current from the wall plate to the patron and operator.
conductor (kôn-dŭk'tẽr): any substance which will attract or allow a current to flow through it easily.
condyle (kŏn'dīl): a rounded articular surface at the extremity of bone.
condyloid (kŏn'dĭ-loid): relating to or resembling a condyle.
congeal (kôn-jēl): to change from a fluid to a solid state.
congenital (kŏn-jĕn'ĭ-tâl): existing at birth; born with.
congestion (kŏn-jĕs'chŭn): overfullness of the capillary and other blood vessels in any locality or organ; local hyperemia.
connecting cords (kôn-ĕkt'ĭng kôrdz): the insulated strands of copper wires which join together the apparatus and the commercial electric current.
connective (kô-nĕk'tĭv): connecting; joining.
consistency (kŏn-sĭs'tĕn-sĭ): the degree of firmness or density.
constituent (kôn-stĭt'ū-ent): that which composes; an essential part of.
constitutional (kŏn-stĭ-tū'shŭn-âl): belonging to or affecting the physical or vital powers of an individual.
constrict (kôn-strĭkt'): bind or press together.
constructive (kôn-strŭk'tĭv): building up; setting in order.
contact (kŏn'tăkt): bringing together so as to touch.
contagion (kôn-tā'jŭn): transmission of specific diseases by contact.
contagiosa, impetigo (kôn-t-jē-ō'să ĭm-pĕt-ĭ-gō): a form of impetigo marked by flat vesicles that first become pustular, then crusted.
contagious (kôn-tā'jŭs): transmittable by contact.
contagium, animatum (kôn-tā'jē-ûm ăn-ĭ-mā'tûm): any living or animal organism that causes the spread of an infectious disease.
contamination (kôn-tăm-ĭ-nā'shŭn): pollution; soiling with infectious matter.
contiguous (kôn-tĭg'ū-û s): in contact; touching; adjoining.
contour (kŏn'tōōr): the outline of a figure or body; **contour of the hair**: shape of the hair, straight or wavy.
contra (kŏn'tră): a prefix denoting against; opposite; contrary.
contract (kôn-trăkt'): to draw together; to acquire by contagion.
contractile (kôn-trăk'tĭl): having the property of contracting.
contractility (kôn-trăk-tĭl'ĭ-tē): the property of contracting or shortening, as in muscular stimulation.
contraction (kôn-trăk'shŭn): having power to become shorter; the act of shrinking, drawing together.
contrary (kŏn'trâ-rē): in opposition.
controller (kôn-trōl'ẽr): magnetic device for the regulation and control of an electric current.
convalesce (kŏn-vă-lĕs'): to recover health and strength gradually after illness.
converter (kôn-vûr'tẽr): an apparatus used to convert the direct current to alternating current.
convex (kŏn'vĕks): curving outward like the segment of a circle.
convolute (kŏn'vŏ-lūt): roll or wound together, one part upon another.
convulsion (kôn-vŭl'shŭn): a violent involuntary muscular contraction.

fāte, câre, ăm, finâl, ärm, ȧsk, sofă; ēve, évent, ĕnd, recênt, evẽr; īce, ĭll; ōld, ṓbey, ôrb, ŏdd, cônnect, sŏft, fōōd, fŏŏt; ūse, ûrn, ŭp, circŭs

copious (kō'pē-ûs): large in amount.
copper (kŏp'ẽr): a metallic element, being a good conductor of heat and electricity.
coracoid (kŏr'ă-koid): a projecting part of the shoulder blade.
core (kôr): the heart or most vital part of anything.
corium (kō'rē-ûm): the derma or true skin.
corkscrew curl (kôrk'skroo kûrl): strands of hair having the form of a corkscrew spiral.
corneum (kôr'nḗ-um): the horny layer of the epidermis.
cornification (kôr-nĭ-fĭ-kā'shŭn): the process of becoming a horny substance or tissue; a callosity.
coronal suture (kŏr'ṓ-nâl sū'tûr): the line of junction of frontal bone with the two parietal bones of the skull.
coronary (kŏr'ṓ-nā-rē): relating to a crown; encircling.
coronoid (kŏr'ṓ-noid): crown-shaped, as the process of the large bone of the forearm or of the jaw.
corpus (kôr'pûs): a body; the human body.
corpuscle (kôr'pŭs-'l): a minute cell; a cell found in the blood.
corpuscles, red (rĕd): cells in blood whose function is to carry oxygen to the cells.
corpuscles, white (whīt): cells in the blood whose function is to destroy disease germs.
corrode (kô-rōd'): to diminish gradually by chemical action; to eat away gradually.
corrosive (kô-rô'sĭv): a substance that eats away or destroys.
corrosive sublimate (sŭb'lĭ māt): an antiseptic, similar to bichloride of mercury.
corrugations (kōr-oo-gā'shŭns): alternate ridges and furrows; wrinkles.
corrugator (kŏr'oo-gā-tẽr): a muscle that draws together the skin, causing it to wrinkle.
corrugator supercilii (sū-pẽr-sĭl'ē-ī): draws eyebrows inward and downward, thus causing vertical wrinkles at the root of the nose.
cortex (kôr'tĕks): the second layer of the hair.
cortical (kôr'tĭ-kăl): pertaining to the cortex.
cosmetic dermatology (kŏs-mĕt'ĭk dûr-mă-tŏl'ṓ-jē): a branch of dermatology devoted to improving the health and beauty of the kin and its appendages.
cosmetic therapy (thĕr'ă-pē): a term used by some State Boards to designate the practice of cosmetology.
cosmeticians (kŏz-mĕ-tĭsh'ănz): those professionally engaged in the art of improving the complexion, skin, and hair.
cosmetics (kŏz-mĕt'ĭks): any external application intended to beautify the complexion, skin, hair, or nails.
cosmetologist (kŏz-mḗ-tŏl'ḗ-jĭst): one skilled in the art of improving beauty.
cosmetology (kŏz-mḗ-tŏl'ō-jē): the treatise or science of beautifying and improving the complexion, skin, hair or nails.
costal (kŏs'tâl): pertaining to a rib.
costal breathing (brēth'ĭng): shallow breathing involving the use of the ribs.
counteract (koun-tẽr-ăkt'): to act in opposition to; to hinder, defeat.
counter-irritant (ĭr'ĭ-tânt): producing artificial irritation, designed to counteract a morbid condition.
cowlick (kou'lĭk): a tuft of hair forming a whorl.
cranial (krā'ne-âl): of or pertaining to the cranium.
cranium (krā'nē-ûm): the bones of the head excluding bones of the face; bony case for the brain.
cream (krēm): a semi-solid cosmetic.

fāte, câre, ăm, finâl, ärm, ȧsk, sofȧ; ēve, ḗvent, ĕnd, recênt, evẽr; īce, ĭll; ōld, ṓbey, ôrb, ŏdd, cônnect, sŏft, food, foot; ūse, ûrn, ŭp, circŭs

create (krē-āt'): to bring into being.
creosol (rē'ó-sōl): a colorless oily liquid resembling phenol.
creosote (krē'ó-sōt): an oily antiseptic liquid obtained from beechwood tar.
cresol (krē'sōl): a colorless, oily liquid or solid derived from coal tar and wood tar and used as a disinfectant.
crepe wool (krāp wōōl): wool made from sheep wool and used to confine hair ends in winding or to fill in for bullk.
crest (krĕst): a ridge, line or thin mark made by folding or doubling, as a crest between two waves, where one begins and the other ends.
criterion (krī-tē'rē-ūn): a standard of judging; rule; test.
croquignole (krō'kĭ-nōl): winding of the hair from ends to the scalp.
crown of the head (kroun): the top part of the head.
crucible (krōō'sĭ-b'l): a pot of clay or other material used for melting substances with great heat.
crude (krōōd): in a natural or unrefined state; imperfect.
crust (krŭst): a scab.
crypt (krĭpt): a small sac or cavity.
cuneiform (kū'nē-ĭ-fôrm): wedge-shaped; a bone of the wrist, or carpus.
curd (kûrd): soap residue found on the hair after an unsatisfactory shampoo.
curd soap (sōp): a white soap of curdy texture, usually containing free alkali.
cure (kūr): to take care of; to heal.
curl (kûrl): a lock of hair that curves spirally; a ringlet.
curler (kûr'lẽr): that which curls anything.
curling (kûr'lĭng): a process of hair waving.
curling, brush (kûr'lĭng): a process of tightly winding a wet strand of hair around the index finger, brushing with a stiff brush, pinning to the scalp with wire pins, and drying with artificial heat.
curling, paper (pā'pẽr): a process of dividing hair into small strands to form flat ringlets held in place by means of a folded piece of paper, and heated between the prongs of pressing irons.
curling, pin (pĭn): the process of forming hair ringlets by winding the hair in a series of concentric circles, fasten in place with hair pins.
curling, poker (pō'kẽr): handing curls having a corkscrew effect; tendril curls.
curling, round: a process of twisting the hair tightly and evenly around a heated curling iron.
curly (kûr'lē): tending to curl; full of curves, twists, or ripples.
current, alternating; A.C. (kŭr'ĕnt, ăl-tẽr-nāt-ĭng): an interrupted current.
current, D'arsonval (d'-är'sôn-vâl): a high-frequency current of low voltage and high amperage.
current, direct; D.C. (dī-rĕkt'): an uninterrupted and even-flowing current.
current, electric (ē-lĕk'trĭk): electricity in motion, or moving within a conductor.
current, faradic (fâ-răd'ik): an induced interrupted current whose action is mechanical.
current, galvanic (găl-văn'ĭk): a direct constant current having a positive and negative pole and producing a chemical action.
current, high-frequency; Tesla (hī-frē-kwên-sē; tĕs'lă): an electric current of medium voltage and medium amperage.
current, sinusoidal (sĭn-û-soi'dâl): an induced interrupted current somewhat similar to faradic current.
curriculum (kû-rĭk'ū-lŭm): the course of study in a school.
cutaneous (kū-tā'nē-ûs): pertaining to the skin.

fāte, câre, ăm, finâl, ärm, ȧsk, sofȧ; ēve, évent, ĕnd, recênt, evẽr; īce, ĭll; ōld, óbey, ôrb, ŏdd, cônnect, sŏft, fōōd, fŏŏt; ūse, ûrn, ŭp, circŭs

cuticle (kū'tĭ-k'l): the very thin outer layer of the skin or hair.
cutis (kū'tĭs): the derma or deeper layer of the skin.
cycle (sī'k'l): circle; a complete wave of an alternating current.
cylinder (sĭl'ĭn-dĕr): a long circular body, solid or hollow, uniform in diameter.
cylindrical (sĭ-lĭn'drĭ-kâl): pertaining to, or having the form of a cylinder.
cyst (sĭst): a closed abnormally developed sac containing fluid, semi-fluid or morbid matter.
cystine (sĭs'tĭn): a sulphur containing amino acid found in hair and nails.
cystoma (sĭs-tō'mă): a tumor containing cysts of pathogenic origin.
cytoplasm (sī'tṓ-plăz'm): the protoplasm of the cell body, exclusive of the nucleus.

D

dandruff (dăn'drŭf): pityriasis; scurf or scales formed in excess upon the scalp.
d'Arsonval current (d'-är'sôn-vâl kŭr'ênt): a high-frequency current of low voltage and high amperage; a bi-terminal current.
de (dē): a prefix denoting from; down or away.
debility (dē-bĭl'ĭ-tē): weakness; feebleness; loss of strength.
debris (dā-brē'; dā'brē): remains; rubbish.
decalvant (dḗ-kăl'vânt): removing the hair; making bald; destroying hair.
decomposition (dḗ-kōm-pṓ-zĭsh'ûn): act or process of separating the constituent parts of.
defective (dḗ-fĕk'tĭv): imperfect; lacking in some physical quality.
deficiency (dḗ-fĭsh'ên-sē): a lacking; something wanting.
deformity (dḗ-fôr'mĭ-tē): abnormal shape of a part of the body.
degenerate (dḗ-jĕn'ēr-āt): to pass to a lower level of mental or physical qualities.
deltoid (dĕl'toid): a muscle of the shoulder.
demarcation (dē-mär-kā'shên): a line setting bounds or limits.
dendrite (dĕn'drīt): a treelike branching of nerve fiber extending from a nerve cell.
dense (dĕns): close; thick; heavy.
dentifrice (dĕn'tĭ-frĭs): a powder, paste or liquid used to clean the teeth.
deodorant (dē-ō'dĕr-ânt): a substance that removes or conceals offensive odors.
deodorize (dē-ō'dĕr-īz): to free from odor.
depilation (dĕp-ĭ-lā'shŭn): removal of hair.
depilatory (dḗ-pĭl'ă-tō-rē): a substance, usually a caustic alkali, used to destroy the hair; having the power to remove hair.
depleted (dḗ-plēt'ĕd): exhausted; reduced.
deportment (dḗ-pōrt'mĕnt): manner of conduct or behavior.
depression (dḗ-prĕsh'ûn): a hollow or sunken area.
depressor (dḗ-pres'ĕr): that which presses or draws down; a muscle that depresses.
depressor alae nasi (ā'lēnā'sī): depressor septi; a muscle which contracts the nostril.
depressor anguli oris (ăng'ā-lī ŏr'ĭs): a muscle that depresses the angle of the mouth.
depressor labii inferioris (lā'bē-ī ĭn-fē-rē-ôr'ĭs): quadratus labii inferioris; a muscle that depresses the lower lip.
derivative (dḗ-rĭv'ă-tĭv): that which is derived; anything obtained or deduced from another.
derma (dûr'mă): the true skin; the corium; the sensitive layer of the skin below the epidermis.
dermal (dûr'mâl): pertaining to the skin.
dermatician (dûr-mă-tĭsh'ân): one skilled in the treatment of the skin.
dermatitis (dûr-mă-tī'tĭs): inflammation of the skin.
dermatitis combustions (kōm-bŭs-tĭ-ō'nēs): a type of dermatitis produced by extreme heat.

fāte, câre, ăm, finâl, ärm, ȧsk, sofă; ēve, ĕvent, ĕnd, recênt, evẽr; īce, ĭll; ōld, ṓbey, ôrb, ŏdd, cônnect, sŏft, fōod, fŏŏt; ūse, ûrn, ŭp, circŭs

dermatitis medicamentosa (mē-dĭk-a-mĕn-tō'sǎ): a type of dermatitis caused by the internal use of medicines, such as bromides.
dermatitis seborrheica (sĕb-ô-rē'ĭ-cǎ): a type of dermatitis found co-existing with seborrhea.
dermatitis venenata (vē-nĕ-na'tǎ): inflammation of the skin caused by the action of an irritant substance such as hair dye.
dermatologist (dûr-mǎ-tŏl'ô-jĭst): a specialist who understands the science of treating skin and its diseases.
dermatology (dûr-mǎ-tŏl'ō-jē): the science which treats of the skin and its diseases.
dermatosis (dûr-mǎ-tō'sĭs): any disease of the skin.
dermis, derma (dûr'mĭs, dûr'mǎ): the layer below the epidermis; the corium or true skin.
desiccation (dĕs-ĭ-kā'shŭn): the process of drying; application for drying up secretions.
desmology (dĕs-mŏl'ō-jē): the science of the ligaments.
desquammation (dĕs-kwä-mā'shŭn): scaling of the superficial epithelial cells of the skin.
destructive (dē-strŭk'tĭv): tending to destroy.
detergent (dē-tŭr'jênt): an agent that cleanses the skin.
deteriorate (dḗ-tē'rḗ-ō-rā t): to make or to grow worse; to become impaired in quality; to degenerate.
deterrent (dē-tĕr'ênt): that which hinders or prevents.
detriment (dĕt'rĭ-mênt): that which injures; reduces in value; causes damage.
device (dḗ-vīs'): an invention or contrivance of a simple nature for a particular use and purpose.
devitalize (dē-vī'tâl-īz): to destroy vitality; to destroy the life of.
dexterity (dĕks-tĕr'ĭ-tē): skill and ease in using the hands; expertness in manual acts.
di (dī): a prefix denoting two-fold; double; twice; separation or reversal.
dia (dī'ǎ): a prefix denoting through; apart; asunder; between.
diagnosis (dī-ǎg-nō'sĭs): the recognition of a disease from is symptoms.
diagram (dī'ǎ-grǎm): a figure for ascertaining or exhibiting certain relations between objects under discussion.
dialysis (dī-ǎl'ĭ-sĭs): the process of separating different substances in solution by diffusion through a moist membrane or septum; separation.
diaphragm (dī'ǎ-frǎm): a muscular wall which separates the thorax from the abdomen.
diathermy (dī'ǎ-thûr-mē): an instrument capable of generating a high-frequency current and elevating of temperature in the deep tissues.
dichromate, bichromate (dī-krō'mǎt; bī -): noting a salt having two parts equivalents of chromic acid to one of the base.
diet (dī'ĕt): a course of food selected with reference to a particular state of health.
diffuse (dĭ-fūz'): to pour out; to spread in every way; to operate.
diffusion (dĭ-fū'zhŭn): a spreading out; dialysis.
digest (dī-jĕst'): to prepare for absorption.
digestion (dī-jĕs'chŭn): the process of converting food into a form which can be readily absorbed by the body.
digital (dĭj'ĭ-tâl): pertaining to the fingers or toes.
digitalis (dĭj-ĭ-tā'lĭs): a drug used as a stimulant.
digits (dĭg'ĭts): fingers or toes.
digitus demonstrativus (dĭj'ĭ-tûs dḗ-mŏn'strǎ-tē'vûs): index finger.
digitus medicus (mĕd'ĭ-kûs): the ring finger.
digitus medius (mē'dē-ûs): the middle finger.
digitus minimus (min'ĭ-mûs): the little finger.

fāte, câre, ăm, finâl, ärm, ȧsk, sofǎ; ēve, ĕ́vent, ĕnd, recênt, evẽr; īce, ĭll; ōld, ŏ́bey, ôrb, ŏdd, cônnect, sŏft, fōod, fŏŏt; ūse, ûrn, ŭp, circûs

dilatator, dilator (dī-lāt′ă-tēr; dī-; dī-lā′tēr; dī-): that which expands or enlarges; an instrument for stretching a cavity or an opening.
dilate (dī-lāt; dī-lāt′): to enlarge ; to expand.
dilator (dī-lā′tēr): that which expands or enlarges.
dilator naris anterior (nā′rĭs ăn-tē′rē-ēr): a muscle which dilates the nostril.
dilute (dī-lūt′; dī-): to make thinner by mixing, especially with water.
dimethylglyoxime (dī-měth″ĭl-glī′ôk-sīm): a compound used in ash testing of dyed hair.
diminish (dĭ-mĭn′ĭsh): to make smaller or less; to reduce.
dimple (dĭm′p′l): a slight natural depression in the skin of the body, especially on the cheek or chin.
dip (dĭp): to slope, turn or hang down as in hair waving.
diphtheria (dĭp-thē′rē-ă): an infectious disease in which the air passages, and especially the throat, become coated with false membrane, caused by a specific bacillus.
diplococcus (dĭ-plŏ́-kŏk′ûs): bacteria exhibiting pairs.
direct current (dī-rěkt′ kŭr′ênt): a current constant in direction, in counter distinction to an alternating current.
dis (dĭs): a prefix denoting apart; away; asunder; between.
disc (dĭsk): a circular plate or surface.
discharge (dĭs-chärj′): to set free; to remove the contents or load; the escape or flowing away of the contents of a cavity.
discharger (dĭs-chärj′ēr): an instrument for setting free electricity.
disconnect (dĭs-kô-někt′): to sever or interrupt.
discretion (dĭs-krěsh′ûn): good judgment.
disease (dĭ-zēz): a pathologic condition of any part or organ of the body, or of the mind.
disease carrier (kăr′ĭ-ēr): a healthy person capable of transmitting disease germs to another person.
disinfect (dĭs-ĭn-fěkt′): to free from infection.
disinfect (dĭs-ĭn-fěk′tânt): an agent used for destroying germs.
disintegrate (dĭs-ĭn′tê-grāt): to separate or decompose into its component parts; to reduce to fragments or powder.
dislocate (dĭs′lŏ́-kāt): to displace, as a bone, from its natural position.
dispensary (dĭs-pěn′sȧ-rī): a place where medicines or other supplies are prepared and dispensed.
dissect (dī-sěkt′): to divide into separate parts, as an animal or plant, for examination; to analyze.
dissolve (dĭ-zŏlv): to make a solution of; to break up.
distal (dĭs′tâl): farthest from the center or median line.
distill (dĭs-tĭl′): to extract the essence or active principle of a substance.
distillation (dĭs-tĭ-lā′shûn): the process of distilling.
distinctive (dĭs-tĭnk′tĭv): marking a difference or distinction; characteristic outstanding.
distributive (dĭs-trĭb′ū-tĭv): tending to divide among several or many.
dormant (dôr′mânt): inactive; asleep.
dorsal (dôr′sâl): pertaining to the back.
dorsal artery of the foot (är′tēr-ē): a vessel which supplies blood to the back of the foot.
dowager's hump (dou′ȧ-jēr): a bony prominence at the back of the neck.
drab (drăb): a yellowish gray color.
dry cell (drī sěl): a metallic cup which generates electricity by chemical action.
dry cleanser (klěn′zēr): an agent such as benzene or orris root powder used to cleanse the hair without the use of soap and water.

fāte, câre, ăm, finâl, ärm, ȧsk, sofă; ēve, évent, ěnd, recênt, evēr; īce, ĭll; ōld, ŏ́bey, ôrb, ŏdd, cônnect, sŏft, fōōd, fŏŏt; ūse, ûrn, ŭp, circûs

duct (dŭkt): a passage or canal for fluids.
duodenum (dū-ŏ-dē'nûm): the part of the small intestines just below the stomach.
durability (dū-ră-bĭl'ĭ-tē): the power of lasting.
dye (dī): to stain or color.
dye remover (rḗ-mōōv'ĕr): a chemical liquid used to remove old dye from the hair.
dynamo (dī'nȧ-m ō): a machine for changing mechanical energy into electrical power.

E

ease (ēz): relief from labor or effort; freedom from pain, trouble, or annoyance.
ectal (ĕk'tâl): external; outer.
ecto (ĕk'tŏ): a prefix denoting without; outside; external.
ectodermic (ĕk-tō-dûr'mĭk): pertaining to the outer layer of cells formed from the inner cell mass in the embryonic cell.
eczema (ĕk'zē-mă): an inflammatory itching disease of the skin.
edema; oedema (ĕ-dē'mă): an abnormal accumulation of clear watery fluid in the lymph spaces of the tissues; dropsy; hydrops.
efferent (ĕf'ĕr-ênt): conveying outward, as efferent nerves conveying impulses away from the central nervous system.
effete (ĕ-fēt'): worn out; incapable of further vital use; exhausted of energy.
efficacious (ĕf-ĭ-kā'shus): possessing the quality of being effective.
efficiency (ĕ-fĭsh'ên-sē): usefulness; quality or degree of being able to produce results; economic productivity.
efficient (ĕ-fĭsh'ênt): characterized by energetic and useful activity.
effile (ĕ-fīl-ĕ'): French term meaning tapered or thinned out, as in shaping a coiffure.
effilate (ĕf'ĭ-lāt): to cut the hair strand by a sliding movement of the scissors.
effileing (ĕ-fīl'ĭng): slithering; the tapering of hair to graduated lengths.
effleurage (ĕ-flû-ràzh'): a stroking movement in massage.
effluvium (ĕ-flōō'vē-ûm): a bad odor; spark discharge from a high frequency current.
effusion (ĕ-fū'shûn): to pour out; the escape of fluid from the blood vessels or lymphatics into the tissue or cavity.
Egyptian henna (ê-jĭp'shân hĕn'ă): a pure vegetable hair dye.
elastic (ê-lăs'tĭk): returning to the original form after being stretched; having ability to stretch.
elasticity (ē-lăs'tĭs'ĭ-tē): the quality of being elastic.
electrical (ē-lĕk'trĭ-kâl): consisting of, containing, producing, or operated by electricity.
electric current (ē-lĕk'trĭk kŭr'ênt): electricity in motion through a conductor.
electric heater (ē-lĕk'trĭk hē'tĕr): as used in permanent waving, a name for a heating device connected to a permanent wave machine.
electricity (ē-lĕk-trĭs'ĭ-tē): a form of energy, which when in motion, exhibits magnetic, chemical or thermal effects.
electricity, animal (ân'ĭ-mâl): the free electricity in the body.
electricity, chemical (kĕm'ĭ-kâl): a kind of electricity which is generated by chemical action in a galvanic cell.
electricity, faradic (fă-răd'ĭk): a kind of electricity produced by the action of a magnetic field in an induction coil.

fāte, câre, ăm, finâl, ärm, ȧsk, sofă; ēve, ĕ́vent, ĕnd, recênt, evẽr; īce, ĭll; ōld, ŏ́bey, ôrb, ŏdd, cônnect, sŏft, fōōd, fŏŏt; ūse, ûrn, ŭp, circŭs

electricity, frictional (frĭk'shûn-âl): a kind of electricity produced by rubbing certain objects together.
electricity, galvanic (găl-văn'ĭk): a kind of electricity which is generated by chemical action in a galvanic cell.
electricity, high-frequency (hī-frē'kwên-sē): a kind of electricity having extremely rapid vibrations, 10,000 cycles or more per second.
electricity, induced or inductive (ĭn-dūst or ĭn-dŭk'tĭv): a kind of electricity produced by proximity to an electrified body.
electricity, magnetic (măg-nĕt'ĭk): a kind of electricity developed by bringing a conductor near the poles of a magnet.
electricity, sinusoidal (sī-nûs-oid'âl): an alternating induced electric current which resembles the faradic current.
electricity, static (stĕt'ĭk): frictional electricity.
electricity, voltaic (vōl-tā'ik): galvanic or chemical electricity.
electrification (ē-lĕk"trĭ-fĭ-kā'shŭn): the application of electricity to the body by holding an electrode in the hand and charging the body with electricity.
electro-coagulation (ē-lĕk'trō-kō-ăg'ū-lā-shŭn): a process employing high-frequency current to removed excess hair from the body.
electrode (ē-lĕk'trōd): a pole of an electric cell; an applicator for directing the use of electricity on a patron.
electrologist (ē-lĕk-tr ō l' ô -jĭst): proposed term for a person versed in electrology, and who may, in addition, be skilled in applying the science.
electrology (ē-lĕk-trŏl'ō-jē): science in relation to electricity.
electrolysis (ē-lĕk-trŏl'ĭ-sĭs): decomposition of a chemical compound or body tissues by means of electricity.
electrolyte (ē-lĕk'trô-līte): any compound which, in solution, conducts a current of electricity and is decomposed by it.
electrolytic (ē-lĕk-trô-lĭt'ĭk): pertaining to electrolysis.
electrolytic cup (ē-lĕk-trô-lĭt'ĭk kŭp): an appliance used to cleanse the skin, before giving a massage.
electromagnet (ē-lĕk"trô-măg'nĕt): a mass of soft iron surrounded by a coil of wire; a current passing through the wire will make the iron core magnetic.
electrometer (ē-lĕk-trŏm'ê-tēr): an instrument which indicates the presence of electricity.
electromotive force (ē-lĕk-trô-mō'tĭv fôrs): the force which by reason of difference in potential, produces electrical currents.
electron (ē-lĕk'trōn): an extremely minute corpuscle or charge of negative electricity, the smallest known to exist.
electrophobia (ē-lĕk-trô-fō'bē-ă): a morbid fear of electricity.
electropositive (ē-lĕk"trô-pŏz'ĭ-tĭv): relating to or charged with positive electricity.
electrotherapeutics (ē-lek-trô-thĕr-ă-pū'tĭks): the treatment of disease with electricity.
element (ĕl'ē-mĕnt): a simple substance, one which is incapable of being split up into other substances.
elementary (ĕl-ê-mĕn'tă-rē): introductory; the first principle of any study.
elimination (ê-lĭm-ĭ-nā'shŭn): act of expelling or excreting.
elongate (ê-lŏn'gāte): to extend; to lengthen; to stretch out.
emaciation (ē-mā"shē-ā'shŭn): make lean; loss of the fat and fullness of the flesh of the body; leanness.
embellish (ĕm-bĕl'ĭsh): to make beautiful or decorate.
embryo (ĕm'brē-ō): in the first stages of development; a bud.

fāte, câre, ăm, finâl, ärm, ȧsk, sofȧ; ēve, évent, ĕnd, recênt, evẽr; īce, ĭll; ōld, ŏbey, ôrb, ŏdd, cônnect, sŏft, fo͞od, fo͝ot; ūse, ûrn, ŭp, circûs

embryology (ĕm-brē-ŏl'ō-jē): science dealing with the development of the embryo.
embryonic (ĕm-brē-ŏn'ĭk): of or pertaining to an organism in the early stages of development.
emesis (ĕm'ĕ-sĭs): the act of vomiting.
eminence (ĕm'ĭ-nĕns): prominence; a circumscribed area raised above the general level of the surrounding surface.
emollient (ē-mŏl'yênt): an agent that softens or soothes the surface of the skin.
emotion (ĕ-mō'shŭn): mental excitement.
emulsifier (ē-mŭl'sĭ-fī-ĕr): an agent used to make an emulsion.
emulsion (ē-mŭl'shŭn): a milky fluid obtained by suspending oil in water.
enamel (ĕn-ăm'êl): gloss; polish.
endo (ĕn'dŏ): a prefix denoting inner; within.
endocrine (ĕn'dō-krĭn): any internal secretion or hormone.
endosteum (ĕn-dŏs'tĕ-ûm): the membrane covering the inner surface of bone in the medullary cavity.
endothelial (ĕn-dŏ-thē-lĕ-âl): a thin lining of the interior of the heart, blood vessels, lymphatics, etc.
energy (ĕn'ĕr-jē): power or capacity for performing work.
enervate (ĕn'ĕr-vāt; ĕ-nûr'vāt): to weaken.
enteric (ĕn-tĕr'ĭk): pertaining to the intestinal tract.
environment (ĕn-vī'rûn-mênt): the surrounding conditions.
enzyme (ĕn'zīm): a substance which induces a chemical change in other substances, without undergoing any change itself.
eosin (ē'ŏ-sĭn): a synthetic organic dye used in lipstick to impart a bluish-red tint to the lips.
epi (ĕp'ĭ): a prefix denoting upon; beside.
epicranium (ĕp-ĭ-krā'nī-ūm): the structure covering the cranium.
epicranius (ĕp-ĭ-krā'nē-ûs): the occipito-frontalis; the scalp muscle.
epidemic (ĕp-ĭ-dĕm'ĭk): common to many people; a prevailing disease.
epidermal (ĕp-ĭ-dûr'mâl): pertaining to or arising from the outer layer of the skin.
epidermis (ĕp-ĭ-dûr'mĭs): the outer epithelial portion of the skin.
epilation (ĕp-ĭ-lā'shŭn): the removal of hair by the roots.
epilepsy (ĕp-ĭ-lĕp'sē): a chronic nervous affection characterized by sudden loss of consciousness with general tonic and clonic convulsions.
epileptic (ĕp-ĭ-lĕp'tĭk): one affected by epilepsy.
epithelial (ĕp-ĭ-thē'lē-âl): relating to or consisting of epithelium.
epithelioma (ĕp-ĭ-thē"lē-ō'mă): a malignant growth consisting of epithelial cells; skin tumor.
epithelium (ĕp-ĭ-thē'-ûm): a cellular tissue or membrane, with little intercellular substance, covering a free surface or lining a cavity.
eponychium (ĕp-ŏ-nīk'ē-ûm): the extension of cuticle at base of nail.
equipment (ĕ-kwĭp'mênt): supplies needed for service.
eradication (ĕ-răd-ĭ-kā'shŭn): act of plucking by the roots; to destroy utterly.
erector (ĕ-rĕk'tĕr): an elevating muscle.
erosion (ĕ-rō'zhûn): the eating away; corrosion.
eructation (ē-rŭk-tā'shŭn): the elimination of gas from the stomach through the mouth.
eruption (ē-rŭp'shŭn): a visible lesion of the skin due to disease, marked by redness or popular condition, or both.
erysipelas (ĕr-ĭ-sĭp'ĕ-lâs): an acute infectious disease accompanied by a diffused inflammation of the skin and mucous membrane.
erythema (ĕr-ĭ-thē'mă): a superficial blush or redness of the skin.

fāte, câre, ăm, finâl, ärm, àsk, sofă; ēve, ĕvent, ĕnd, recênt, evẽr; īce, ĭll; ōld, ŏbey, ôrb, ŏdd, cônnect, sŏft, foōd, foŏt; ūse, ûrn, ŭp, circûs

erythrasma (ĕr-i-thră z'mă): an eruption of reddish brown patches, in the axillae and groins especially due to the presence of a fungus.
erythrocyte (ĕ-rĭth'rṓ-sīt): a red blood cell; red corpuscle.
eschar (ĕs'kȧr): a dry slough, crust, or scab following a burn.
esophagus; oesophagus (ê-sof'ă-gôs): the canal leading from the pharynx to the stomach.
essential oil (ĕ-sĕn'shȧl oil): natural or synthetic product having a fragrant odor and used in the making of perfumes.
esthetic; aesthetic (ĕs-thĕt'ĭk): relating to sensation, either mental or physical.
ether (ē'thẽr): a substance obtained from distilling alcohol with sulphuric acid; used as an anaesthetic.
ethics (ĕth'ĭks): principles of good character and proper conduct.
ethmoid (ĕth'moid): resembling a sieve; a bone forming part of the walls of the nasal cavity.
etiology (ĕ-tē-ŏl'ṓ-jē): the science of the causes of disease.
evaporation (ê-văp-ṓ-rā'shŭn): change from liquid to vapor form.
evolution (ĕv-ô-lū'shŭn): the process of developing from a simple to a complex form.
ex (ĕks): a prefix denoting out of; from; away from;
exaggerate (ĕg-zăj'ẽr-ăt): to enlarge or increase beyond the normal.
excitation (ĕk-sī-tā'shŭn): the act of stimulating or irritating.
excoriation (ĕks-kō-rē-ā'shŭn): act of stripping or wearing off the skin; an abrasion.
excrescence (ĕks-krĕs'ĕns): a disfiguring outgrowth.
excretion (ĕks-krē'shŭn): that which is thrown off or eliminated from the body.
excretory (ĕks'krḗ-tṓ-rē): pertaining to or serving for excretion.
exercise (ĕk'sẽr-sīz): a putting into action, use or practice; exertion for the sake of improvement.
exfoliation (ĕks-fō-lē-ā'shŭn): the process of throwing off scales from the skin as in dandruff.
exhalation (ĕks-hȧ-lā'shŭn): the act of breathing outward.
exhaustion (ĕg-z ô s'chŭn): loss of vital and nervous power from fatigue or protracted disease.
expansion (ĕks-jăn'shôn): distention; dilation or swelling.
expert (ĕks'pûrt): an experienced person; one who has special knowledge or skill in a particular subject.
exposure (ĕks-pō'shûr): act of being open to view; unprotected, as from the weather.
extensibility (ĕks-tĕn-sĭ-bĭl'ĭ-tĭ): capable of being extended or stretched.
extensor (ĕks-tĕn'sôr): a muscle which serves to extend or straighten out a limb or part.
exterior (ĕks-tē'rē-ẽr): outside.
external (ĕks-tûr'nâl): pertaining to the outside.
externus (ĕks-tûr'nŭs): external; pertaining to the outside.
extract (ĕks'trăkt): a solid obtained by evaporating a solution of a drug.
extreme (ĕks-trēm'): to a very great or to the greatest degree; to the farthest point.
extremity (ĕks-trĕm'ĭ-tē): the distant end or part of any organ; a hand or foot.
exudation (ĕks-û-dā'shŭn): act of discharging from a body through pores or incisions as sweat, moisture or other liquid; oozing out.
eye (ī): organ of vision.
eyeball (ī'bôl): the globe of the eye.
eyebrow (ī'brou): the hair, skin, and tissue above the eye.
eyelashes (ī'lĕsh-ês): the hair of the eyelids.
eyelid (ī'lĭd): the protective covering of the eyeball.
eye shadow (ī'shăd"ō): a cosmetic applied on the eyelids to accentuate their brilliance.

fāte, câre, ăm, finâl, ärm, ȧsk, sofă; ēve, ĕvent, ĕnd, recênt, evẽr; īce, ĭll; ōld, ṓbey, ôrb, ŏdd, cônnect, sŏft, fo͞od, fo͝ot; ūse, ûrn, ŭp, circŭs

F

facial (fā'shâl): pertaining to the face; the seventh cranial nerve.
Fahrenheit (fä'rên-hīt): pertaining to the Fahrenheit thermometer or scale; water freezes at 32°F and boils at 212°F.
faradic current (fă-răd'ĭk kŭr'ênt): relating to an induced interrupted current of electricity.
faradism (făr'ă-dĭz'm): a form of electrical treatment used for stimulating activity of the tissues.
fascia (făsh'ē-ă): a sheet of connective tissue covering, supporting, or binding together internal parts of the body.
fascial (făsh'ē-âl): relating to a fascia.
fascicle (făs'ĭ-k'l): a small band or a bundle of muscle or nerve fibers.
fasciculus (fâ-sĭk'û-lûs): a fascicle.
fat (făt): a greasy soft-solid material found in animal tissue.
fatigue (fă-tēg'): body or mental exhaustion.
favus (fā'v û s): a contagious parasitic disease of the skin, with crusts.
feather edge (fĕth'ẽr ĕj): a very thin fringe of hair resembling the edge of a feather.
fecal (fē'kâl): relating to the matter discharged from the bowel during defecation.
felon (fĕl'ûn): paronychia of the nail.
felt protector (fĕlt prô-tĕk'tẽr): a felt disk or rectangle used to protect the scalp from heat and fluid in permanent waving.
fertilization (fûr'tĭ-lī-zā-'shûn): the union of the male and female reproductive cells.
fermentation (fûr-mĕn-tā'shûn): a chemical decomposition of organic compounds into more simple compounds, brought about by the action of an enzyme.
fetid (fĕt'ĭd; fē'tĭd): having a foul smell; stinking.
fever (fē'vẽr): rise of body temperature.
fever blister (blĭs'tẽr): an acute skin disease characterized by the presence of vesicles over an inflammatory base; herpes simplex.
fiber; fibre (fī'bẽr): a slender thread or filament; thread-like in structure.
fiber rod (rŏd): a rod composed of fibrous material, not metal.
fibrin (fī'brĭn): the active agent in coagulation of the blood.
fibrinogen (fī'brĭn'ô-jĕn): a substance capable of producing fibrin.
fibroma (fī-brō'mă): a tumor composed mainly of fibrous or fully developed connective tissue.
fibrous (fī'brûs): containing, consisting of, or like fibers.
fibula (fĭb'û-là): the slender bone at the outer part of the leg.
filament (fĭl'ă-mênt): a thread-like structure.
file (fīl): a hardened steel instrument having cutting ridges, for the removal of fine shavings; nail file, used to remove portion of the free edge of the nail.
film (fĭlm): a membranous covering, causing opacity; thin skin.
filter (fĭl'tẽr): anything porous through which liquid is pass4ed to cleanse or strain it.
finesse (fĭ-nĕs'): delicate skill.
finger (fĭn'gẽr): one of the digits of the hand.
finishing cream (fĭn'ĭsh-ĭng krēm): a special cream used before applying make-up.
fish-kettle sterilizer (fĭsh-kĕt'l stẽr'ĭ-lī-zẽr): a special container used to dip objects into a disinfectant solution.
fission (fĭsh'ŏn): reproduction of bacteria by cellular division.
fissure (fĭsh'ûr): a narrow opening made by separation of parts; a furrow; a slit.
fixative (fĭk'sa-tĭv): a hair dressing used to keep hair in place; in cold waving, it stops the chemical action of the cold waving solution and sets or hardens the hair.
flabby (flăb'ē): lacking firmness; flaccid.

fāte, câre, ăm, finâl, ärm, àsk, sofă; ēve, évent, ĕnd, recênt, evẽr; īce, ĭll; ōld, ṓbey, ôrb, ŏdd, cônnect, sŏft, fo͞od, fo͝ot; ūse, ûrn, ŭp, circŭs

flaccid (flăk′sĭd): flabby; relaxed; being without bone.
flagella (flă-jĕl′ă): slender whip-like processes which permit locomotion in certain bacteria.
flannel (flăn′êl): a strip of flannel is used in permanent waving, as a cover for the curl to be steamed; it helps to retain moisture and prevents burning the hair.
flat winding (flăt wĭn′dĭng): winding the hair on a rod without twisting.
flatter (flăt′ĕr): to beguile; soothe; to charm.
flexible (flĕk′sĭ-b′l): that which may be bent; pliable; not stiff.
flexor (flĕk′sôr): a muscle that bends or flexes a part or a joint.
florid (flŏr′ĭd): flushed with red.
fluctuate (fluk′tû-āt): to roll back and forth; to cause to move as a wave.
fluid (floo′ĭd): a non-solid substance, liquid or gas.
foam (fōm): white bubbles forming on the surface of a liquid as a result of mixing or decomposition.
foil (foil): a sheet of metal (such as aluminum or tin) used in the construction of the permanent wave sachet or pad.
follicle (fŏl′ĭ-k′l): a small secretory cavity or sac; the depression in the skin containing the hair root.
folliculitis (fŏ-lĭk-û-lī′tĭs): an inflammation of any follicle.
folliculose (fŏ-lĭk′ū-lōs): full of follicles.
folliculosis (fŏ-lĭk-ū-lō′sĭs): a disease in which there is excessive development of the follicles.
food (food): nutriment; material capable of being utilized for the growth and the repair of the tissues.
foramen (fô-rā′mĕn): a passage or opening through a bone or membrane.
forceps (fŏr′sĕps): pincers or pliers for extracting, especially for delicate operations.
formaldehyde (for-măl′dê-hīd): a pungent gas possessing powerful disinfectant properties.
formalin (fôr′mă-lĭn): a 37% to 40% solution of formaldehyde.
formula (fôr′mă-lă): a prescribed method or rule; a recipe or prescription.
fossa (fŏs′ă); pl., **fossae** (-ē): a depression, furrow or sinus, below the level of the surface of a part.
foundation (foun-dā′shûn): the lowest and supporting layer of a structure.
fragilitas (fră-jĭl′ĭ′tăs): brittleness.
fraud (frôd): deceit; trickery.
fraudulent claim (frôd′û-lênt clām): characterized by, founded on, or obtained by fraud.
frayed (frād): worn away by friction or use.
freckle (frĕk″l): a yellow or brown spot on the skin; lentigo.
free edge (frē ĕj): part of the nail body extending over the finger tip.
frequency (frē′kwên-sē): the number of complete cycles of current produced by an alternating current generator per second. Standard frequencies are 25 and 60 cycles per second.
friction (frĭk′shûn): the resistance encountered in rubbing one body on another.
frontal (frŭn′tâl): in front; relating to the forehead; the bone of the forehead.
frontalis (frŏn-tă′lĭs): anterior portion of the epicranium; muscle of the scalp.
fulguration (fŭl-gû-rā′shûn): act of flashing or of sparking with special electrode and high frequency current, in treating malignant tumors.
fuller's earth (fool′ĕrz ûrth): a soapy clay often used as a foundation for packs and masks.
fulling (fool′ĭng): a massage movement in which the limb is rolled back and forth between the hands.
full twist (fool twĭst): a rope-like winding of the hair on the rod in spiral permanent waving.
fume (fūm): a vaporous or odorous smoke.

fāte, câre, ăm, finâl, ärm, ȧsk, sofȧ; ēve, évent, ĕnd, recênt, evẽr; īce, ĭll; ōld, ŏbey, ôrb, ŏdd, cônnect, sŏft, food, foot; ūse, ûrn, ŭp, circûs

fumigate (fū'mĭ-gāt): disinfect by the action of smoke or fumes.
function (fŭnk'shôn): a normal or special action of a part.
fundamental (fŭn-dă-měn'tâl): essential; basic rule or principle.
fundus (fŭn'dŭs): the bottom or lowest part of a sac or hollow organ.
fungus (fŭn'gŭs): a vegetable parasite; a spongy growth of diseased tissue on the body.
funny bone (fŭn'ē bōn): the bone on the inner side of the forearm; the ulna; a tingling sensation is felt when the nerve is struck.
furfurol (fûr'fû-rol): a colorless aromatic fluid obtained from the distillation of bran with dilute sulphuric acid.
furrow (fŭr'ō): a groove; wrinkle.
furuncle (fū-rŭn'k'l): a boil.
fuscin (fŭs'ĭn): the black pigment of the retina.
fuse (fūz): to liquefy by heat; a special device which prevents excesive current from passing through a circuit.

G

galea (gā'lê-ă): a form of head-bandage; headache extending all over the head; the aponeurotic portion of the occipito-frontalis muscle.
galvanic current (găl-văn'ĭk kŭr'rent): a direct constant and silent current having a positive and a negative pole; named for Galvani (1737-1798).
galvanism (găl'vă-nĭz'm): a constant current of electricity the action of which is chemical.
ganglion (găn'glē-ôn); pl., **ganglia** (-ă): subcutaneous tumors; bundles of nerve cells in the brain, in organs of special sense, or forming units of the sympathetic nervous system; circumscribed cystic swellings connected with tendon sheaths.
gangrene (găn-grēn'): the dying of tissue due to interference with local nutrition.
gasoline (găs'ô-lēn): an inflammable liquid used as a cleansing fluid.
gastric (găs'trĭk): pertaining to the stomach.
gastric juice (jo͞os): the digestive fluid secreted by the glands of the stomach.
gastrocnemiuis muscle (găs-trōk-nē'mĭ-ŭs mŭs'l): the largest and most superficial muscle of the calf of the leg.
gastro-intestinal (găs-trô-ĭn-těs'tĭ-nâl): pertaining to both the stomach and the intestines.
gauze (gôz): a thin open-meshed cloth used for dressings.
gelatin (jěl'ă-tĭn): jelly-like substance; glutinous matter obtained from animal tissues by prolonged boiling.
general system, blood (jěn'ěr-âl sĭs'těm): blood circulation from the heart throughout the body and back again.
generator (jěn'ěr-ā-těr): a machine for changing mechanical energy into electrical energy; a dynamo.
genesiology (jē-nē'sē-ŏl'ô-jē): the science of reproduction.
gentian violet jelly (jěn'shăn vī'ô-lět jěl'ĭ): an antiseptic used in the first aid treatment of a scalp burn.
genus (jē'nŭs): the knee; kind; order.
germ (jûrm): a bacillus; a microbe; an embryo in its early stages.
germicidal (jûr-mĭ-sī'dâl): destructive to germs.
germicide (jûr'mĭ-sīd): any chemical, especially a solution that will destroy germs.
germination (jûr-mĭ-nā'shŭn): the formation of an embryo from an impregnated ovum; the first act of growth in a germ, seed or bud.

fāte, câre, ăm, finâl, ärm, ȧsk, sofă; ēve, évent, ěnd, recênt, evĕr; īce, ĭll; ōld, ó̆bey, ôrb, ŏdd, cônnect, sŏft, fo͞od, fo͝ot; ūse, ûrn, ŭp, circŭs

germinative (jûr′mĭ-nâ-tĭv): having power to grow or develop.
germinative layer (lā′ẽr): stratum germinativum; the inner layer of the epidermis resting on the corium.
germitabs (jûr′mĭ-tăbs): a trade name; special tablets, which, when dissolved in water, form an antiseptic solution.
glabrous (glā′brûs): smooth; without hair.
gland (glănd): a secretory organ of the body.
glandular (glăn′dû-lăr): pertaining to a gland.
glint (glĭnt): brightness; luster; shine.
globule (glōb′ūl): a small round body.
glossa (glŏs′ă): tongue; lingua.
glossy (glŏs′ē): smooth and shining; highly polished.
glossopharyngeal (glŏs-ô-fâ-rĭn′jê-âl): pertaining to the tongue and pharynx; the ninth cranial nerve.
glycerin; glycerine (glĭs′ẽr-ĭn): sweet oily fluid, used as an application for roughened and chapped skin; also used as a solvent.
glycogen (glī′kô-jĕn): animal starch.
goiter (goi′tẽr): enlargement of the thyroid gland.
gonads (gŏn′ăds): essential sexual glands; ovaries and testes.
gonococcus (gŏn-ō-kŏk′ûs); pl., **gonococci** (-s ē): the germ causing gonorrhea.
gonorrhea (gŏn-ō-rē′ă): a contagious venereal disease.
gracious (grā′shŭs): kindly, pleasant.
graduation (grăd-ū-ā′shŭn): regular progress, step by step.
granular layer (grăn′û-lăr lā′ẽr): the stratum granulosum of the skin.
granules (grăn′ūlz): small grains; small pills.
granulosum (grăn′ū-lōs′ûm): granular layer of the epidermis.
great auricular (grāt ô-rĭk′û-lăr): a nerve affecting the face, ear, neck, and parotid gland.
greater multangular (mŭl-tăn′gû-lăr): trapezium; bone of the wrist.
greater occipital (grăt′ẽr ŏk-sĭp′ĭ-tâl): sensory and motor nerve affecting the splenius, complexus, and scalp.
gristle (grĭs″l): cartilage.
groom (grōōm): to make neat or tidy.
groove (grōōv): of a marcel iron, the long hollow part of the iron into which the rod fits.
ground wire (ground wīr): a wire which connects an electric current to a ground (waterpipe or radiator).
gumma (gŭm′ă): the gummy tumor in the tertiary stage of syphilis.
guttate (gŭt′āt): drop-like in form, characterizing certain cutaneous lesions.

H

habit (hăb′ĭt): an acquired tendency to repetition.
hacking (hăk′ĭng): a chopping stroke made with the edge of the hand in massage.
hair (hâr): pilus; a slender thread-like outgrowth on the body of animals.
hair, superfluous (sŭ-pûr′flōō-ûs): unwanted hair found on the face of women and girls.
hair bobbing (bŏb′ĭng): the term commonly applied to the cutting of women's and children's hair.
hair bulb (bŭlb): the lower extremity of the hair.

---

fāte, câre, ăm, finâl, ärm, ȧsk, sofă; ēve, ĕvent, ĕnd, recênt, evẽr; īce, ĭll; ōld, ŏ́bey, ôrb, ŏdd, cônnect, sŏft, fōōd, fŏŏt; ūse, ûrn, ŭp, circŭs

hair clipping (klĭp′ĭng): removing the hair by the use of hair clippers; removing split hair ends of the hair with the scissors.
haircutting (hâr′kŭt-ĭng): shortening and thinning of the hair, and molding the hair into a becoming style; hair shaping.
hair dressing (hār drĕs′ĭng): art of arranging the hair into various becoming shapes or styles.
hair dyeing (dī′ĭng): to give the hair new and permanent color by impregnating it with a coloring agent.
hair follicle (fŏl′ĭ-k′l): the depression in the skin containing the root of the hair.
hairline (hâr′līn): the edge of the scalp at the brow where the hair growth of the head begins.
hair papilla (hâr pă-pĭl′ă): a small cone-shaped elevation at the bottom of the hair follicle.
hair piece (pēs): curl, braid or other hair section worn over the hair.
hair pressing (prĕs′ĭng): a method of straightening curly or kinky hair by means of a heated iron or comb.
hair pressing oil (oil): an oily or waxy mixture used in hair pressing.
hair restorer (rē-stōr′ĕr): a preparation containing a metallic dye.
hair root (rōōt): that part of the hair contained within the follicle.
hair shaft (shăft): the portion of the hair which projects beyond the skin.
hair straightener (strāt′n-ĕr): a physical or chemical agent used in straightening kinky or over-curly hair.
hair test (tĕst): a sampling of how the hair will react to a particular treatment.
hair tint (tĭnt): to give a coloring to the hair; color or shade of hair.
hair trim (trĭm): trimming; cutting the hair lightly over the already existing formed lines.
half twist (häf twĭst): a term used in spiral permanent waving to designate a type of winding, flat on one side of the rod and twisted on the other side in each revolution.
halitosis (hăl″ĭ-tō′sĭs): offensive odor from the mouth; foul breath.
hamamelis (hăm-ă-mē′lĭs): a shrub of eastern North America; witch-hazel is an extract of this plant, and is used as an astringent.
hamate (hā′māt): hooked; unciform; a bone of the wrist.
hanging curls (hăng′ĭng kûrlz): curls suspended from the head with a downward slope or inclination.
hangnail (hăng′nāl): a tearing up of a strip of epidermis at the side of the nail; agnail.
hard water (härd wô′tĕr): water containing certain minerals; does not lather with soap.
Haversian canals (hă-vûr′shân): small channels through which the blood vessels divide in the bone.
heal (hēl): to cure.
health (hĕlth): state of being hale or sound in body and mind.
heart (härt): a hollow muscular organ which, by contracting rhythmically keeps up the circulation of the blood.
heating coil (hēt coil): an electric coil which heats the air in a hair dryer.
heat regulation (hēt rĕg-û-lā′shûn): temperature controlled.
helical (hĕl-ĭ-kâl): shaped like a spiral.
heliotherapy (hē-lĭ-ô-thĕr′ȧ-pĭ): the use of sun rays to treat disease.
hemal; haemel (hē′mâl): relating to the blood or blood vessels.
hematidrosis; hemidrosis (hĕm″ă-tĭ-drō′sĭs, hĕm-ĭ-drō′sĭs): the excretion of sweat stained with blood or blood pigment.
hematocyte (hĕ′mă-tô-sīt): a blood corpuscle.
hemi (hĕm′ĭ): a prefix signifying half.
hemoglobin; haemoglobin (hē″mô-glō′bĭn): the coloring matter of the blood.

fāte, câre, ăm, finâl, ärm, ȧsk, sofă; ēve, évent, ĕnd, recênt, evẽr; īce, ĭll; ōld, ŏbey, ôrb, ŏdd, cônnect, sŏft, fōōd, fŏŏt; ūse, ûrn, ŭp, circûs

hemorrhage (hĕm′ô-râj): bleeding; a flow of blood, especially when profuse.
henna (hĕn′ă): the leaves of an Asiatic thorny tree or shrub used as a dye, imparting a reddish tint; it is also used as a cosmetic.
henna, compound (kŏm′pound): Egyptian henna to which has been added one or more metallic preparations.
henna, white (whīt): a mixture of magnesium carbonate, peroxide and ammonia used in giving a bleach retouch.
hereditary (hê-rĕd′ĭ-tâ-rē): descending from ancestor to heir.
heredity (hê-rĕd′ĭ-tĭ): the transfer of qualities or disease from parents to offspring.
herpes (hûr′pēz): an inflammatory disease of the skin having small vesicles in clusters.
herpes simplex (sĭm′plĕks): fever blister; cold sore.
hidrosis (hī-drō′sĭs): abnormally profuse sweating.
high-frequency, Tesla (hī-frē′kwĕn-sē): violet ray; an electric current of medium voltage and medium amperage.
hirsute (hûr′sūĭt; hēr-sūt′): hairy; having coarse, long hair; shaggy.
histologists (hĭs-tŏl′ô-jĭsts): experts in the science of histology.
histology (hĭs-tŏl′ô-je): the science of the minute structure of organic tissues; microscopic anatomy.
hives (hīvz): urticarial; a skin eruption.
honey (hŭn′ē): mel; the product of the honey bee.
horizontal (hŏr-ĭ-zŏn′tâl): parallel to the horizon; level.
hormone (hôr′mōn): a chemical substance formed in one organ or part of the body and carried in the blood to another organ or part which it stimulates to functional activity or secretion.
horny (hôr′nē): composed of or resembling horns; hard.
humerus (hū′mēr-ûs): the bone of the upper part of the arm.
humidity (hû-mĭd′ĭ-tĭ): moisture; dampness.
hyaline (hī′ă-lĭn): transparent like glass.
hydrate (hī′drāt): a compound formed by the union of water with some other substance.
hydration (hī-drā′shûn): the chemical union of a substance with water.
hydro (hī′drô): a prefix denoting water; hydrogen.
hydro-carbon (hī-drô -kär′bôn): charcoal; any compound composed only of hydrogen and carbon.
hydrochloric acid (hī″-drô-klō′rĭk ă-s′ĭd): a compound of hydrogen and chlorine.
hydrocyst (hīd′rō-sĭst): a cyst containing a water-like liquid.
hydrocystoma (hīd-rō-sĭs-tō′mă): a variety of sudamina appearing on the face, especially of women in middle and advanced life.
hydrofluoric acid (hī″drô-floo-ŏr′ĭk ăs′ĭd): a compound of hydrogen and fluorine.
hydrogen (hī′drô-jên): a colorless, odorless and tasteless gaseous inflammable element, lighter than any other known substance.
hydrogen peroxide (pĕr-ŏk′sīd): a powerful oxidizing agent; in liquid form is used as an antiseptic.
hydrolysis (hī-drŏl′ĭ-sĭs): chemical decomposition involving the addition of water.
hydroscope (hī′drô-skōp): hygroscope; water clock.
hydrotherapeutics (hī′drŏthĕr-ȧ-pū′tĭks): treating disease by baths and mineral waters.
hygiene (hī-jēn): the science of preserving health.
hygroscopic (hī-grō′skŏp′ĭk): readily absorbing and retaining moisture.
hyoid (hī′oid): the "u" shaped bone at the base of the tongue.
hyper (hī′pĕr): a prefix denoting excessive; above normal; above; beyond.

fāte, câre, ăm, finâl, ärm, ȧsk, sofă; ēve, évent, ĕnd, recênt, evẽr; īce, ĭll; ōld, ŏ́bey, ôrb, ŏdd, cônnect, sŏft, fōod, foŏt; ūse, ûrn, ŭp, circûs

hyperacidity (hī″pĕr-ă-sĭd′ĭ-tē): an excess of acidity.
hyperemia (hi″pĕr-ē′mē-ă): the presence of an excessive quantity of blood in a part of the body; congestion.
hyperhidrosis, hyperhidrosis (hī″pĕr-ĭ-drō′sĭs): excessive sweating.
hyperostosis (hī-pĕr-ŏs-tō′sĭs): general hypertrophy of bone tissues.
hyperplasia (hī-pĕr-plā′zhē-ă; -zē-ă): an increase in number of the individual tissue elements, excluding tumor formations, whereby the bulk of the part or organ is increased.
hypersecretion (hī″pĕr-sê-krē′shûn): excessive secretion.
hypertrichosis; hypertricosis (hī″pĕr-trĭ-kō′sĭs): a condition of excessive development or abnormal growth of the hair; superfluous hair.
hypertrophica (hī″pĕr-trŏf′ĭ-kă): a form of acne in which the lesions leave conspicuous pits and scars upon healing.
hypertrophy (hī″pĕr-trō′fē): abnormal increase in the size or a part of an organ; overgrowth.
hypo (hī′pō): a prefix denoting under; beneath; lower state of oxidation.
hypodermic (hī″pō-dûr′mĭk): beneath the skin; a liquid injection into the subcutaneous tissues.
hypoglossal (hi″pô-glŏs′âl): under the tongue; the twelfth cranial nerve.
hyponychium (hi″pô-nīk′ē-ûm): the extension of the skin underneath the free edge of the nail.
hypothenar (hī-pŏth′ê-năr): the fleshy eminence on the palm of the hand over the metacarpal bone at the base of the fingers.
hypothesis (hī-pŏth′ê-sĭs): a specific or detailed statement of a topic of discourse; a theory assumed as true.
hysteria (hĭs-tē′rĭ-à): a nervous disorder peculiar to women.

I

ichthyosis (ĭk-thē-ō′sĭs): a skin disease in which the skin becomes rough with diminished sweat and sebaceous secretion; fish skin disease.
ide (īd): a word termination forming names of compounds, such as chlorides.
identical (ī-děn-tĭ-kâl): exactly alike.
idiosyncrasy (ĭd-e-ô-sĭn′kră-sē): an individual characteristic or peculiarity; a susceptibility, peculiar to the individual due to the action of certain drugs, articles of diet, etc.
illicit (ĭ-lĭs′ĭt): not allowed; improper.
imbecile (ĭm′bê-sĭl): mentally deficient; a weak minded person.
imbibition (ĭm-bĭ-bĭsh′ûn): the act of sucking up moisture.
imbrication (ĭm-brĭ-kâ′shûn): overlapping of the edges like that of the shingles.
imbrications of hair: tiny overlapping scales found on the hair cuticle.
immerse (ĭ-mûrs′): to plunge into; dip; submerge in a liquid.
immiscible (ĭ-mĭs′ĭ-b′l): a liquid that will not mix with another liquid.
immune (ĭ-mūn′): safe from attack; protected by vaccination.
immunity (ĭ-mūn′ĭ-tē): freedom from or resistant to disease.
impermeable (ĭm-pūr′mê-ă-b′l): impenetrable; not permitting passage.
impervious (ĭm-pûr′vē-ûs): impenetrable; especially passage of liquids.
impetigo (ĭm-pḗ-tī′gō): an eruption of pustules, which soon rupture or become crusted, occurring chiefly on the face around the mouth and the nostrils.
impetigo contagiosa (kôn-tā″jē-ō′să): scrumpox; a contagious disease, characterized by an eruption of flat vesicles which may develop into pustules.
implement (ĭm′plê-mênt): an instrument or tool used by man to accomplish a given work.
impregnate (ĭm-prĕg′nāt): to mix with an active agent.
in (ĭn): a prefix denoting not; negative; within; inside.

fāte, câre, ăm, finâl, ärm, àsk, sofă; ēve, évent, ĕnd, recênt, evẽr; īce, ĭll; ōld, ŏbey, ôrb, ŏdd, cônnect, sŏft, fōod, fŏot; ūse, ûrn, ŭp, circûs

incision (ĭn-sĭzh′ŭn): a cut; a division of the soft parts made with a knife.
incandescent (ĭn-kăn-dĕs′ĕnt): giving forth light and heat.
incisor teeth (ĭn-sī′zẽr; -sẽr tēth): the four anterior teeth in each jaw.
inclined (ĭn-klīnd′): bowed forward; bent.
incubation (ĭn-kû-bā′shŭn): the period of a disease between the implanting of the contagion and the development of the symptoms.
indemnity (ĭn-dĕm′nĭ-tē): compensation for loss.
indent (ĭn-dĕnt′): a cut in a margin.
index (ĭn′dĕks): the forefinger; the pointing finger.
indigo (ĭn′dĭ-go): a blue dyestuff.
indispensable (ĭn-dĭs-pĕn′să-b′l): absolutely necessary.
individually (ĭn-dĭ-vĭd′ŭ-ăl-ē): each by itself.
induction (ĭn-dŭk′shŭn): the transfer of electricity from a current to a magnetized object.
indurate, acne (ĭn-dû-rā′tă): deeply seated popular eruptions with hard tubercular lesions.
induration (ĭn-d û -rā′sh û n): the process or act of hardening; a spot or area of hardened tissue.
inefficiency (ĭn″ĕ-fĭsh′ên-sē): quality, state or fact of being incapable.
inert (ĭn-ûrt): inactive.
infect (ĭn-fĕkt): to cause infection.
infection (ĭn-fek′shŭn): the invasion of the body tissues by disease germs.
infection, general (jĕn′ẽr-ĕl): the result of the disease germs gaining entrance into the blood stream and thereby circulating throughout the entire body.
infection, local (lō′kâl): confined to only certain portions of the body, such as an abscess.
infectious (ĭn-fĕk′shŭs): capable of spreading infection.
inferior (ĭn-fē′rē-ẽr): situated lower down, or nearer the bottom or base.
inferioris (ĭn-fē″rē-ŏr′ĭs): below; lower.
infiltration (ĭn-f ĭ l-trā′sh û n): the act of passing one substance into another.
inflammation (ĭn-flâ-mā′shŭn): the reaction of the body to irritation with accompanying redness, pain, heat, and swelling.
influenza (ĭn-floo-ĕn′ză): a contagious epidemic catarrhal fever, with great prostration an varying symptoms; grippe.
infra (ĭn′fră): a prefix denoting below; lower.
infra-mandibular (ĭn″fră-măn-dĭb′û-lăr): below the lower jaw.
infra-mental (mĕn′tâl): below the chin.
infra-orbital (ôr′bĭ-tâl): below the orbit; in the floor of the orbit; a sensory and motor nerve affecting the cheek muscles, nose, and upper lip.
infra-red (ĭn″fră-rĕd′): pertaining to that part of the spectrum lying outside of the visible spectrum and below the red rays.
infra-trochlear (trŏk′lē-ăr): sensory nerve affecting the lacrimal sac, the skin of the nose and the inner muscle of the eye.
ingestion (ĭn-jĕs′chŭn): the act of taking substances, especially food, into the body.
ingredient (ĭn-grē′dē-ênt): any constituent part of a compound.
ingrown hair (ĭn′grōn hâr): a wild hair that has grown underneath the skin, thereby causing an infection.
ingrown nail (ĭn′grōn nāl): the growth of the nail into the flesh instead of toward the tip of the finger or toe, thereby causing an infection.
inhalation (ĭn-hă-lā′shŭn): the inbreathing of air or other vapors.
inhibition (ĭn-hĭ-bĭsh′ŭn): the diminution or arrest of the function in an organ.

fāte, câre, ăm, finâl, ärm, ȧsk, sofȧ; ēve, ĕvent, ĕnd, recĕnt, evẽr; īce, ĭll; ōld, ŏ́bey, ôrb, ŏdd, cônnect, sŏft, fōōd, fŏŏt; ūse, ûrn, ŭp, circŭs

innervation (ĭn-ẽr-vā'shûn): distribution of the nerves in a part.
innominate veins (ĭ-nŏm'ĭ-nât vāns): veins of the neck.
inoculation (ĭn-ŏk-û-lā'shûn): the process by which protective agents are introduced into the body.
inorganic (ĭn-ôr-găn'ĭk): composed of matter not relating to living organisms.
insanitary; unsanitary (ĭn-săn'ĭ-tā-rē; ŭn-): not sanitary or healthful; injurious to health; unclean.
insanity (ĭn-săn'ĭ-tĭ): unsoundness or derangement of mind.
insertion (ĭn-sûr'shûn): act of inserting; that which is set in.
insidious (ĭn-sĭd'ē-ûs): treacherous; hidden or stealthy.
insolation (ĭn-sō-lā'shûn): exposure to the rays of the sun; sunstroke.
insoluble (ĭn-sŏl'ū-b'l): incapable of being dissolved or very difficult to dissolve.
instantaneous (ĭn-stăn-tā'nē-ŭs): acting immediately.
insulation (ĭn-sû-lā'shûn): the non-conducting substance by which electricity or heat is prevented from escaping.
insulator (ĭn'sū-lā-tẽr): a non-conducting material or substance. Materials used to cover electric wires.
insulin (ĭn'sŭ-lĭn): a hormone which regulates carbohydrate metabolism.
insurance (ĭn-shoor'ăns): protection against loss, damage or injury.
insure (ĭn-shoor'): to make sure or secure.
integument (ĭn-tĕg'û-mênt): a covering, especially the skin.
inter (ĭn'tẽr): a prefix denoting amid; between; among.
intercellular (ĭn-tẽr-sĕl'ū-lăr): between or among cells.
interior (ĭn-tē'rē-ẽr): inside.
intermediate (ĭn-tẽr-mē'dē-ăt): between two extremes.
intermittent heat (ĭn-tẽr-mĭt'ênt hēt): interrupted heating period; electric current turned on and off during the steaming period.
internal (ĭn-tûr'nâl): pertaining to the inside; inner part.
internus (ĭn-tûr'nûs): internal; pertaining to the inside.
interosseous (ĭn-tẽr-ŏs'ế-ûs): lying between or connecting bones.
interstice (ĭn-tûr'stĭs): a small gap or hole in the substance of an organ or a tissue; pore.
interval (ĭn'tẽr-vâl): a time or space between two periods or objects.
intestinal (ĭn-tĕs'tĭ-nâl): pertaining or relating to the intestines.
intestine (ĭn-tĕs'tĭn): the digestive tube from the stomach to the anus.
intolerance (ĭn-tŏl'ẽr-ăns): quality or state of being unable to endure, especially refusal to allow others the enjoyment of their opinions.
invasion (ĭn-va'zhûn): the beginning of a disease.
inversion (ĭn-vûr'shûn): the act of turning inward.
involution (ĭn-vŏ-lū'shûn): that in which anything is folded or wrapped; the return of an enlarged part or organ to its normal size.
involuntary muscles (mŭs"ls-z): function without the action of the will.
iodine (ī'ố-dīn; -dĭn): a non-metallic element used as an antiseptic for cuts, bruises, etc.
iodoform (ī-ō'dô-fôrm): a yellow crystalline compound formed by the action of iodine on alcohol and potash; a valuable antiseptic for wounds and sores.
ion (ī'ŏn): an atom or group of atoms carrying an electric charge.
ionization (ī-ŏn-ī-zā'shûn): the separating of a substance into ions.
iontophoresis (ī-ŏn-tō-fố-rē'sĭs): the introduction of ions into the body by the electric current.
iridescence (ĭr-i-dĕs'êns): the rainbow-like play of colors, as in mother of pearl.

fāte, câre, ăm, finâl, ärm, ȧsk, sofă; ēve, ếvent, ĕnd, recênt, evẽr; īce, ĭll; ōld, ỗbey, ôrb, ŏdd, cônnect, sŏft, fōod, foŏt; ūse, ûrn, ŭp, circŭs

iris (ī'ris): the colored muscular disk-like diaphragm of the eye which regulates the pupil or opening in the center.

iron (ī'ûrn): ferrum; a metallic element.

irradiation (ĭ-rā″dĭ-ā'shŭn): the process of exposing an object to the natural or artificial sunlight.

irregularity (ĭ-rĕg'-ū-lăr-tē): quality or state of being uneven or not uniform.

irreparable (ĭ-rep'ă-ră-b'l): damaged beyond repair.

irritability (ĭr-ĭ-tȧ-bĭl'ĭ-ĭ): readily excited or stimulated.

irritant (ĭr'ĭ-tȧnt): causing irritation; an irritating agent; a stimulus.

itinerant beauty operator (ī-tĭn'ẽr-ȧnt bū'tē ŏp'ẽr-ā-tẽr): an operator who does work from house to house.

ive (īv): a word termination signifying relating or belonging to, such as active.

ize (īz): a word termination forming transitive verbs, such as sterilize.

J

jaundice (jôn'dĭs): a morbid condition, characterized by yellowness of the eyes, skin and urine, constipation, loss of appetite, and general languor.

jowl (jōl): the hanging part of a double chin.

joint (joint): a connection between two or more bones.

jugular (jŭ'gū-lăr): pertaining to the neck or throat; the large vein in the neck.

K

kaolin; kaoline (kā'ô-lĭn; kä-): fuller's earth; porcelain clay; employed occasionally as a dusting powder, but chiefly in the form of a poultice with glycerine (mud pack).

karaya gum (kă-ră'ă-gŭm): Indian gum; a gum obtained in India and Africa from the trees of the genus Sterculia; used to make mucilages and wave set preparations.

keloid (kē'loid): a skin disease marked by whitish indurated patches surrounded by a pinkish or purplish border; a fibrous growth arising from irritation and usually from a scar.

keratoma (kĕr-ă-tō'mă): a callosity; a horny tumor; an acquired thickened patch of the epidermis.

keratosa, acne (kĕr-ă-tō 'să): horny plugs projecting from the hair follicles, accompanied by inflammation.

keratosis (kĕr-ă-tō'sĭs): any disease of the epidermis, especially one marked by the presence of circumscribed overgrowths of the horny layer; callous or keratoma.

key (kē): in permanent waving, a device used to tighten the hair wound on the rod.

kidney (kĭd'nē): a glandular organ which excretes urine.

kilowatt (kĭl'ô-wŏt): one thousand watts of electricity.

kinky (kĭnk'ĭ): very curly hair.

knead (nēd): to work and press with the hands as in massage.

knowledge (nŏl'ĕj): instruction; learning; practical skill.

kohl (kōl; kō″l): a preparation used to darken the edges of the eyelids.

kolsterol (kōl'stê-rōl): a trade name; a prepared germicide.

---

fāte, câre, ăm, finâl, ärm, ȧsk, sofȧ; ēve, évent, ĕnd, recênt, evẽr; īce, ĭll; ōld, ȯbey, ôrb, ŏdd, cônnect, sŏft, fōod, fŏŏt; ūse, ûrn, ŭp, circûs

L

labial (lā'bē-āl): pertaining to the lips'
labii (lā'bē-ī): of or pertaining to the lip
labium (lā'bē-ûm); pl., **labia** (-ă): lip
laboratory (lăb'ô-ră-tô-rē): a room containing apparatus for conducting experiments
laceration (lăs'ĕr-ā'shûn): a tear of the skin or tissues
lachrymal; lacrimal (lăk'rĭ-măl): pertaining to tears or weeping; bone at the front of the orbits
lacquer, nail (lăk'ĕr nāl): a thick liquid which forms a glossy film on the nail.
lacteals (lăk'tē-ālz): any one of the lymphatics of the small intestines that take up the chyle.
lacuna (lă-kū'nă): a small cavity or hollow space; a gap or defect.
lamina (lăm'ĭ-nă): a thin layer or scale.
lamp black (lămp blăk): a fine black substance, almost pure carbon, made by burning coal oils in an atmosphere deficient in oxygen.
lanolin (lân'ô-lĭn): purified wool fat.
languor (lăn'gĕr): not inclined to take bodily exercise; dullness; lack of vigor.
lanugo (lă-nū'gō): the fine hair which covers most of the body.
larkspur (lärk'spûr): the seeds of the Delphinium plant; its tincture is used to treat head lice.
laryngeal (lă-rĭn'jê-ăl): pertaining to the larynx.
laryngitis (lă-rĭn-jī'tĭs): inflammation of the larynx.
larynx (lăr'ĭnks): the upper part of the trachea or wind pipe; the organ of voice production.
lateral (lăt'ĕr-âl): on the side.
lather (lăth'ĕr): froth made by mixing soap and water.
latissimus dorsi (lă-tĭs'ĭ-mŭs dôr'sī): a broad, flat superficial muscle of the back.
laxative (lăk'să-tĭv): a medicinal agent which relieves constipation
layer cutting (lā'ĕr kŭt'ĭng): shortening the hair into many thin layers.
lecithin (lĕs'ĭ-thĭn): a yellowish-brown waxy solid occurring in various animal and vegetable tissues; used as an emulsifier.
legislation (lĕj-ĭs-lā'shŭn): the making of laws by an authority.
legitimate (lḗ-jĭt'ĭ-mât): real; genuine; lawful.
lemon rinse (lĕm'ûn rĭns): a product containing lemon juice or citric acid; used to lighten the color of the hair.
lentigo (lĕn-tī'gō); pl., **lentigines** (lĕn-tĭ-jī'nēz): a freckle; circumscribed spot or pigmentation in the skin.
lepothrix (lĕp'ō-thrĭks): a bacterial infection resulting in dry and scaly hair.
lesion (lē'zhûn): a structural tissue change caused by injury or disease.
lesser multangular (lĕs'ĕr mŭl-tăn'gū-lăr): trapezoid; bone of the wrist.
lesser occipital (lĕs'ĕr ŏk-sĭp'ĭ-tâl): the nerve supplying muscles at the back of the ear.
leuco (lū'kô): a prefix denoting white; colorless.
leucocyte (lū'kô-sīt): a white corpuscle; white blood cell.
leukoderma (lū'kô-dûr'mă): abnormal white patches on the skin; absence of pigment in the skin.
leukonychia (lū'kôn-ĭk'ē-ă): a whitish discoloration of nails; white spots.
levator (lê-vā'tôr): a muscle that elevates a part.
levator anguli oris (âng'ū-lī ŏr'ĭs): caninus; muscle that raises the angle of the mouth and draws it in.
levator labii superioris (lā'bē-ī sû-pē-ŏr'ĭs): quadratus labii superioris; muscle that elevates upper lip and dilates the nostrils.
levator palpebrae (păl'pê-brē): muscle that raises upper eyelid.

fāte, câre, ăm, finâl, ärm, ȧsk, sofă; ēve, évent, ĕnd, recênt, evẽr; īce, ĭll; ōld, ŏ́bey, ôrb, ŏdd, cônnect, sŏft, fōod, fŏot; ūse, ûrn, ŭp, circŭs

liability insurance (lī-ă-bĭl'ĭ-tē ĭn-shoo'âns): the act or system of insuring against personal damage.
lichen (lī'kên): a dry, popular eruption of the skin.
ligament (lĭg'ă-mênt): a tough band of fibrous tissue, serving to connect bones, or to hold an orgn in place.
ligation (lī-gā'shŭn): the operation of tying together, especially an artery.
light therapy (līt thĕr'ă-pē): the application of light rays for treatment of diseases.
lime (līm): a white powder containing calcium oxide.
limp (lĭmp): weak; lacking firmness or strength.
linear (lĭn'ē-ăr): composed of lines; straight.
lingual (lĭn'gwăl): shaped like or pertaining to the tongue.
liniment (lĭn'ĭ-mênt): a liquid intended for application to the skin by gentle friction.
linseed (lĭn'sēd): the dried seeds of flax; contains a mucilage which is used as an emollient in hand preparations.
lipomatodes (lĭ-pō-mȧ-tō'dēs): a birth mark of a fatty nature.
liquefy (lĭk'wḗ-fī): to reduce to the liquid state said of both solids and gases.
liquid (lĭ'kwĭd): flowing like water; a fluid that is not solid or gaseous.
liquor cresolis compound (lĭk'ẽr krē'sōl'ĭs kŏm'pound): a powerful germicide.
listerine (lĭs-tẽr-ēn): a trade name; a mild antiseptic in liquid form.
litmus paper (lĭt'mûs pāpẽr): a blue coloring matter that is reddened by acids and turned blue again by alkalies.
liver (lĭ'vẽr): an internal organ which secretes bile for digestion.
liver spots (lĭv'ẽr spŏts): the lesions of chloasma.
lobe (lōb): a branch extending from a body; ear lobe.
lock-jaw (lŏk'jôw): tetanus; specifically trismus; a firm closing of the jaw due to tonic spasm of the muscles of mastication.
locomotion (lō-kô-mō'shŭn): animal movement.
logical (lŏj'ĭ-kâl): the result of correct reasoning; correct thinking.
lotion (lō'shûn): a liquid solution used for bathing the skin.
louse (lous); pl., **lice** (līs): pediculus; an animal parasite infesting the hairs of the head.
lubricant (lū'brĭ-kânt): anything that makes things smooth and slippery, such as oil.
lucid (lū'sĭd): clear; distinct; marked by mental clarity.
lucidum (lū'sĭ-dûm): the clear layer of the epidermis.
luminous (lū'mĭ-nŭs): full of light; brilliant.
lunate (lū'nāt): crescent-shaped.
lunate bone (bōn): semi-lunar; a bone of the wrist.
lung (lŭng): one of the two organs of respiration.
lunula (lū'nū-lă): the half-moon-shaped area at the base of the nail.
lustre (lŭs'têr): glossy; shining.
lusterless lŭs'têr-lĕs): without brightness; dull.
luxuriant (lŭks-ū'rē-ânt): very abundant; strong vigorous growth.
lymph (lĭmf): a clear yellowish or light straw colored fluid, which circulates in the lymph spaces. or lymphatics of the body.
lymphatic (lĭm-făt'ĭk): pertaining to, containing or conveying lymph.
lymphatic system (sĭs'tĕm): consists of lymph flowing through the lymph spaces, lymph vessels, lacteals, and lymph nodes or glands.
Lysol (lī'sōl): a trade name; a disinfectant and antiseptic; a mixture of soaps and phenols.

M

machineless (mă-shēn′lĕss): without a machine; heated by chemicals.
macroscopic (măk′-rô-skŏp-ĭk): visible to the unaided eye.
macula (măk′û-lă); pl., **maculae** (-le): a spot or discoloration level with skin; a freckle; macule.
madarosis (măd-ă-rō′sĭs): loss of the eyelashes or eyebrows.
magnesia (măg-nā′zhē-ă; -zhă): a fine white odorless powder of an earthy taste, insoluble in water, antacid and laxative
magnet (măg′nĕt): a body having the power to attract iron bodies.
magnetize (măg′nĕt-īz): convert into a magnet; to communicate magnetic properties to.
magnify (măg′nĭ-fī): to increase the size or importance of.
magnum (măg′nûm): largest bone of the wrist.
major (mā′jĕr): greater; larger; most important.
makeup (māk′ŭp): the way in which one is dressed, painted, etc., for a part.
mal (măl): a prefix denoting ill; evil.
malaise (mȧ-lâz′; măl′āz): discomfort; an indefinite feeling of bodily uneasiness.
malar (mā′lăr): of or pertaining to the cheek; the cheek bone.
malassimilation (măl-â-sĭm-ĭ-lā′shûn): faulty or incomplete assimilation.
malformation (măl-fôr-mā′shûn): an abnormal shape or structure; badly formed.
malignant (mă-lĭg′nânt): resistant to treatment; growing worse; occurring in severe form; a tumor recurring after removal.
malingerer (mȧ-lĭn′gĕr-ẽr): one who falsifies illness or inability.
malnutrition (măl-nū-trĭsh′ûn): poor nutrition resulting from malassimilation.
malpighian (măl-pĭg′ê-ân): stratum nucosum; the deeper portion of the epidermis.
mammal (măm′ăl): a warm-blooded animal who nourishes its young with milk.
management (măn′āj-mênt): directing; carrying on; control.
mandible (măn′dĭ-b′l): the lower jaw bone.
mandibular (măn′dĭb′ū-lăr): pertaining to the lower jaw.
mandibular nerve (nûrv): the fifth cranial nerve which supplies the muscles and skin of the lower part of the face
manicure (măn′ĭ-kūr): the artful care of the hands and nails.
manicurist (măn′ĭ-kūr-ĭst): one who professionally attends to the care of the hands and nails.
manipulation (mă-nĭp-ū-lā′shûn): act or process of treating, working or operating with the hands or by mechanical means, especially with skill.
mantilla (măn-tĭl′ȧ): a Spanish veil which covers the head and falls down upon the shoulders.
mantle (măn′t'l): nail mantle, the fold of the skin into which the nail root is lodged.
manus (mā′nûs); pl., **mani** (-nī): the hand.
marcel wave (mär-sĕl′wäv): resembling a perfect natural wave, produced by means of a heated iron; originated by Francois Marcel, a French hairdresser.
marrow (măr′ō): a soft fatty substance filling the cavities of bone.
mascara (măs-kă′ră): a preparation used to darken the eyelashes.
mask (mȧsk): a special cosmetic formula used to beautify the face.
massage (mă-säzh): manipulation of the body by rubbing, pinching, kneading, tapping, etc., to increase metabolism, promote absorption, relieve pain, etc.
masseter (mă-sē′tẽr): a chewer; one of the muscles of the jaw used in mastication.
masseur (mă-sûr′): a man who practices massage.
masseuse (mă-sûz′): a woman who practices massage.
mastication (măs-tĭ-kā′shûn): the act of chewing.
mastoid (măs′toid): breast shaped; relating to the mastoid process.

fāte, câre, ăm, finâl, ärm, ȧsk, sofă; ēve, ĕvent, ĕnd, recĕnt, evẽr; īce, ĭll; ōld, ŏbey, ôrb, ŏdd, cônnect, sŏft, food, foot; ūse, ûrn, ŭp, circŭs

mastoid process (prŏs'ĕs): a conical nipple-like projection of the temporal bone.
materia medica (mă-tĕ'rē-ă mĕd'ĭ-kă): the branch of medical science treating of drugs.
matrix (mā'trĭks): the formative portion of a nail or a tooth; the intercellular substance of a tissue.
matter (măt'ẽr): pus; a substance that occupies space and has weight.
matured (mă-tūrd'): fully developed; completely worked out.
maxilla (măk-sĭl'ă): jaw bone.
maxilla, inferior (ĭn-fē'rē-ẽr): lower jaw bone or mandible.
maxilla, superior (sû-pē'rē-ẽr): upper jaw bone.
maxillary (măk'sĭ-lā-rē): pertaining to the jaws.
maximum (măk'si-mum): the greatest or highest degree or amount of anything.
measles (mē'z'lz): an acute contagious respiratory disease marked by fever and other constitutional disturbances, usually in children.
meatus (mē-ā'tûs): passage or channel of the ear.
mechanical (mē-kăn'ĭ-kâl): relating to a machine; performed by means of some apparatus not manual.
mechanism (mĕk'ă-nĭs'm): mechanical construction; parts of a machine.
mechanotherapy (mĕk-à-nō-thēr'à-pĭ): the treatment of disease by special machines which bring about forced movements of the body.
medial; median (mē'dē-âl; -ân): pertaining to the middle.
medicament (mē-dĭk'ă-mênt): a medicinal application; a remedy.
medicamentosus (mē-dĭk"ă-mên-tō'-sûs): dermatitis; a term characterizing an eruption caused by a drug.
medication (mĕd-ĭ-kā'shûn): the act of treating disease with drugs.
medicine (mĕd'ĭ-sĭn): a drug; the art of preventing or curing disease.
medius (mē'-dē-ûs): the middle finger.
medulla (më-dŭl'ă): the marrow in the various bone cavities; the pith of the hair.
medulla oblongata (ŏb-lŏn-gā'tă): the lowest, or posterior, part of the brain, continuous with the spinal cord.
medullary (mĕd'û-lā-rē): pertaining to the marrow, or medulla.
medullary space (spās): the cavity through the shaft of the bones.
mega (mĕg'ă): a prefix denoting great; extended; powerful; a million.
megascopic (mĕg-ă-skŏp'ĭk): enlarged; magnified.
mel (mĕl): honey.
melanin (mĕl'ă-nĭn): the dark or black pigment in the epidermis and hair, and in the choroid or coat of the eye.
membrane (mĕm'brān): a thin sheet or layer of pliable tissue, serving as a covering.
menopause (mĕn'ō-pôz): the physiological cessation of menstruation.
menstruation (mĕn-stroo-ā-shŭn): the periodic discharge of blood from the female sex organ.
mental (mĕn'tâl): pertaining to the mind; pertaining to the chin.
mental nerve (nûrv): a nerve which supplies the skin of the lower lip and chin.
mentalis (mĕn-tā'lĭs): the muscle that elevates the lower lip, and raises and wrinkles the skin of the chin.
menthol (mĕn'thōl): peppermint camphor; often employed for its marked cooling effect.
menthyl salicylate (mĕn'thĭl să-lĭs'ĭ-lāt): an organic compound which is used as a filtering agent in subburn preventives; produces an even tan by removing the majority of the ultraviolet rays.
mentum (mĕn'tûm); pl., **menti** (-i): of or pertaining to the chin.

fāte, câre, ăm, finâl, ärm, ȧsk, sofă; ēve, évent, ĕnd, recênt, evẽr; īce, ĭll; ōld, ŏbey, ôrb, ŏdd, cônnect, sŏft, food, foot; ūse, ûrn, ŭp, circûs

mercurochrome (mĕr-kū′rṓ-krōm): a trade name; ;a germicide.
mercury bichloride (mûr′kŭ-rē bī-klō′rīd): a powerful germicide, poisonous and also corrosive to metal.
mercury cyanide (sī′ă-nīd): a powerful germicide, very poisonous.
meso (mĕs′ṓ): a prefix denoting in the middle; intermediate.
mesoblast (mĕs′ṓ-blĕst): middle germinal layer of the embryo.
mesodermic (mĕs′-ō-dûr′mĭk): relating to the mesoderm, the middle layer of the skin.
meta (mĕt′ă): a prefix signifying over; beyond; among.
metabolism (mĕ-tăb′ō-lĭz′m): the constructive and destructive life process of the cell.
metacarpus (mĕt-ă-kär′pûs): the bones of the palm of the hand.
metatarsus (mĕt-ȧ-tär′sŭs): the bones which comprise the instep of the foot.
metal curler (mĕt′ȧl kûr′lẽr): a metal device upon which the hair is rolled while wet, to make curls.
metallic (mė-tăl′ĭk): relating to, or resembling metal.
metal salts (mĕt′ȧl sôlts): a compound of a base and an acid.
metamorphosis (mĕt-ȧ-môr′fō-sĭs): structural change
meter (mē′tẽr): an instrument used for measuring; a measure of length, the basis of the metric system.
methyl salicylate (mĕth′ĭl să-lĭs′ĭ-lāt): the chief constituent of oil of wintergreen.
meticulosis (mē-tĭk′ū-lŭs): unduly careful of small details.
metric (mĕt′rĭk): pertaining to the meter as a standard of measurement.
mica (mīkă): a mineral occurring in the form of thin, shining plates.
micro (mī′krō): a prefix denoting very small; slight; millionth part of.
microbe (mī′krōb): a micro-organsism; a minute one-celled animal or vegetable bacterium.
micrococcus (mī-krō-kŏk′ûs): a minute bacterial cell having a spherical shape.
micron (mī′krŏn): a colloid particle visible under the microscope; one millionth of a meter.
micro-organism (mī-krō-ôr′gân-ĭz′m): microscopic plant or animal cell; a bacterium.
microscope (mī′krō-skōp): an instrument for making enlarged views of minute objects.
microspira (mī-krō-spī′ră): pathogenic bacteria which causes cholera.
mid (mĭd): a prefix denoting the middle part.
midway (mĭd-wā′): halfway.
milliampere (mĭl′-ē-ăm-pâr): one thousandth of an ampere.
milliamperemeter (-mē′tẽr): an electrical instrument which registers the amount of current required for a given treatment.
miliaria (mĭl-ē-ā′rē-ă): an eruption of minute vesicles due to retention of fluid at the mouths of the sweat glands.
miliaria rubra (ro͞ob′ră): prickly heat; burning and itching usually caused by exposure to excessive heat.
miliary fever (mĭl′ē-ă-rē fē′vẽr): sweating sickness; an infectious disease characterized by fever profuse sweating, and sudamina.
milium (mīl′ē-ûm); pl., **milia** (-ă): a small whitish pimple due to a retention of sebum, beneath the epidermis; a whitehead.
millimeter (mĭl′ĭ-mē-têr): one thousandth of a meter.
mineral (mĭn′ẽr-ȧl): any inorganic material found in the earth's crust.
mineral salts (sôlts): salts derived from an inorganic chemical compound.
minor (mī′nẽr): lesser; contrary to greater.
minute (mī-nūt′): very small; tiny.
miscible (mĭs′ĭ-b'l): the property of certain liquids to mix with each other in equal proportions.

fāte, câre, ăm, finâl, ärm, ȧsk, sofă; ēve, ĕvent, ĕnd, recênt, evẽr; īce, ĭll; ōld, ṓbey, ôrb, ŏdd, cônnect, sŏft, fo͞od, fo͝ot; ūse, ûrn, ŭp, circŭs

mitosis (mī-tō'sĭs): indirect nuclear division, the usual process of cell reproduction of the human tissues.
mobility (mō-bĭl'ĭ-tĭ): being easily moved.
modality (mō-dăl'ĭ-tē): any condition influencing or modifying drug action or electricity.
mode (mōd): fashion; way; style.
modification (mŏd-ĭ-fĭ-kā'shŭn): the result of slight change in form.
modified swirl (mŏd'ĭ-fīd swŭrl): the back of the head waved on a slant, waves not connected symmetrically.
mold; mould (mōld): to form into a particular shape.
mole (mōl): a small brownish spot on the skin.
molecule (mŏl'ḗ-kūl): the smallest possible unit of existence of any substance.
monilethrix (mṓ-nĭl'ḗ-thrĭks): beaded hair; a condition in which the hairs show a series of constrictions, giving the appearance of a string of fusiform beads.
mono (mŏn'ō): a prefix denoting unit singly.
monoterminal (mŏn-ṓ-tûr'mĭ-nâl): one terminal of an alternating current.
morbid (môr'bĭd): diseased.
mordant (môr'dânt): a substance, such as alum, used to make fast a dye.
motile (mō'tĭl): having the power of movement, as certain bacteria.
motor (mō'tĕr): moving or causing motion.
motor nerves (nûrvz): carry impulses from nerve centers to muscles for certain motions.
motor oculi (ŏk'ū-lī): third cranial nerve; the nerve controlling most of the eye muscles.
mould (mōld): to conform to a given shape.
mucosa (mû-kō'să): mucous membrane.
mucosum, stratum (mû-kō'sŭm strā-tûm): mucous or Malpighian layer of the epidermis; a deeper portion of the skin.
mucous membrane (mū'kŭs mĕm'brân): a membrane secreting mucus, which lines passages and cavities communicating with exterior.
mucus (mū'kŭs): the clear viscid secretion of mucous membrane.
mug (mŭg): a cup used for shaving purposes.
mumps (mŭmps): a specific infectious disorder characterized by an inflammation of the parotid and other salivary glands.
muscle (mŭs"l: the contractile tissue of the body by which movement is accomplished.
muscle curl (kûrl): shaped like a muscle shell; larger at the head and tapering toward the end, hanging at an angle.
muscle oil (oil): an oil, vegetable or mineral, in which eithr lecithin or cholesterin is dissolved; used in conjunction with massage to relieve fatigue and sore muscles.
muscle strapping (străp'ĭng): a heavy massage treatment used to reduce fatty deposits.
muscle tone (tōn): the normal degree of tension in a healthy muscle.
myelin (mī'e-lĭn): a white substance forming the covering for certain nerve fibers.
mylohyoid (mī-lô-hī'oid): relating to the molar teeth, or posterior portion of the lower jaw, and to the hyoid bone.
myocardium (mī-ō-kär'dē-ûm): the muscular substance of the heart.
myology (mī-ŏl'ô-jē): the science of the function, structure, and diseases of muscles.

N

naevus; nevus (nē'vŭs); pl. **naevi; nevi** (vī): a birthmark; a congenital skin blemish.
nail (nāl): unguis; the horny protective plate located at the end of the finger or toe.
nail-bed (bĕd): that portion of the skin on which the body of the nail rests.

fāte, câre, ăm, finâl, ärm, ȧsk, sofă; ēve, ĕvent, ĕnd, recênt, evēr; īce, ĭll; ōld, ṓbey, ôrb, ŏdd, cônnect, sŏft, fōōd, fŏŏt; ūse, ûrn, ŭp, circŭs

nail-body (bŏd'ē): the horny nail blade resting upon the nail-bed.
nail-fold (fōld): nail-wall.
nail-grooves (grōōvz): the furrows between the nail-walls and the nail-bed.
nail matrix (mā'trĭks): the portion of the nail-bed extending beneath the nail-root.
nail-root (rōōt): located at the base of the nail, imbedded underneath the skin.
nail-wall (wôl): cuticle covering the sides and base of the nail body.
nape (nāp): the back part of the neck.
narcotic (när-kŏt'ĭk): a drug, which in moderate doses relieves pain, but in large doses produces stupor and convulsions.
naris (nā'rĭs); pl., **nares** (-rēz): a nostril.
nasal (nā'zâl): pertaining to the nose.
nasalis (nā-sā'lĭs): a muscle of the nose.
nasitis (nâ-sī'tĭs): rhinitis; inflammation of the nasal mucous membrane of the nose.
nasociliary (nā-zô-sĭl'yă-rē): a nerve affecting the mucous membrane of the nose.
nasus (nā'sûs); pl., **nasi-** (-si): the nose.
natural neckline (năt'û-râl nêk-līn): not in a definite outline, retaining the natural tendency of hair growth.
nausea (nô'shê-ă): sickness of the stomach; with a desire to vomit.
navicular (nă-vĭk'û-lăr): boat-shaped; a bone of the wrist.
neck duster (nĕk dŭs'tĕr): a brush used to brush the hair from the neck after cutting; in most states its use is prohibited because it is not sanitary.
neckline (nĕk'līn): in hair cutting, where the hair growth of the head ends and the neck begins;; hair line.
necrosis (nĕk-rō'sĭs): the death of cells surrounded by living tissue.
negative (nĕg'ă-tĭv): the opposite of positive; expressing denial.
negative pole, N. (pōl N): the pole from which negative current flows.
negative terminal (tûr'mĭ-nâl): the end of the conducting circuit of the electric current manifesting alkaline reaction; the zinc plate in a battery.
neoplasm (nē'ō-plăz'm): a new growth or turnor.
nerve (nûrv): a whitish cord, made up of bundles of nerve fibers, through which impulses are transmitted.
nerve papillae (pă-pĭl'ē): a bundle of nerve tissue in the true skin.
nervous (nûr'vûs): easily excited.
Nettle rash (nĕt'l răsh): a skin eruption caused by the sting from the nettle plant.
network (nĕt'wûrk): any system of lines crossing each other at certain intervals.
neuralgia (nū-răl'jē-ă): a severe pain along the course of a nerve.
neurasthenia (nû-răs-thē'nē-ă): nerve tire; nervous exhaustion.
neuritis (nû-rī'tis): inflammation of nerves, marked by neuralgia.
neurology (nū-rōl'ô-jē): the science of the structure, function, and pathology of the nervous system.
neuron (nū'rŏn): the unit of the nervous system, consisting of the nerve cell and its various processes.
neurosis (nû-rō'sĭs): a functional nervous disorder.
neutral (nū'trâl): exhibiting no positive properties; indifferent; in chemistru, neither acid nor alkaline.
neutralization (nū-trâl-ĭ-zā'shûn): the rendering ineffective of any action or process; a chemical reaction between an acid and a base.
neutralizer (nū'trâl-īz-ĕr): an agent capable of neutralizing another substance.

fāte, câre, ăm, finâl, ärm, ȧsk, sofȧ; ēve, évent, ĕnd, recênt, evẽr; īce, ĭll; ōld, ŏ́bey, ôrb, ŏdd, cônnect, sŏft, fōod, fŏŏt; ūse, ûrn, ŭp, circûs

nevus (nē'vŭs): a birthmark.
nicotine (nĭk-ō-tēn'): a poisonous alkaloid in tobacco.
nimble (nĭm'b'l): light and quick in motion.
nit (nĭt): the egg of a louse, usually attached to a hair.
nitric acid (nī'trĭk ăs'ĭd): concentrated acid employed as a caustic for the removal of warts.
nitro-celluose (nī-trô-sĕl'û-lōs): pyroxylin; gun cotton; a granulaar, yellowish mass formed in the chemical reaction between cellulose and nitric acid; used in nail polishes.
nitrogen (nī'trô-jĕn): a colorless gaseous element, tasteless and odorless found in air and living tissue.
nitrous (nī'trûs): designating a compound of nitrogen in the lower valence.
node (nôd): a knot or knob; a circumscribed swelling; a knuckle or ringer joint.
nodosa (nô-dōs'ă): having nodes or knot-like swellings.
nodule (nŏd'ūl): a small node.
non (nŏn): a prefix denoting not.
non-conductor (nŏn-kôn-dŭk'tĕr): any substance that resists the passage of electricity, light, or heat towards or through it.
non-pathogenic (nŏn-păth-ô-jĕn'ĭk): non-disease producing; growth promoting.
non-striated (strī'āt-ĕd): involuntary muscle function without the action of the will; consists of spindle-shaped cells without striations; smooth muscle.
non-vascular (văs'kû-lăr): not supplied with blood vessels.
normal (nŏr'mâl): regular; natural.
nose (nōz): the organ of smell.
nostril (nŏs'trĭl): an external opening of the nose.
nourish (nŭr'ĭsh): to feed; to furnish with whatever promotes growth.
nourishment (nŭr'ĭsh-mênt): anything which nourishes; ;nutriment; food.
noxious (nŏk'shŭs): harmful; poisonous.
nozzle (nŏz'l): the projecting end.
nucleus (nū'klê-ûs); pl., **nuclei** (-ī): the active center of cells.
nude (nūd): naked; bare; unclothed.
nutriment (nū'trĭ-mênt): that which nourishes; food.
nutrient (nū'trē-ênt): nutritious; a food constituent.
nutrition (nū-trĭsh'ûn): the process of nourishment.
nutritious (nū-trĭsh'ûs): yielding nourishment.
nutritive (nū'trĭ-tĭv): pertaining to nutrition.

O

obese (ô-bēs'): extremely fat.
objective (ôb-jĕk'tĭv): a goal; aim; existing independently of mind.
objective symptom (sĭmp'tûm): symptom that can be seen, as in pimples, pustules, etc.
oblique (ŏb-lēk'; -lik); **obliquis** (-ūs): slanting or inclined.
oblongata (ŏ b-lŏn-gā'tă): medulla oblongata; the lowest part of the btain near the spinal cord.
obnoxious odor (ôb-nŏk'shŭs ō'-dĕr): offensive; hateful.
observation (ŏb-zĕr-vā'shûn): respectful attention; act of observing; also the information or record so obtained.
obsolete (ŏb'-sô-lēt): old; gone out of date.
occipital (ŏk-sĭp'ĭ-tâl): pertaining to the back part of the head; the bone which forms the back and lower part of the cranium.
occipital nerve (nûrv): a nerve which supplies the occipito-frontalis muscle.

fāte, câre, ăm, finâl, ärm, åsk, sofă; ēve, évent, ĕnd, recênt, evẽr; īce, ĭll; ōld, ŏbey, ôrb, ŏdd, cônnect, sŏft, fōod, fōot; ūse, ûrn, ŭp, circûs

occipito-frontalis (ŏk-sĭp'ĭ-tō-frŏn-tā'lĭs): epicranius; the scalp muscle.
occiput (ŏk'sĭ-pŭt): the back of the head.
occupational disease (ŏk-û-pā'shŭn-âl dĭ-zēz'): due to certain kinds of employment, such as coming into contact with chemicals, dyes, etc.
ocular (ŏk'û-lăr): pertaining to the eye; the eyepiece of a microscope; the lenses at the upper end of the microscope.
oculist (ŏk'û-lĭst): a specialist in diseases of the eyes.
oculomotor (ŏk"û-lô-mō'tĕr): third cranial nerve; controlling the motion of the eye.
oculus (ŏk'û-lûs); pl., **oculi** (-lī): the eye.
odor (ō'dĕr): scent; smell.
offensive (ŏ-fĕn'sĭv): giving offense, disagreeable; obnoxious; distasteful.
ohm (ōm): a unit of measurement used to denote the amount of resistance in an electrical system or device.
Ohm's Law (ōmz lô): the simple statement that the current in an electric circuit is equal to the pressure divided by the resistance.
oil (oil): a greasy liquid.
ointment (oint'mênt): a fatty, medicated mixture used externally.
ol (ôl): a word ending denoting that the name of the substance to which the ending is added, belongs to the series of alcohols, or hydroxyl derivatives, such as carbonol, glycerol.
oleaginous (ō-lê-aj'ĭ-nûs): oily; greasy.
olecranon (ō-lê-krā'nŏn): tip of the elbow; the prominent curved upper extremity of the ulna.
oleum (ō'lê-ûm); pl., **olea** (ă): oil.
olfactory (ŏl-făk'tô-rē): relating to the sense of smell; first cranial nerve, the special nerve of smell.
oma (ō'mă): a word ending properly added to words derived from Greek roots, denoting a tumor, such as cystoma.
omohyoid (ō-mô-hī'oid): connected with the hyoid and scapula bones.
onychatrophia (ŏn-ĭ-kă-trō'fê-ă): atrophy of the nails.
onychauxis (ōn-ĭ-kôk'sĭs): enlargement of the nails.
onychia (ô-nĭk'ē-ă): inflammation of the matrix of the nail with pus formation and shedding of the nail.
onycho (ôn'ĭ-kô): a prefix meaning relating to the nails.
onychoclasis (ŏn-ĭ-kô-klā'sĭs): breaking of the nail.
onychocryptosis (ŏn-ĭ-kô-krĭp-tō'sĭs): ingrowing nail.
onychogryposis (ŏn-ĭ-kô-grī-pō'sĭs): denotes enlargement with increased curvature of the nail.
onycholysis (ŏn-ĭ-kôl'ĭ-sĭs): loosening of the nail without shedding.
onychomycosis (ŏn-ĭ-kô-mī-kō'sĭs): refers to any parasitic disease of the nails.
onychophagy (ŏn-ĭ-kŏf'ă-jē): the morbid habit of eating or biting the nails.
onychophosis (ŏn-ĭ-kŏf-ō'sĭs): growth of horny epithelium in the nail-bed.
onychophyma (ŏn-ĭ-kŏf-ī'mă): a morbid degeneration of the nail.
onychoptosis (ŏ n-ĭ-kô-kŏp-tō'sĭs): falling off of the nails.
onychorrhexis (ŏn-ĭ-kô-rĕk'sĭs): abnormal brittleness of the nails with splitting of the free edge.
onychosis; onychonosus (ŏn-ĭ-kô'sĭs; ŏn-ĭ-kṓ-nō'sûs): any disease of the nails.
onyx (ṓ'-nĭks): a nail of the fingers or toes.
onyxis (ô-nĭk'sĭs): ingrowing of the nails.
opacity (ô-păs'ĭ-tĭ): the quality of being shaded or obscure.
opaque (ṓ-pāk'): not transparent to light.
operative (ŏp'ĕr-â-tĭv): relating to, or affected by means of an operation; active, effective.

fāte, câre, ăm, finâl, ärm, ȧsk, sofă; ēve, ĕvent, ĕnd, recênt, evẽr; īce, ĭll; ōld, ṓbey, ôrb, ŏdd, cônnect, sŏft, fōod, fŏŏt; ūse, ûrn, ŭp, circŭs

operator (ŏp'ẽr-â-tẽr): one who is able to perform correctly any service rendered professionally in the care of the face, hair, etc.
ophthalmic (ŏp-thăl'mĭk): pertaining to the eye.
opsonin (ŏp'sô-nĭn): a blood constituent which renders invading germs more susceptible to the action of white blood cells.
optic (ŏp'tĭk): second cranial nerve; the nerve of sight; pertaining to the eye, or to vision
optional (ŏp'shûn-âl): left to one's discretion or choice; not compulsory.
optician (ŏp'tĭsh'ân): a maker of optical instruments pursuant to an oculist's prescription.
optimistic (ŏp'tĭ-mĭs'tĭk): hoping for the best.
orangewood stick (ŏr'ĕnj-wo͞od stĭk): a stick made of orangewood used in manicuring the nails.
optometrist (ŏp-tŏm'é-trĭst): a trained person who fits glasses to correct visual defects.
orbicular (ŏr-bĭk'ū-lăr): circular; a muscle whose fibers are circularly arranged.
orbicularis oris (ŏr-bĭk-ū-lă'rĭs ō'rĭs): orbicular muscle; muscle of the mouth.
orbicularis palpebral (păl'pé-brăl): a muscle of the eyelid.
orbit (ôr'bit): the bony cavity of the eyeball; the eye-socket.
orbital (ôr'bĭ-tâl): pertaining to the orbits.
orbital nerve (nûrv): a sensory nerve supplying the temple and cheek.
organ (ôr'gân): any part of the body exercising a specific function.
organic (ŏr-gân'ĭk): relating to an organ; pertaining to substances derived from living organisms.
organism (ŏr'gân-ĭz'm): any living being, either animal or vegetable.
orifice (ŏr'ĭ-fĭs): a mouth; an opening.
origin (ŏr'ĭ-jĭn): the beginning; the starting point of a nerve; the place of attachment of a muscle to a bone.
originate (ŏ-rĭj'ĭ-nāt): to produce as new.
oris (ŏ'rĭs): pertaining to the mouth; an opening.
orris root (or'is-ro͞ot): a special powder used to give a dry shampoo.
os (ŏs): a bone.
oscillation (ŏs'ĭ-lā'shûn): movement like a pendulum; a swinging or vibration.
osis (ō'sĭs): a word ending denoting an abnormal or a diseased condition.
os magnum (ŏs măg'nûm): bone in the lower rfow of the carpus.
osmidrosis (ŏs-mĭ-drō'sĭs; ŏz): bromidrosis; foul smelling perspiration.
osmosis (ŏs-mō'sĭs; ŏz): the passage of fluids and solutions through a membrane or other porous substance.
osseous; osseus (ŏs'ê-ûs): bony.
osteology (ŏs-té-ŏl'ó-jē): science of the anatomy structure and function of bones.
ottoman (ŏt'ó-mân): foot pedal of a chair.
Oudin current (o͞o'dĭn kŭr'rênt): high frequency current of high voltage and low amperage.
ounce (ouns): a unit of measure of weight; one-sixteenth of a pound.
ovarian (ó-vā'rē-ân): relating to the ovary.
ovary (ō-vă'rē): one of the two reproductive glands in the female, containing the ova or germ cells.
overlap (ō-vẽr-lăp'): to lie or be folded partly upon.
ovular (ō'vū-lăr): egg-like in shape; pertaining to the ovum, or egg.
oxidation (ŏk-sĭ-dā'shûn): the act of combining oxygen with another substance, with or without generation.
oxide (ŏk'sīd): a compound of oxygen with another element or radical.

fāte, câre, ăm, finâl, ärm, ȧsk, sofă; ēve, évent, ĕnd, recênt, evẽr; īce, ĭll; ōld, óbey, ôrb, ŏdd, cônnect, sŏft, fo͞od, fo͝ot; ūse, ûrn, ŭp, circûs

oxidize (ŏk'sĭ-dīz): the process of combining oxygen with another substance.
oxygen (ŏk'sĭ-jên): a gaseous element, essential to animal and plant life.
oxygenation (ŏk″sĭ-jê-nā'shŭn): saturation with oxygen, noting especially the aeration of the blood in the lungs.
ozone (ō'zōn): a form of oxygen used as a disinfectant.

P

pack (păk): a special cosmetic formula used to beautify the face.
palate (păl'ăt): the roof of the mouth and the floor of the nose.
palatine bones (bōnz): situated at the back part of the nasal fossae.
palmar (păl'măr): referring to the palm of the hand.
palpebral (păl'pê-bră); pl. **palpebrae** (-brē): eyelids.
palpebrarum (păl-pê-bră'rûm): of or pertaining to the eyelids.
panacea (păn-ă-sê'ă): a remedy that is claimed to be curative for all diseases; a universal remedy.
pancreas (păn'crê-ăs): a gland connected with the digestive tract.
panicula (pă-nĭk'û-lă): a swelling or a tumor.
panidrosis (păn-ĭ-drō'sĭs): general perspiration.
paper curl (pā'pêr kûrl): a curl rolled up on a stick encased in a triangle of special paper and pinched with a warm iron.
papilla (pă-pĭl'ă): a small, nipple-like process.
papilla, hair (hăr): a small cone-shaped elevation at the bottom of the hair follicle in the dermis.
papillary (păp'ĭ-lâ-rē; pă-pĭl'ă-rē): relating to, resembling, or provided with papillae.
papillary layer (lā'ĕr): the outer layer of the dermis.
papilloma (păp-ĭ-lō'mă); pl. **papillomata** (păp-i-lo-mātă): an epithelial tumor formed by hypertrophy of the papillae of the skin.
papular (păp'ū-lăr): characterized by papules.
papule (păp'ûl): a pimple; a small, circumscribed elevation on the skin containing no fluid.
papulous (păp'û-lûs): covered with papulae or pimples.
para (pă'ră): a prefix denoting alongside of; beyond; beside; against; near.
paraffin (păr'â-fĭn): a white mineral wax consisting of hydrocarbons and extracted from petroleum.
paralysis (pă-râl'ĭ-sĭs): loss of physical or mental functions through nerve injury or disease.
para-phenylene-diamine (păr-ă-fēn-ĭ-lēn-dĭ-âm'ĭn; dī'ă-mēn): an aniline derivative used in hair dyeing.
parasite (păr'ă-sīt): a vegetable or animal organism which lives on or in another organism, and draws its nourishment therefrom.
parasiticide (păr-ă-sīt'ĭ-sīd): a substance that destroys parasites.
parathyroid (păr-ă-thī'roid): a endocrine gland located near the thyroid.
parchment paper (pärch'mĕnt pā'pêr): thin paper used to wrap hair in permanent waving.
parietal (pă-rīē-tâl): pertaining to the wall of a cavity; a bone at the side of the head.
paronychia (păr-ô-nĭk'ē-ă): felon; an inflammation of the tissues surrounding the nail.
parotid (păr-ô-tĭd): near the ear; a gland near the ear.
patch test (păch tĕst): a skin test used to determine individual reaction to a chemical substance
patella (pà-tĕl'ă): a flat movable bone forming the front part of the knee.
pathogenic (păth-ô-jĕn'ĭk): causing disease; disease producing.
pathological (păth-ô-lôj'ĭ-kâl): relating to pathology; morbid; diseased.

fāte, câre, ăm, finâl, ärm, àsk, sofă; ēve, évent, ĕnd, recênt, evẽr; īce, ĭll; ōld, ồbey, ôrb, ŏdd, cônnect, sŏft, fōod, fŏot; ūse, ûrn, ŭp, circûs

pathology (păth-ŏl'ṓ-jē): the science which treats or modifications of the functions and changes in structure caused by disease.
patron (pâ'trŭn): the person to whom service is rendered.
patter (pât'ẽr): a mechanical device used during muscle strapping treatments.
pectoralis (pĕk-tṓ-rā'lĭs): a muscle of the breast.
pediculosis (pĕ-dĭk"ū-lō'sĭs): lousiness; state of being infected with pediculi or lice.
pediculosis capitis (kăp'ĭ-tĭs): lousiness of the hair of the head.
pediculous (pḗ-dĭk'ū-lûs): infested by pediculi; lousy.
pedicure (pĕd'ĭ-kūr): the care of the feet and toe nails.
pelada (pĕ-lā'dă): a disease of the hair causing circumscribed patches of baldness; alopecia areata.
pelage (pĕl'ăj): the hair covering of the body of man and the lower animals.
pellagra (pĕ-lăg'ră): a skin affection manifesting digestive disturbances, followed by scaling or peeling of the skin, and nervous symptoms.
pellicle (pĕl'ĭ-k'l): thin skin; cuticle.
penetrate (pĕn'ḗ-trāt): to pierce; to pass into the deeper tissues.
pepsin (pĕp'sĭn): an enzyme which digests protein.
per (pẽr): a prefix denoting through.
percussion (pẽr-kŭsh'ûn): a form of massage consisting of repeated blows or taps of varying force.
perforate (pûr'fṓ-rāt): to pierce with holes.
perfume (pûr-fūm'; pẽr-fūm'): a fluid preparation, as of the essence of flowers, used for scenting.
pH: symbol for hydrogen; ion concentration; the relative degree of acidity or alkalinity.
peri (pẽr'ĭ-): a prefix denoting about; near; around.
pericardium (pĕr-ĭ-kär'dē-ûm): the membranous sac around the heart.
perionychium (pĕr-ĭ-ô-nĭk'ĭ-ûm): the epidermis about the nail.
periosteum (pĕr-ĭ-ôs'tê-ûm): the fibrous membrane covering the surface of the bones.
peripheral system (pê-rĭf'ẽr-âl sĭs'tĕm): consists of the nerve endings in the skin and sense organs.
periphery (pê-rĭf'ẽr-ē): the outer part or surface.
peristalsis (pêr-ĭ-stâl'sĭs): muscular movements of the digestive tract.
permalite (pûr'mâ-līt): a trade name; a light for drying the permanent wave after the wave has been set.
permanent wave, cold (pûr'mă-nĕnt wāv, kōld): a system of permanent waving employing chemicals rather than heat.
permanent wave, heat: accomplished by changing the hair structure from an ordinary and natural straightness to one of permanent curliness or waviness.
permanent wave, pin curl (pĭn kûrl): a cold or heatless permanent in which the hair is set n pin curls insteadof being rolled on curlers.
permeable (pûr'mê-â-b'l): permitting the passage of liquids.
peroneus muscle (pêr-ō-nē-ŭs mŭs'l): one of several muscles of the lower leg.
peroneal nerve (pĕr-ō-nē'ăl nŭrv): a nerve which supplies the lower leg and foot.
peroxide (pêr-ŏk'sīd): an oxide with the highest amount of oxygen.
peroxide of hydrogen (hī'drô-jên): a powerful oxidizing agent; in liquid solutions is used as an antiseptic.
peroxide rinse (rĭns): it is used to lighten the color of the hair.
perpendicular (pûr-pên-dĭk'û-lăr): being perfectly upright.
personality (pûr-sŭn-ăl'ĭ-tĭ): the sum total of physical and mental qualities in a person.

fāte, câre, ăm, finâl, ärm, ȧsk, sofă; ēve, ĕvent, ĕnd, recênt, evẽr; īce, ĭll; ōld, ṓbey, ôrb, ŏdd, cônnect, sŏft, fo͞od, fo͝ot; ūse, ûrn, ŭp, circŭs

personality bob (pûr′sŭn-ăl′ĭ-tĭ bŏb): a type of bob which constitutes distinction of individuality.
perspiration (pûr′spĭ-rā′shŭn): sweat; the fluid excreted from the sweat glands of the skin.
pessimistic (pĕs-ĭ-mĭs′tĭk): hoping for the worst.
petrissage (pĕt-rĭ-säj′): the kneading movement in massage,
petrolatum (pĕt-rô-lā′tûm): petroleum jelly; Vaseline; a purified, yellow mixture of semi-solid hydrocarbons obtained from petroleum.
petroleum (pḗ-trō′lê-ûm): an oily liquid coming from the earth and consisting of a mixture of hydrocarbons.
petrous (pĕt′rûs): of stony hardness.
phagocyte (făg′ṓ-sīt): a cell possessing the property of ingesting bacteria, particles, and other cells.
phalangette; phalanget (fă-lăn′jĕt): the last phalanx or terminal bone of a finger or toe.
phalanx (fā′lănks); pl., **phalanges** (fă-lăn′jēz): the long bone of the finger or toe.
pharmacologist (fär-mă-kŏl′ṓ-jĭst): one versed in the science of the nature and properties of drugs.
pharynx (făr′ĭnks): the upper portion of the digestive tube, behind the nose and mouth.
phenol (fē′nōl): carbolic acid; caustic poison; in dilute solution is used as an antiseptic and disinfectant.
phenomenon (fê-nŏm′ê-nŏn): observing facts or events that which appeals to one as strange or unusual.
phobia (fō′bĭ-ȧ): a morbid fear of anything.
phoresis (fô-rē′sĭs): the process of introducing solutions into the tissues through the skin by the use of galvanic current.
phosphoric (fŏs-fôr′ĭk): pertaining to compounds containing phosphorus.
phosphorus (fŏs′fôr-ûs): an element found in the bones, muscles, and the nerves.
phototherapy (fō-tō-thĕr′ă-pĭ): the application of light for the treatment of disease.
phyma (fī′mă); pl., **phymata** (fī′mă-tă): a circumscribed swelling one the skin larger than a tubercle.
physic (fĭz′ĭk): a medicine, especially a laxative; drugs in general.
physical (fĭz′ĭ-kâl): relating to the body, as distinguished from the mind.
physics (fĭz′ĭks): the branch of science that deals with matter and motion and comprises the study of light, heat, electricity, sound, and mechanics.
physiology (fĭz-ē-ŏl′ô-jē): the science of the functions of living things.
physio therapy (fĭz′ē-ō thĕr′ă-pē): the use of natural forces such as light, heat, air, water, and exercise in the treatment of disease.
picric acid (pĭk′rĭk ăs′ĭd): an organic acid used as an antiseptic.
pigment (pĭg′mênt): any organic coloring matter, as that of the red blood cells, of the hair, skin, iris, etc.
pigmentation (pĭg″mên-tā′shûn): the deposition of pigment in the skin or tissues.
pilary (pī′lă-rē): pertaining to hair.
pilocarpine (pī-lô-kär′pĭn; -pēn): an alkaloid obtained from the leaves of pilocarpus; stimulates the tissues and increases secretion of the glands.
pilose (pī′lōs): covered with hair.
pilosebaceous (pī‴lô-sê-bā′shûs): pertaining to the hair follicles and the sebaceous glands.
pilus (pī′lûs); p., **pili** (-lī): hair.
pimple (pĭm′p′l): any small pointed elevation of the skin; a papule or small pustle.
pin curl permanent (pĭn kûrl pûr′mă-nênt): a cold or heatless permanent in which the hair is set in pin curls instead of being rolled on curlers; basic curl permanent; foundation curl.
pineal (pĭn′ḗ-âl): a ductless gland located in the region of the brain.

fāte, câre, ăm, finâl, ärm, ȧsk, sofȧ; ēve, ė́vent, ĕnd, recênt, evẽr; īce, ĭll; ōld, ṓbey, ôrb, ŏdd, cônnect, sŏft, fōod, fo͝ot; ūse, ûrn, ŭp, circûs

pinna (pĭn′ă): wing; the external ear, exclusive of meatus.
pipette (pī-pĕt′): a slender tube for measuring liquids.
pisiform (pī′sĭ-fôrm): pea-shaped; a bone of the wrist.
pit (pĭt): a surface depression or hollow.
pith (pĭth): the marrow of bones; the center of the hair.
pituitary (pĭ-tū′ĭ-tĕr-ē): a ductless gland located at the bass of the brain.
pityriasis (pĭt-ĭ-rī′ă-sĭs): dandruff; an inflammation of the skin characterized by the formation and flaking of the fine branny scales.
pityriasis capitis (kăp′ĭ-tĭs): a scale inflammation marked by dry dandruff or branny exfoliation.
pityriasis pilaris (pī-lă′rĭs): characterized by an eruption of papules surrounding the hair follicles, each papule pierced by a hair, and tipped with a horny plug or scale.
pityriasis steatoides (stē-ă-toy′dēz): a scalp inflammation marked by fatty type of dandruff characterized by yellowish to brownish waxy scales or crusts on the scalp.
pityroid (pĭt′ĭ-roid): branny.
plantar artery (plăn′tȧr är′tĕr-ē): a blood vessel which extends across the sole and around the toes of the foot.
plasma (plăz′mă): the fluid part of the blood and lymph.
plasticizer (plăs′tĭ-sī-zĕr): a compound which keeps a substance soft and thick as in nail polishes.
plastic surgeon (plăs′tĭk sûr′jŭn): a surgeon who builds up or molds tissue or repairs physical skin defects.
platelets (plāt′lĕts): blood cells which aid in the formation of clots.
platinum nail polish (plăt′ĭ-nŭm nāl pŏl′ĭsh): a liquid nail enamel, silver white in appearance.
platinum rinse (rĭns): used on extremely light hair to give it a beautiful white blonde effect.
platysma (plă-tĭz′mă): a broad thin muscle of the neck.
pledget (plĕj′ĕt): a compress or small flat mass of lint, absorbent cotton, or the like.
plexus (plĕk′sŭs): a network of nerves or veins.
pluck (plŭk): to pull with sudden force.
pneumogastric (nū-mô-găs′trĭk): relating to the lungs and stomach.
pneumogastric nerve (nûrv): vagus nerve; tenth cranial nerve.
pneumonia (nū-mŏ′nē-ă): inflammation of the lungs.
podiatrist (pō′dĭ-ȧ-trĭst): one who treats disease of the feet.
point (point): a sharp end or apex; an abscess, the wall of which becomes thin and is about to break.
poise (poiz): the manner in which the head or body is carried.
poison (poi′z′n): a substance, which when taken internally is injurious to health, or dangerous to life.
poison ivy (ī′vĭ): a harmful plant which is poisonous to the touch.
poisoning, blood (poi′z′n-ĭng, blŭd): a diseased condition due to the presence of germs or harmful substances in the blood.
polarity (pô-lăr′ĭ-tē): the property of having two opposite poles, as that possessed by a magnet or galvanic current.
poliosis (pŏl-ē-ō′sĭs): a condition characterized by absence of pigment in the hair.
pollex (pŏl-eks): the thumb.
poly (pō′lĭ): a prefix denoting many; much.
pomade (pô-mâd′; -mäd′): a medicated ointment for the hair.
pomphus (pŏm′fŭs): a whitish or pinkish elevation of the skin; a wheal.
pore (pôr): a small opening of the sweat glands of the skin.
porous (pō′rŭs): full of pores.

fāte, câre, ăm, finȧl, ärm, ȧsk, sofă; ēve, ĕvent, ĕnd, recênt, evẽr; īce, ĭll; ōld, ŏbey, ôrb, ŏdd, cônnect, sŏft, fōod, fŏot; ūse, ûrn, ŭp, circŭs

portability (pôr-tă-bĭl'ĭ-tē): quality or state of being easily carried about.
portable (pōr'tà-b'l): easily carried.
positive (pŏz'ĭ-tĭv): affirmative; not negative; the presence of abnormal condition; having a relative high potential in electricity.
positive pole, P. or + (pōl): the pole from which positive electricity flows.
positive terminal (tûr'mĭ-nâl): the end of a conducting circuit manifesting acid reaction; the carbon plate in a battery.
post (pōst): a prefix denoting back; after.
posterior (pŏs-tē'rē-ẽr): situated behind; coming after or behind.
posterior auricular (ô-rĭk'û-lăr): a nerve which supplies muscles in the posterior surface of the ear.
postiche (pôs-tēsh): artificial hair piece; curls, braids, or other extra hair piece used in creating coiffures.
posture (pŏs'tûr): the position of the body as a whole.
potassium (pô-tăs'ē-ûm): an element, the salts of which are used in medicine.
potassium hydroxide (hī-drŏk's-īd): a powerful alkali, used in the manufacture of soft soaps.
potassium permanganate (pẽr-măn'gă-nāt): a salt of permanganate acid; used as an antiseptic and deodorant.
potential (pô-tĕn'shâl): indicting possibility; tension in an electrical source enabling it to do work under suitable conditions.
pouch (pouch): a cyst or sac containing fluid.
poultice (pōl'tĭs): a medicinal preparation used as a local stimulant on the skin.
powder (pou'dẽr): a dry mass of extremely fine particles.
precaution (prê-kô'shûn): to warn or advise beforehand.
precipitation (prê-sĭp-ĭ-tā'shûn): the formation of an insoluble substance which settles out as a result of a chemical reaction between substances in solution.
predicament (prê-dĭk'ă-mênt): condition; especially unpleasant, unfortunate, or trying position.
predisposition (prē-dĭs-pô-zĭsh'ûn): a condition of special susceptibility to disease; allergy.
pregnant (prĕg'nânt): a female bearing a child.
prehension (prḗ-hĕn'shûn): grasping; taking hold of, as in eating.
preliminary (prḗ-lĭm'ĭ-nâ-rē): introductory; preparatory.
premature (prē'mă-tūr): happening before the usual time.
presenilis (prē-sê-nĭl'ĭs): prematurely old.
pressing (prĕs'ĭng): a method of straightening over-curly or kinky hair with a heated comb or iron.
preventive (prê-vĕn'tĭv): a prophylactic; warding off disease.
primary (prī'mă-rē): first; primitive.
prism (prĭz'm): a transparent solid with triangular ends and two converging sides it breaks up white light into its component colors.
procerus (prṓ-sē'rûs): pyramidalis nasi muscle.
process (prŏ'sĕss): a course of development; a projecting part.
profession (prô-fĕsh'ûn): vocation; those engaged in work which requires special knowledge to serve the public in a particular art.
profuse (prṓ-fūs): to spend too liberally; abundant.
prognosis (prŏg-nô-sĭs): the foretelling of the probable course of a disease.
progressive dyes (prṓ-grĕs'ĭv dīz): hair restorers requiring time to oxidize; color develops gradually.
proliferate (prô-lĭf'ẽr-āt): to grow by reproduction of similar forms.
prominences (prŏm'ĭ-nên-sēz): projections.

fāte, câre, ăm, finâl, ärm, àsk, sofă; ēve, évent, ĕnd, recênt, evẽr; īce, ĭll; ōld, ṓbey, ôrb, ŏdd, cônnect, sŏft, fo͞od, fo͝ot; ūse, ûrn, ŭp, circûs

pronate (prō'nāt): to bend forward.
prong (prŏng): the round rod of the marcel iron.
prophylactic (prō-fĭ-lăk'tĭk): preventing disease; relating to prophylaxis.
prophylaxis (prō-fĭ-lăk'sĭs): prevention of disease.
proportion (prŏ-pōr'shŭn): comparative relation of one thing to another.
prostration (prŏs-trā'shŭn): the state of being weak or destroyed.
protection (prô-tĕk'shŭn): the act of shielding from injury.
protein (prō'tê-ĭn): a complex organic substance present in all living tissues, both animal and vegetable, necessary in the diet.
protoplasm (prō'tŏ-plăz'm): the material basis of life; a substance found in all living things.
protozoa (prō'tŏ-zō'ă): subkingdom of animals, including all the uni-cellular animall organisms.
protrude (prŏ-trōōd'): to project; to push forward or outward.
proximal (prŏk'sĭ-măl): nearest.
pruritus (prōō-rī'tŭs): itching; a symptom of various skin and scalp diseases.
psoriasis (sô-rī'ă-sĭs): a skin disease with circumscribed red patches, covered with adherent white scales.
psychic (sī'kĭk): relating to the mind.
psychology (sī-kŏl'ô-jē): the science of the mind and its operations.
pterygium (tê-rĭj'ē-ûm): a forward growth of the eponychium with adherence to the surface of the nail.
pterygoid (tĕr'ĭ-goid): wing-shaped.
pterygoideus (tĕr-ĭ-goid'ê-ûs): internus and externus muscle between mandible and cheek bone, draws mandible forward.
ptomaine (tō'mā-ĭn; -ēn): a poison produced during the decomposition of dead animal or vegetable matter.
ptyalin (tī'ă-lĭn): a starch splitting enzyme found in the saliva.
puberty (pū'bẽr-tē): the period of life in which the organs of reproduction are developed.
pull burn (pōōl bûrn): scalp irritation resulting from pulling the hair during permanent waving.
pulmonary (pŭl'mŏ-nā-rē): relating to the lungs.
pulmonary circulation (sûr-kū-lā'shŭn): blood circulation from heart to lungs and back to heart.
pulse (pŭls): stroke; the rhythmical dilation of an artery, produced by the increased volume of blood that is thrown into the vessel by the contraction of the heart.
pumice (pŭm'ĭs): hardened volcanic glass froth, white or gray in color, used for polishing in manicuring; called also pumice stone.
punctata, acne (pŭnk-tā'tă): a form of acne in which the lesions are pointed papules with a comedone in the center.
pungent (pŭn'jĕnt): producing a sharp sensation; painful; caustic.
purgative (pûr'gă-tĭv): an agent causing active movement of the bowels.
pupil (pū'pĭl): a small opening in the iris of the eye through which light enters.
purification (pū-rĭ-fĭ-kā'shŭn): the act of cleaning or removing foreign matter.
purpura (pûr'pū-ră): a disease characterized by the formation of purple patches on the skin and the mucous membrane.
pus (pŭs): a fluid product of inflammation, consisting of a liquid containing leucocytes and the debris of dead cells and tissue elements.
pusher (pōōh'ẽr): a steel instrument used to loosen the cuticle from the nail.
push wave (pōōsh wăv): a wave which is pushed into place with the hands.
postulation (pŭs-tû-lā'shŭn): the formation or the presence of pustules.

fāte, câre, ăm, finâl, ärm, ȧsk, sofă; ēve, ḗvent, ĕnd, recênt, evẽr; īce, ĭll; ōld, ŏbey, ôrb, ŏdd, cônnect, sŏft, fōōd, fŏŏt; ūse, ûrn, ŭp, circûs

pustule (pūs′tūl): an inflamed pimple containing pus.
pustulosa acne (pŭs-tû-lō′să): a form of acné characterized by pustules.
putrefaction (pū-trê-făk′shûn): decomposition; decay; the splitting up of the molecule of a protein into less complex substances.
pyloric (pĭ-lŏr′ĭk): pertaining to an opening found between the stomach and small intestine.
pyogenic (pī-ṓ-jĕn′ĭk): pus forming.
pyosis (pī-ō-sĭs): the formation of pus.
pyramidal (pĭ-răm′ĭ -dăl): shaped like a pyramid; relating to the pyramidal bone.
pyramidal bone (bōn): the wedge-shaped bone of the carpus.
pyramidalis nasi (pĭ-răm-ĭ-dā′lĭs nā′sī): pocerus; muscle of the nose.
pyro (pī′rō): a prefix denoting fire; prepared by fire.
pyrogallic acid (pī-rô-găl′ĭk ăs′ĭd): pyrogallol.
pyrogallol (pī-rô-găl′ŏl;-ōl): a substance obtained from gallic acid by the action of heat, employed externally in the treatment of psoriasis, ringworm, and other skin affections.
pyrogenic (pī-rṓ-jĕn′ĭk): producing fever.

Q

quadratus (kwod-rā′tûs): a square-shaped muscle; a muscle of the lower jaw.
quadratur labii superioris (lā′bē-īsû-pē′rē-ŏr′ĭs): a muscle of the upper lip.
quality (kwŏl′ĭ-tĭ): distinctive kind, trait, or character.
quarantine (kwŏr′ân-tēn): the isolation of a person to prevent spread of a contagious disease.
quince seed (kwĭns sēd): the dried seeds of Pyrus Cydonia which yield a mucilage used in the making of hand lotions.
quinine (kwī′nīn; kwĭ-nēn): enters into the composition of many hair lotions in small quantities; its effect is slightly antiseptic.

R

rabies (rā′bēz): an acute infectious disease of dogs, wolves, and other animals, corresponding to hydrophobia in human beings.
race (rās): a family, people or nation having a common ancestor.
radical (răd′ĭ-kâl): in chemistry, a group of atoms behaving like a single atom.
radial artery (rā′dĭ-ăl är′tĕr-ē): a blood vessel which supplies the lower arm and hand.
radial nerve (nûrv): a nerve which affects the arm and hand.
radiation (rā-dĭ-ā′shŭn): the process of giving off light or heat rays.
radius (rā′dē-ûs): the outer and smaller bone of the forearm.
ramus (rā′mûs): a branch of an artery, vein, or nerve.
rash (răsh): a skin eruption having little or no elevation.
rat-tail comb (răt-tāl kōm): a comb having a thick handle and used to push a wave in place.
ray (rā): a beam or light or heat.
re (rē): a prefix denoting back to the original or former state or position.
reaction (rē-ăk′shŭn): a response.
reagent (rê-ā′jĕnt): any substance used in detecting, examining, or measuring other substances.
receptacle (rē-sĕp′tâ-k′l): a utensil used for storage.
recondition treatment (rē-k û n-d ĭ sh′ û n trēt′mênt): a treatment to bring the hair back to a healthy condition; an oil treatment.

fāte, câre, ăm, finâl, ärm, ȧsk, sofă; ēve, évent, ĕnd, recênt, evẽr; īce, ĭll; ōld, ṓbey, ôrb, ŏdd, cônnect, sŏft, fo͞od, fo͝ot; ūse, ûrn, ŭp, circûs

rectifier (rĕk'tĭ-fī-ẽr): an apparatus to change an alternating current of electricity into a direct current.
rectum (rĕk'tûm): the terminal portion of the digestive tube.
rectus (rĕk'tûs): in a straight line; the name of small muscles of the eye.
recuperate (rê-kû'pẽr-āt): to recover health or strength.
red corpuscle (rêd kôr'pŭs-'l): red blood cell.
reddish cast (rĕd'ish kȧst): a tinge of red.
reflex (rē'flĕks): an involuntary nerve reaction.
rejuvenate (rê-jōō'vê-nāt): to make young or vigorous again.
relapse (rê-lăps): a slipping back, especially to a former bad condition.
relaxation (rē-lăk-sā'shûn): the act of being loose and less tense.
renal (rē'nâl): relating to a kidney.
reproductive (rē-prô-dŭk'tĭv): pertaining to reproduction or the process by which plants and animals give rise to offspring.
research (rê-sûrch): a careful search for facts or principles.
residue (rĕz'ĭ-dū): that which remains after a part is taken; remainder.
resilient (rê-zĭl'ĭ-ĕnt): elastic.
resistance (rê-zĭs'tȧns): opposition; act or capacity of striving against defeat; in electricity the opposition of a substance to the passage hrough it of an electric current.
respiration (rĕs-pĭ-rā'shûn): the act of breathing; the process of inhaling air into the lungs and expelling it
respiratory system (rê-spĭr'ă-tô-rē sĭs'tĕm): consists of the nose, pharynx, larynx, bronchi, and lungs which assist in breathing.
resorcin (rĕz-ôr'sin): resorcinal.
resorcinal (rĕz-ôr'sĭ-nâl): chiefly used as an external antiseptic in psoriasis, eczema,seborrhea, and ringworm.
restorative (rḗ-stôr'ă-tĭv): a food or medicine which helps to regain normal health and vigor.
restore (rḗ-stōr): to bring back to former strength;; repair; rebuild.
retard (rḗ-tärd'): to hinder or delay.
rete (rē-tḗ): any interlacing of either blood vessels or nerves.
reticular (rê-tĭk'û-lăr): having form of a network.
reticular layer (lā'ẽr): the inner layer of the corium.
retina (rĕt'ĭ-nă): the sensitive membrane of the eye which receives the image formed by the lens.
retinitis (rê-tĭn-ī'tĭs): inflammation of the retina.
retouch (rē'-tŭch): application of hair dye to new growth of hair.
retrahens aurem (rē'tră-hĕnz ôr'êm): a muscle back of the ear.
revivification (rḗ-vĭv-ĭ-fī-kā'shûn): to cause to revive or restore.
revolution (rĕv-ô-lū'shŭn): progressive motion of a body around a center.
rewave (rē'wāv): a permanent wave given to hair which still retains some of the former permanent.
rhagades (răg'ă-dẽz): cracks, fissures or chaps on the skin.
rheostat (rē-ō-stăt): a resistance coil; an instrument used to regulate the strength of an electric current.
rheumatism (rōō-mă-tĭz'm): a painful disease of the muscles and joints, accompanied by swelling and stiffness.
rhinitis (rī-nī'tĭs): inflammation of the nasal mucous membrane.
rhythm (rĭth'm): regular recurring movements.

fāte, câre, ăm, finâl, ärm, ȧsk, sofă; ēve, ḗvent, ĕnd, recênt, evẽr; īce, ĭll; ōld, ṓbey, ôrb, ŏdd, cônnect, sŏft, fōōd, fŏŏt; ūse, ûrn, ŭp, circûs

rickets (rĭk'ĕts): a disease of childhood, due chiefly to deficient nutrition, in which the bones become soft and cause deformity.
rickettsia (rĭk-ĕt'sĭ-ă): a type of pathogenic microorganism, capable of producing disease.
ridge (rĭj): crest of a wave.
ringed hair (rĭngd hâr): a variety of canities in which the hair appears white or colored in rings.
ringlet (rĭng'lĕt): a curl of hair.
ringworm (rĭng'wûrm): a vegetable parasitic disease of the skin and its appendages which appears in circular lesions and is contagious.
rinse (rĭns): to cleanse with a second or repeated application of water after washing; a prepared rinse water.
risorius (rĭ-zôr'ē-ûs): muscle at the side of the mouth.
rod (rŏd): the round solid prong of a waving iron; a slender bar on which hair is wound for curling or permanent waving.
rolling (rōl'ĭng): a massage movement in which the tissues are pressed and twisted.
root (root): in anatomy the base; the foundation or beginning of any part.
rosacea, acne (rô-zā'shē-ă): an eruption on the cheeks and nose.
rotate (rō'tāt): to turn; to revolve.
rouge (roozh): a cosmetic to color the skin pink or red.
ruffing (rŭf'ĭng): back combing; teasing.
round curling (round kûrl-ĭng): process of winding the hair tightly and evenly around a heated curling iron.

S

Sabouraud Rousseau (să'boo-rōroo'-sō): a discoverer of a 24-hour skin test used in hair dyeing to determine whether or not a patron can tolerate an aniline derivative hair dye.
saccular (săk'ū-lăr): shaped like a sac.
sachet (să-shā'): shaped like a sac.
sage tea rinse (sāj tē rĭns): given to darken the hair.
salicylic acid (săl-ĭ-sĭl'ĭk ăs'ĭd): white crystalline acid; it is used as an antiseptic in treating rheumatism.
saline (sā'līn): salty; containing salt.
saliva (să-lī'vă): the secretion of the salivary glands; spittle.
salivary gland (săl'ĭ-vă-rē glănd): the gland in the mouth secreting spittle.
sallow (săl'ō): having a yellowish color; of a pale, sickly color.
salt (sôlt): the union of a base with an acid, used to season food.
saturate (săt'ū-rāt): to cause to become soaked or completely penetrated; that which has absorbed all that it can hold.
scab (skăb): a crust formed on the surface of a sore.
scabies (skā'bĭ-ēz): a skin diseases caused by an animal, parasite, attended with intense itching; the itch.
scale (skāl): any thin plate of horny epidermis; regular markings used as a standard in measuring and weighing.
scalp (skălp): the skin covering of the cranium.
scalpial (skăl'pē-âl): the technical term for general all around treatment of the scalp.
scaphoid bone (skăf'oid bōn): the boat-shaped bone of the tarsus and the carpus.
scapula (skăp'ū-lă): the shoulder blade; a large flat triangular bone of the shoulder.
scar (skär): a mark remaining after a wound has healed.

fāte, câre, ăm, finâl, ärm, ȧsk, sofă; ēve, ĕvent, ĕnd, recênt, evẽr; īce, ĭll; ōld, ŏbey, ôrb, ŏdd, cônnect, sŏft, food, foot; ūse, ûrn, ŭp, circŭs

scarf skin (skärf ĭn): epidermis.
scarlet fever (skär'lĕt fē'vẽr): a contagious disease accompanied by fever and scarlet eruption
sciatica (sī-ăt'ĭ-kă): a painful inflammation of the sciatic nerve running down the back of the leg.
science (sī'êns): knowledge duly arranged and systematized.
scientific (sī-ên-tĭf'ĭk): pertaining to, or used in science.
sclerosis (sklẽr-ō'sĭs): hardening of tissue as a result of chronic inflammation.
scrum-pox (skrŭm'pŏks): impetigo contagiosa.
scrupulous (skroo'pû-lûs): careful; cautious.
sculpture curl (skŭlp'tūr kûrl): a curl placed close to the head, to appear as if it were carved.
scurf (skûrf): thin dry scales or scabs on the body, especially on the scalp; dandruff.
sebaceous (sêbā'shûs): oily; fatty.
sebaceous cyst (sĭst): a distended oily or fatty follicle or sac.
sebaceous glands (glăndz): oil glands of the skin.
seborrhea (sĕb-ô-rē'ă): over-action of the sebaceous glands.
seborrhea capitis (kăp'ĭ-tĭs): seborrhea of the scal, commonly called dandruff; pityriasis.
seborrhea oleosa (ō-lē-ō'să): excessive oiliness of the skin, particularly the forehead and nose.
seborrhea sicca (sĭk'ă): an accumulation on the scalp, of greasy scales or crusts, due to over-action of the sebaceous glands; dandruff or pityriasis.
seborrheic (sĕb-ô-rē'ĭk): seborrheal; pertaining to the over-action of the sebaceous glands.
seborrheic alopecia (ăl-ô-pē'shē-ă): baldness caused by diseased sebaceous glands.
sebum (sē'bŭm): the fatty or oil secretions of the sebaceous glands.
secondary (sĕk'ûn-dâ-rē): second in order.
secretion (sê-krē'shûn): a product manufactured by a gland for a special purpose.
secretory (sê-krē'tó-rē): relating to secretion or the secretions.
sectioning (sĕk'shûn-ĭng): dividing the hair into separate parts.
sedative (sĕd'ă-tĭv): tending to quiet or allay nervous excitement.
sedentary (sĕd'ên-tâ-rē): occupied in sitting; settled; inactive.
seep (sēp): to ooze out slowly.
segment (sĕg'mênt): to divide and re-divide into minute equal parts.
selector switch (sé-lĕk'tẽr swĭch): an apparatus used to select the kind of current desired for a treatment.
semilunar bone (sĕm-ĭ-lū'năr bōn): a crescent-shaped bone of the wrist.
senility (sê-nĭl'ĭ-tē): quality or state of being old.
sensation (sĕn-sā'shûn): a feeling or impression arising as the result of the stimulation of an afferent nerve.
sensitive (sĕn'sĭ-tĭv): easily affected by outside influences.
sensory (sĕn'sô-rē): relating to or pertaining to sensation.
sensory nerve (nûrv): afferent nerve; a nerve carrying sensations.
sentient (sĕn'shĭ-ênt): sensitive; capable of sensation.
sepsis (sĕp'sĭs): the presence of various pus forming and other pathogenic organisms, or their toxins, in the blood or tissues; septicemia.
septal artery (sĕp'tâl är'tẽr-ē): supplies the nostrils.
septic (sĕp'tĭk): relating to or caused by sepsis.
septicemia (sēp'tĭ-sē-mē-ă): the condition which exists when the pathogenic bacteria enter the bloodstream and circulate through the body, causing a general infection.
septum (sĕp'tûm): a dividing wall; a partition.
serous (sē'rûs): relating to, or containing serum.

fāte, câre, ăm, finâl, ärm, ȧsk, sofă; ēve, évent, ĕnd, recênt, evẽr; īce, ĭll; ōld, óbey, ôrb, ŏdd, cônnect, sŏft, food, foŏt; ūse, ûrn, ŭp, circûs

serratus (sē-rā'tûs): a muscle of the chest assisting in breathing and in raising the arm.
serum (sē'rum): the fluid portion of the blood obtained after coagulation; an antitoxin as prepared for therapeutic use.
sewage (sū'āj): the waste mater, solid and liquid, passing through a sewer.
shadow weaving (shăd'ō wāv'ĭng): a very soft wave for resistant hair which does not readily take finger waving.
shaft (shăft): slender stem-like structure; the long slender part of the hair above the scalp.
shampoo (shăm-pōō'): to subject the scalp and hair to washing and rubbing with some cleansing agent such as soap and water.
sheath (shēth): a covering enclosing or surrounding some organ.
sheen (shēn): gloss; brightness.
shingling (shĭng'lĭng'): cutting the hair close to the nape of the neck and gradually longer toward the crown.
shock (shŏk): a marked lowering of the vital activities from an injury or operation; a blow to the feelings.
short circuit (shôrt sûr'kĭt): to shut or break off an electric current before it has completed its course.
siccant; siccative (sĭ'kănt; sĭk'ă-tĭv): drying; tending to make dry.
silica (sĭl'ĭ-kă): dioxide of silicon used in the making of glass.
silicon (sĭl'ĭ-kŏn): a very abundant non-metallic element.
silver dye (sĭl'vẽr dī): a hair restorer, containing a silver salt used as a dye.
simplex (sĭm'plĕks): common; simple.
simplex, acne (ăk'nē): common pimple.
Singeing (sĭnj'ĭng): process of lightly burning hair ends with a lighted wax taper.
sinus (sī'nûs): a cavity or depression; a hollow in bone or other tissue.
sinusoid (sī'nûs-oid): resembling a sinu; a blood space in certain organs, as the liver, pancreas, etc.
sinusoidal current (sī-nûs-oid'ăl kûr'ênt): an induced interrupted current similar to faradic current.
skeletal muscles (skĕl'ĕ-tâl mŭs'l'z): muscles connected to the skeleton.
skeleton (skĕl'ĕ-tûn): the bony framework of the body.
skin (skĭn): the external covering of the body.
skull (skŭl): the bony case or the framework of the head.
slake (slāk): to become mixed with water in chemical combination.
sleek (slēk): to render smooth, soft, and glossy.
slip (slĭp): a smooth and slippery feeling imparted by talc to face powder.
slithering (slĭth'ĕr-ĭng): tapering the hair to graduated lengths with scissors.
slough (slŭf): to separate as dead matter from living tissues; to discard.
small pox (smôl pŏks): a contagious skin disease resulting in the production of pock marks.
smaller occipital (smôl'ẽr ŏk-sĭp'ĭ-tâl): sensory nerve affecting skin behind the ear.
snarls (snarlz): tangles, as of hair.
soap (sōp): compound of fatty acid with an alkaline base.
soapless shampoo (sōp'lĕs shăm-pōō'): a shampoo made with sulfonated oil, alcohol, mineral oil and water; this type of shampoo does not foam and is usually slightly acid in reaction.
socket (sŏk'ĕt): a cavity in which a movable part is inserted.
sodium (sō'dē-ûm): a metallic element of the alkaline group.
sodium bicarbonate (bī-kär'bôn-āt): baking soda: bicarbonate of soda; it relieves burns, bites; is often used in bath powders as an aid to cleansing oily skin.

fāte, câre, ăm, finâl, ärm, ȧsk, sofă; ēve, ĕvent, ĕnd, recênt, evẽr; īce, ĭll; ōld, ŏbey, ôrb, ŏdd, cônnect, sŏft, fōōd, fŏŏt; ūse, ûrn, ŭp, circŭs

sodium carbonate (kär′bôn-āt): washing soda; used to prevent corrosion of metallic instruments when added to boiling water.
sodium hydroxide (hī-drŏk′sīd): powerful alkali used in the manufacture of hard soaps.
sodium thiosulphat (thī-ō-sŭl′fât): it is used in solutions for impetiginous conditions and parasitic alopecias of the beard.
soft water (sŏft wô′tẽr): water which readily lathers with soap.
solar (sō′lẽr): pertaining to the sun.
solarium (sô-lă′rē-ûm): a sun parlor.
sole (sōl): the plantar surface of the foot.
soluble (sŏl′û-b′l): capable of being dissolved.
solution (sō-lū′shûn): the act or process by which a substance is absorbed into a liquid.
solvent (sŏl′vĕnt): an agent capable of dissolving substances.
somnolence (sŏm′nō-lêns): sleepiness; drowsiness.
sparsely (spärs′lē): pertaining to the hair, thinly scattered.
spatula (spăt′ū-lă): a flexible, knife-like implement for handling creams and drugs, etc.
specialist (spĕsh′ă-lĭst): one who devotes himself to some special branch of learning, art, or business.
specific gravity (spĕ-sĭf′ĭk grăvĭ-tĭ): the measured weight of a substance compared with an equal volume of another taken as a standard.
spectrum (spĕk′trûm): the band of rainbow colors produced by decomposing light by means of a prism.
spermaceti (spŭr-mă-sĕt′ē): cetaceum; an animal wax obtained from the head of the sperm whale; used to give body to creams.
sphere (sfẽr): a ball or globular body.
spherical (sfẽr′ĭ-kâl): relating to or having the shape of a sphere.
sphenoid (sfē′noid): wedge-shaped; a bone in the cranium.
sphincter (sfĭnk′tẽr): a muscle which surrounds and closes a natural opening of the body.
spinal (spī′nâl): pertaining to the spine or vertebral column.
spinal accessory (ăk-sĕs′ō̆-rē): eleventh cranial nerve.
spinal column (kŏl′ŭm): the backbone or vertebral column.
spinal cord (kôrd): the portion of the central nervous system contained within the spinal or vertebral canal.
spinal nerves (nûrvz): the nerves arising from the spinal cord.
spindle-shaped (spĭn′d′l-shāpt): tapering toward each end.
spine (sp n): a short process of bone; the backbone.
spiral (spī′râl): coil; winding around a center, like a watch spring.
spiral rod (rŏd): a rod upon which the hair is wound in a spiral manner for a permanent wave.
spiral winding (wīnd′ĭng): winding the hair on a rod, like the thread of a screw, from the scalp to the ends.
spirillum (spĭ-rĭl′ûm); pl., **spirilla** (-ă): curved bacterium.
spirocheta pallida (spī-rō̆-kē′ta păl′ĭ-dă): pathogenic bacteria responsible for syphilis.
spleen (splēn): a large vascular ductless gland between the stomach and the diaphragm.
splenius (splē′nē-ûs): a muscle or a group of muscles at the side and back of the neck.
spongy (spŭn′jē): elastic; porous.
spore (spōr): a tiny bacterial body having a protective wall to withstand unfavorable conditions.
spray (sprā): to discharge liquid in the form of fine vapor.
squama (skwā′mă): an epidermic scale made up of thin, flat cells.
squamous (skwā′mûs): scaly.
stagnation (stăg-nā′shûn): lack of action; cessation of activity.

fāte, câre, ăm, finâl, ärm, ȧsk, sofȧ; ēve, ĕvent, ĕnd, recênt, evẽr; īce, ĭll; ōld, ō̆bey, ôrb, ŏdd, cônnect, sŏft, fōōd, fŏŏt; ūse, ûrn, ŭp, circûs

staphylococcus (stăf′ĭ-lṓ-kŏk′ŭs): cocci which are grouped in clusters like a bunch of grapes; found in pustules and boils.
static electricity (stăt′ĭk ē-lĕk-trĭs′ĭ-tē): electricity produced by friction.
steamer, facial (stēm′ĕr fā′shâl): an apparatus, used in place of hot towels, for steaming the scalp or face.
steam pocket (stēm pŏk′ĕt): pertaining to permanent waving, a special folding of the permanent wave pad to make a closed steam chamber, to protect the scalp from steam burns.
stearate (stē′ă-rāt): a salt of stearic acid.
stearic acid (stê-ăr′ĭk ăs′-ĭd): a white fatty acid, occurring in solid animal fats and in some of the vegetable fats.
steatoma (stē-ă-tō′mă): a sebaceous cyst; a fatty tumor.
steatosis (stē-ă-tō′sĭs): fatty degeneration; adiposis.
sterile (stĕr′ĭl): barren; free from all living organisms.
sterility (stê-rĭl′ĭ-tē): a condition of being unfruitful; barren.
sterilization (stêr-ĭ-lī-zā′shŭn): the process of making sterile; the destruction of germs.
sterilizer (stĕr′ĭ-lī-zĕr): an agent or receptacle for sterilization.
sterno (stûr′nṓ): a prefix denoting connection with the sternum (breast bone).
sterno-cleido-mastoideus (stûr″nṓ-klī-dṓ-măs′-toid′ē-ŭs): a muscle of the neck which depresses and rotates the head.
sternomastoid (stûr-nṓ-măs′toid): pertaining to the sternum and the mastoid process.
sternum (stûr′nŭm): the flat bone of the breast.
stimulant (stĭm′ū-lânt): an agent that arouses organic activity.
stimulation (stĭm-ū-lā′shûn): the act arousing increasesd functional activity.
stimulus (stĭm′ū-lŭs): an agent which causes stimulation.
stomach (stŭm′ŭk): the dilated portion of the alimentary canal, in which the first process of digestion takes place.
strand (strănd): a fiber, hair or the like.
stratum (strā′tûm); pl., **strata** (-ă): layer of tissue.
stratum corneum (kôr′nḗ-ŭm): horny layer of the skin.
stratum granulosum (grăn-û-lo′sum): granular layer of the skin.
stratum lucidum (lū′sĭ-dûm): clear layer of the skin.
stratum mucosum (mū-kō′sŭm): mucous or malpighian layer of the skin.
streptococcus (strĕp-tṓ-kŏk′ûs): pus-forming bacteria that arrange in curved lines resembling a string of beads; found in erysipelas and blood poisoning.
striated (strī′āt-ĕd): marked with parallel lines or bands; striped; voluntary muscle.
stroking (strōk′ĭng): a gliding movement over a surface; to pass the finger or any instrument gently over a surface; effleurage.
stroma (strō′mă): the framework, usually of connective tissue of an organ, gland, or other structure.
Strontium sulphide (strŏn′shē-ûm sŭl′fĭd): a light gray powder capable of liberating hydrogen sulphide in the presence of water; used as a depilatory.
structure (strŭk′tûr): construction; manner of building or form.
sty, stye (stī); pl., **sties, styes** (stīz): inflammation of one of the sebaceous glands of the eyelid.
styptic (stĭp′tĭk): an agent causing contraction of living tissue; used to stop bleeding; an astringent.
sub (sŭb): a prefix denoting under; below.
subcutaneous (sŭb-kŭ-tā′nē-ûs): under the skin.
subcutis (sŭb-kū′tĭs): subdermis; subcutaneous tissue; under or beneath the corium or dermis, the true skin.

fāte, câre, ăm, finâl, ärm, ȧsk, sofä; ēve, évent, ĕnd, recênt, evẽr; īce, ĭll; ōld, ṓbey, ôrb, ŏdd, cônnect, sŏft, fo͞od, fo͝ot; ūse, ûrn, ŭp, circûs

subdermis (sŭb-dûr′mĭs): subcutis or subcutaneous tissue of the skin.
subjective (sŭb-jĕk′tĭv sĭmp-tūm): sensed by the individual and not by the examiner
sublingual (sŭb-lĭn′gwăl): under the tongue
submerge (sûb-mûrj′): sink or plunge anything under water or other fluid
submental artery (sŭb-mĕn′tăl är′tĕr-ē): supplies blood to the chin and lower lip.
subsidiary (sŭb-sĭd′ē-ā-rē): supplementary; furnishing assistance.
substance (sŭb′stăns): matter; material.
sudamen (sū-dā′mĕn); pl., **sudamina** (sū-dăm′ĭ-nă): a disorder of the sweat glands with obstruction of their ducts.
sudor (sū′dôr): sweat; perspiration.
sudoriferous ducts (dŭkts): the excretoary ducts of the sweat glands.
sudoriferous glands (glăndz): sweat glands of the skin.
sudorific (sū-dôr-ĭf′ĭk): causing or inducing perspiration.
sulcus (sŭl′kŭs): a furrow or groove.
sulfonated oil (sŭl′fûn-āt-êd oil): an organic substance prepared by reacting oils with sulphuric acid; has a slightly acid reaction and is miscible with water; used as a base in soapless shampoos.
sulphide (sŭl′fīd): a compound of sulphur with a base.
sulphur (sŭl′fûr): a chemical element whose compounds are used in bleaching and in medicine.
sulphuric acid (sŭl-fū′rĭk ăs′ĭd): oil of vitriol; colorless and nearly odorless, heavy oil, corrosive liquid; employed as a caustic.
sunburn (sŭn′bûrn): inflammation of the skin caused by excessive exposure to the sun.
sunlight (sŭn′līt): the light rays coming from the sun.
suntan (sŭn′tăn): a brownish coloring of the skin as a result of sun exposure.
super (sū′pẽr): a prefix denoting over; above; beyond.
superciliary (sū-pẽr-sĭl′ē-â-rē): pertaining to or in the región of the eyebrow.
supercilii (sū-pẽr-sĭl′ē-ī): of or pertaining to the eyebrown.
supercilium (sū′pẽr-sĭl′ē-ûm); pl., **supercilia** (-ă): the eyebrow.
superficial (sū-pẽr-fĭsh′ăl): pertaining to or being on the surface.
superficial cervical (sûr′vĭ-kăl): a cranial nerve which supplies the muscle and skin of the neck.
superfluous (sû-pûr′floo-ûs): excessive; more than is wanted or needed.
superior (sû-pē′rē-ẽr): higher; upper; better or of more value.
superior maxillary (măk′sĭ-lâ-rē): the upper jaw bone.
superioris (sû-pē-rê-ŏr′ĭs): a muscle which elevates a part of the body.
supinate (sū′pĭ-nāt): to turn the forearm and hand so that the palm faces upward.
supinator (sū′pĭ-nāt-ôr): a muscle which produces supination of the forearm.
supine (sû-pīn′): lying flat or on the back.
suppuration (sŭp-ū-rā′shûn): the formation of pus.
supra (sū′pră): a prefix denoting on top of, above, over, beyond, besides; more than.
supraorbital (sū-pră-ôr′bĭ-tăl): above the orbit or eye.
supra-trochlear (sū-pră-trŏk′lē-ă): above the trochlea or pulley of the superior oblique muscle.
sural nerve (sū′răl nûrv): supplies the outer side and back of leg and foot.
susceptible (sû-sĕp′tĭ-b′l): capable of being influenced or easily acted on.
suspension (sû-spĕn′shûn): a mixture of a liquid and insoluble particles which have a tendency to settle out on standing.
suture (sū′tûr): a uniting; a stitch.

fāte, câre, ăm, finâl, ärm, àsk, sofă; ēve, évent, ĕnd, recênt, evẽr; īce, ĭll; ōld, ŏbey, ôrb, ŏdd, cônnect, sŏft, fōod, fŏot; ūse, ûrn, ŭp, circûs

swirl (swûrl): formation of a wave in a diagonal direction from back to side of head.
switch (swĭch): a separate tress of hair, or of some substitute, worn by women, to increase the apparent mass of hair.
swooning (swōō'ĭng): fainting.
sycosis (sī-kŏ'sĭs): a chronic pustular inflammation of the hair follicles.
sycosis barbae (bär'bē): a chronic inflammation of the hair follicles of the beard; barber's itch.
sycosis, tinea (tĭn'ē-ă): parasitic ringworm of the beard; barber's itch.
symbol (sĭm'bŏl): a mark representing an atom of an element or a molecule of a radical.
sympathetic (sĭm-pă-thĕt'ĭk): relating to or exhibiting sympathy; noting the nerves in organic life.
sympathetic nervous system (nûr'vûs sĭs'tĕm): controls the involuntary muscles which affect respiration, circulation, and digestion.
symptom (sĭmp'tûm): a change in the body or its functions which indicates disease.
symptom, objective (ŏb-jĕk'tĭv): that which can be seen, as in pimples, pustules, etc.
symptom, subjective (sŭb-jĕc'tĭv): can be felt, as in itching.
symptomatic (sĭmp-tûm-ăt'ĭk): relating to a symptom or symptoms; indicative.
symptomatica alopecia (sĭmp-tûm-ăt'ĭ-kă ăl-ō-pē'shē-ă): loss of hair from illness.
symptomatica chloasma (klŏ-ăz'mă): a form of chloasma accompanying disease.
syn (sĭn): a prefix denoting along with; together; at the same time.
synovia (sĭ-nō'vē-ă): a transparent viscid lubricating fluid secreted by the lining membranes of joints.
synthetic (sĭn-thĕt'ĭk): made artificially by the unin of simpler compounds or elements.
syphilis (sĭf'ĭ-lĭs): a chronic, infectious venereal disease.
system (sĭs'tĕm): a group of organs which especially contribute toward one of the more important vital functions; an assemblage of objects united by regular interdependence.
systematic (sĭs-tĕm-ăt'ĭk): proceeding according to system or regular method.
systemic (sĭs-tĕm'ĭk): pertaining to a system or to the body as a whole.
systole (sĭs'tṓ-lē): the period of the heart's contraction.

T

tactile (tăk'tĭl): pertaining to touch.
tactile corpuscle (kôr'pŭs'l): touch nerve endings found within the skin.
tan (tăn): sunburn; pigmentation of the skin from exposure to the sun.
tannic acid (tăn'ĭk ăs'ĭd): a plant extract used as an astringent.
taper (tā'pẽr): regularly narrowed to a point.
tapering (tā'pẽr-ĭng): shortening and thinning the hair at the same time.
tapotement (tȧ-pṓt-män'): a massage movement using a short, quick slapping or tapping movement
tapping (tăp'ĭng): a massage movement; striking lightly with the partly flexed fingers.
tar (tär): a thick, semi-solid blackish brown mass, of complex composition, obtained by the destructive distillation of the wood of various species of pine.
tarsus (tär'sûs): the root of the foot or instep; the seven bones of the instep.
taut (tôt): tensely stretched; not slack.
teasing (tēz'ĭng): back combing; combing the short hair toward the scalp while the hair strand is held in a vertical position.
technic; technique (tĕk'nĭk; tĕk'nēk): manner of performance; a skill; a process.
technical (tĕk'nĭ-kȧl): relating to a technic.

fāte, câre, ăm, finȧl, ärm, ȧsk, sofă; ēve, ḗvent, ĕnd, recênt, evẽr; īce, ĭll; ōld, ṓbey, ôrb, ŏdd, cônnect, sŏft, fōōd, fŏŏt; ūse, ûrn, ŭp, circûs

tela (tē′lă): a web-like structure.
temperature (tĕm′pẽr-ă-tûr): the degree of heat or cold.
temple (tĕm′p'l): the flattened space on the side of the forehead.
temporal (tĕm′pṓ-râl): of or pertaining to the temple.
temporal bone (bōn): the bone at the side and base of the skull.
temporalis (tĕm-pṓ-ră′lĭs): the temporal muscle.
tendon (tĕn′dŭn): fibrous cord or band connecting muscle with bone.
tension (tĕn′shŭn): stress caused by stretching or pulling.
tepid (tĕp′ĭd): neither hot nor cold; lukewarm; about blood heat.
teres (tē′rēz): cylindrical muscles attached to the scapula and capable of moving the arm.
terminal (tûr′mĭ-nâl): of or pertaining to the end or extremity.
tertiary (tûr′shē-ȧ-rē): third in order.
Tesla, Nikola (tĕs′lă, nĭ-kō′lă): American electrician of Hungarian birth (1857).
Tesla current (kŭr′ênt): high-frequency current.
test curl (tĕst kûrl): a sample curl, by which the correct treatment for the hair under consideration is ascertained.
testes (tĕs′tês): the male reproductive glands.
test for color (tĕst for kŭl′ẽr): to dye a strand of hair to determine the result of the color used.
test, hair dye (hâr dī): a test made upon the scalp, behind the ear, or in the bend of the arm, for predisposition to the dye agent used; a test to determine the reaction of the dye upon the sample strand, regarding both color and breakage.
tetanus (tĕt′ă-nŭs): a disease with spasmodic and continuous contraction of the muscles; lockjaw.
textometer (tĕks′tŏm′ē-tẽr): a device used to measure the elasticity and reaction of the hair to alkali solutions.
texture (tĕks′tûr): the composition or structure of a tissue or organ.
thenar (thē′när): the fleshy prominence of the palm corresponding to the base of the thumb.
theory (thē′ṓ-rē): an hypothesis; a reasoned and probable explanation.
therapeutic lamp (thĕr′ă-pū′tĭk lămp): an electrical apparatus producing any of the various rays of the spectrum; used for skin and scalp treatments.
therapeutics (thĕr-ă-pū′tĭks): branch of medical science concerned with the treatment of disease.
therapy (thĕr′ă-pē): the science and art of healing.
thermal (thûr′mâl): pertaining to heat.
thermometer (thĕr-mŏm′ḗ-tẽr): any device for measuring temperature.
thermostat (thûr′mṓ-stăt): an automatic device for regulating temperature.
thinning hair (thĭn′ĭ ng): decreasing the thickness of the hair where it is too heavy.
thoracic (thô-răs′ĭk): pertaining to the thorax.
thorax (thō′răks): the part of the body between the neck and the abdomen; the chest.
thrombocyte (thrŏm′bṓ-sīt): a blood platelet which aids in clotting.
thymol (thĭm′ŏl; -ŏl): a substance extracted from oil of thyme and used as a medicine for skin and scalp diseases.
thymus (thī′mŭs): a ductless gland situated in the upper part of the chest.
thyroid gland (thī′roid glănd): a large ductless gland situated in the neck.
tibia (tĭb′ĭ-ȧ): the inner bone of the leg between the knee and the ankle.
tincture (tĭnk′tûr): an alcoholic solution of a medicinal substance.
tinea (tĭn′ē-ă): a skin disease, especially ringworm.
tinea barbae (bär′bē): tinea sycosis.
tinea capitis (kăp′ĭ-tĭs): tinea tonsurans; ringworm of the scalp.

fāte, câre, ăm, finâl, ärm, ȧsk, sofă; ēve, ĕvent, ĕnd, recênt, evẽr; īce, ĭll; ōld, ṓbey, ôrb, ŏdd, cônnect, sŏft, fōod, fŏot; ūse, ûrn, ŭp, circŭs

tinea sycosis (sī-kō′sĭs): parasitic sycosis; ringworm of the beard; barber's itch.
tinea tonsurans (tŏn-sū′rănns): tinea capitis; ringworm of the scalp.
tinea unguium (ŭn′gwē-ŭm): ringworm of the nail.
tinge (tĭnj): a degree, usually slight, of some color, addewd to something.
tint (tĭnt): to give a coloring to; as used in beauty culture, pertaining to hair dyeing; to color the hair by means of a hair dye, color rinse, or hair tint.
Tirrell burner (tĭ-rĕl′bûr′nẽr): an apparatus used to burn the hair in ash testing.
tis; sis (tĭs; sĭs): a word ending added to the name of a part to denote inflammation of that part, such as pityriasis, dermatitis.
tissue (tĭsh′ū): a collection of similar cells which perform a particular function.
tissue, connective (kŏ-nĕk′tĭv): binding and supporting tissue.
titanium dioxide (tī-tā′nē-ûm dī-ŏk′sīd): a white substance in face powder used for its covering power.
tone (tōn): healthy functioning of the body or its parts.
tong (tŏng): an instrument for lifting or holding an object.
tonic (tŏn′ĭk): increasing the strength or tone of the system.
torsade (tôr-sād): a twisted fringe of hair.
torso (tôr′sō): the trunk of the human body.
toupee (tōō-pā): a small wig used to cover the top or crown of the head.
toxemia (tŏk-sē′mē-ă): a form of blood poisoning.
toxic (tŏk′sĭk): due to, or of the nature of poison; poisonous.
toxin; toxine (tŏk′sĭn; -sēn): a poisonous substance of undetermined chemical nature, elaborated during the growth of pathogenic micro-organisms.
trachea (trā′kē-ă; tră-kē′ă): wind-pipe.
trachoma (tră-kō′mă): a contagious disease of the eyelids characterized by small granular elevations on the lids.
tragacanth (trăg′ă-kănth): a gummy exudation from the stems of Astragalus gummifier; used as a thickener and as an emulsifier.
transformation (trăns-fŏr-mā′shûn): a change in the external appearance of an object; an artificial band of hair worn over a person's own hair.
transformer (trăns-fôr′mẽr): used for the purpose of increasing or decreasing the voltage of the current used; it can only be used on an alternating current.
transmission (trăns-mĭsh′ûn): passing on by anything, often said of disease.
transmit (trăns-mĭt′): to cause to go across; to send over; dispatch.
transmitter (trăns-mĭt′ẽr): one who or that which transmits.
transparent (trăns-pâr′ênt): admitting the passage of light.
transverse (trăns-vûrs′): lying or being across or crosswise.
transverse facial (fā′shâl): an artery supplying the skin, the parotid gland and the masseter muscle.
trapezium (tră-pē′zē-ûm): the first bone of the second row of the carpus.
trapezius (tră-pē′zē-ûs): muscle that draws the head backward and sideways.
trapezoid (trăp′ē-zoid): a small bone ini the second row of the carpus.
trauma (trô′mă): a wound or injury.
treatise (trē′tĭs): a learned or scientific discourse on a subject.
tremor (trē′mor; trĕm′ ŏ r): an involuntary trembling or quivering.
Treponema pallidum (trĕp- ő -nē′mă păl′ ĭ -d û m): the pathogenic parasite of syphilis.
triangular (tr ī -ăn′g ū -lăr): having three angles or corners; bone of the wrist.

fāte, câre, ăm, finâl, ärm, ȧsk, sofă; ēve, évent, ĕnd, recênt, evẽr; īce, ĭll; ōld, ȍbey, ôrb, ŏdd, cônnect, sŏft, fōōd, fŏŏt; ūse, ûrn, ŭp, circûs

triangularis (trī-ăn-gū-lā′rĭs): depressor anguli oris; a muscle that pulls down corners of the mouth.
triceps (trī′sĕps): three-headed.
trichology (trĭ-kŏl′ŏ-jē): the science of the care of the hair.
trichonosus (trĭk-ō-nō′sûs): any disease of the hair.
trichophyton (trĭ-kŏf′ĭ-tŏn): a fungus parasite responsible for ringworm.
trichophytosis (trĭ-kŏf′ĭ-tō′sĭs): ringworm of the skin and scalp, due to growth of a fungus parasite.
trichoptilosis (trĭ-kŏp-tĭ-lō′sĭs): a splitting of the hair ends, giving them a feathery appearance.
trichorrhexis (trĭk-ô-rĕk′sĭs): brittleness of the hair.
trichosis (trĭ-kō′sĭs): abnormal growth of hair.
tricuspid (trī-kŭs′pĭd): having three points, as the right auriculo-ventricular valve of the heart.
trifacial (trĭ-fā′shâl): the fifth cranial nerve; trigeminus nerve.
trigeminal (trī-jĕm′ĭ-nâl): relating to the fifth cranial or trigeminus nerve.
trismus (trĭz′mûs, trĭs′-): lock jaw; usually associated with, and due to the same cause of eneral tetanus.
trochlea (trŏk′le-ă): a pulley-like process; a smooth articular surface of bone upon which another glides.
true skin (troo skĭn): the corium.
tubercle (tū′bĕr-k'l): a rounded, solid elevation on the skin or membrane.
tuberculosis (tū-bûr′kū-lō′sĭs): an infectious disease due to a specific bacillus, characterized by the formation of tubercles, usually in the lungs.
tumor (tū′mĕr): a swelling; an abnormal enlargement; a mass of new tissue which persists and grows independently of its surrounding structures, and which has no physiological use.
turbinal; turbinate (tûr′bĭ-nâl, -nāt): a bone in the nose; turbinated body.
turbinated (tûr′bĭ-nāt-ĕd): shaped like a top; scross-shaped.
tweezers (twēz′ĕrz): a pair of small forceps to remove or extract hair.
typhoid (tī′foid): a continued acute infectious fever, with intestinal lesions and an eruption of rose-colored spots on the chest and abdomen.

U

ulcer (ŭl′sĕr): an open sore not caused by a wound.
ulna (ŭl′nă): the inner and larger bone of the forearm.
ultra (ŭl′tră): a prefix denoting beyond; on the other side; excessively.
ultra-violet (ŭl′tră-vī′ō-lĕt): invisible rays of the spectrum which are beyond the violet rays.
un (ŭn): a prefix denoting not; contrary.
unadulterated (ŭn-ă-dŭl′tĕr-āt-ĕd): pure.
unciform (ŭn′sĭ-form): hook-shaped; the bone on the inner side of the second row of the carpus.
unctuous (ŭnk′tū-ûs): greasy; oily.
undulation (ŭn-dû-lā′shûn): a wave-like movement or shape.
unguentum (ŭn-gwĕn′tûm); pl., **unguenta** (-ă): a salve or ointment.
unguis (ŭn′gwĭs); pl., **ungues** (gwēz): the nail of a finger or toe.
umguium tinea (ŭn′gĭvĕ-ŭm tĭn′é-ă): ringworm of the nails.
uni (ūn′i): a prefix denoting one; once.
unipolar (ū-nĭ-pōlăr): a term used when oone electrode of a direct current is applied to the body.

fāte, câre, ăm, finâl, ärm, ȧsk, sofă; ēve, évent, ĕnd, recênt, evẽr; īce, ĭll; ōld, ŏbey, ôrb, ŏdd, cônnect, sŏft, foōd, foŏt; ūse, ûrn, ŭp, circŭs

unit (ū'nĭt): a single thing or value.
United States Pharmacopeia (ū-nīt'ĕd stāts fär-má-kō-pē-yä): an official book of drug and medicinal standards.
unsanitary (ŭn-săn'ĭ-tâ-rē): not sanitary; injurious to health.
urea (ū'rē-ă): a crystalline substance found in urine.
uric acid (ū'rik ăs'-ĭd): a crystalline acid contained in the urine.
uridrosis (ū-rĭ-drō'sĭs): the presence of urea in sweat.
urine (ū'rĭn): the fluid secreted by the kidneys.
urticaria (ûr-tĭ-kā'rē-ă): a skin disease in which wheals and severe itching develops; hives; nettle rash.
uterine (ū'tĕr-ĭn; -īn): pertaining to the uterus, an organ of the female mammals in which the young is contained and nourished before birth.
utilize (ū'tĭ-līz): to make useful.
uvula (ū'vū-lă): the conical projection from the posterior edge of the middle of the soft palate.

V

vaccination (văk-sĭ-nā'shûn): inoculation with the virus of cowpox, or vaccma as a means of producing immunity against small pox.
vaccine (văk'sĭn; -sēn): any substance used for preventive inoculation.
vaccum (văk'ū-ûm): a space entirely devoid of matter; a space from which the air has been exhausted.
vagus (vā'gûs): pneumogastric nerve; tenth cranial nerve.
valence (vā'lĕns): the degree of combining power of an element or radical.
valve (vălv): a structure which temporarily closes a passage or orifice or permits flow in one direction only.
vapor (vā'pĕr): the gaseous state of a liquid or solid.
vaporization (vā-pĕr-ī-zā'shûn): act or process of converting water into steam or a vapor.
varicose veins (văr'ĭ-cōs-vāns): swollen or knotted veins.
varicosis (văr-ĭ-kō'sĭs): a dilated or varicose state of a vein or veins.
vascular (văs'kû-lăr): supplied with small blood vessels; pertaining to a vessel for the conveyance of a fluid as blood or lymph.
vascularization (văs-kû-lăr-ī-zā'shûn): the formation of new blood vessels in a part of the body.
vaseline (văs'ĕ-lĭn; ēn): a trade name; petrolatum; a semi-solid greasy or oily mixture of hydrocarbons obtained from petroleum.
vaso-constrictor (văs-ŏ-kôn-strĭk'tĕr): a nerve which, when stimulated, causes narrowing of blood vessels.
vaso-dilator (văs-ŏ-dī-lā'tĕr): a nerve which, when stimulated, causes expansión of the blood vessels.
vegetable dyes (vĕj'ê-tă-b'l dīz): comprised of Egyptian henna, indigo, and camomile used as hair dyes or hair rinses.
vegetation (vĕj-ĕ-tā'shûn): morbid or fungus growths; of or pertaining to growths.
vehicle (vē'hĭ-k'l): a means of conveyance; a substance in which medicaments are carried into the deeper tissues.
vein; vena (vān; vē'nă): a blood vessel carrying blood toward the heart.
vena cava (kā'vă): one of the large veins which carry the blood to the right auricle of the heart.
venenata, dermatitis (vē-nĕn-ă'tă): skin inflammation produced by local action of irritating substances.
venenation (vĕn-ĕ-nā'shûn): the condition due to poisoning.

fāte, câre, ăm, finâl, ärm, àsk, sofă; ēve, évent, ĕnd, recênt, evẽr; īce, ĭll; ōld, ŏbey, ôrb, ŏdd, cônnect, sŏft, fōod, fŏot; ūse, ûrn, ŭp, circûs

venereal (vḗ-nē′rḗ-âl): pertaining to a disease arising from illicit sexual indulgence with an infected person.
venter (věn′tẽr): belly; the abdomen.
ventilate (věn′tĭ-lāt): to renew the air in a place; to oxygenate the blood in the capillaries of the lungs.
ventral (věn′trâl): pertaining to the belly.
ventricle (věn′trĭ-k′l): a small cavity; particularly in the brain or heart.
vermin (vûr′mĭn): parasitic insects, as lice and bedbugs.
verruca (vě-roo′kă): a wart; a circumscribed hypertrophy of the papillae and epidermis.
verrucose; verrucous (věr′oo-kōs; -kûs): warty; presenting wart-like elevations.
vertebra (vûr-tê-bră); pl., **vertebrae** (bre): a bony segment of the spinal column.
vertebrate (vûr′tê-brāt): having a backbone or spinal column.
vertex (vûr′těks): the crown or top of the head.
vesicle (věs′ĭ-k′l): a small blister or sac; a small elevation on the skin.
vesicular (vḗ-sik′û-lăr): relating to or containing vesicles.
vessel (věs′l): tube or canal in which blood, lymph, or other fluid is contained and conveyed or circulated.
vibration (vī-brā′shûn): shaking; a to and fro massage movement.
vibrator (vi′brā-tẽr): an electrically driven massage apparatus causing a swinging, shaking sensation on the body, producing stimulation.
vibrissae (vī-brĭs′à): stiff hairs in the nostrils.
vibroid (vī′broid): a vibratory movement in massage.
villus (vĭl′ŭs); pl., **villi** (-ī): minute finger-like processes covering the surface of the mucous membrane of the small intestine.
vinegar (vĭn′ḗ-gẽr): a sour liquid used as a condiment or as a preservative, formed by fermentation of dilute alcoholic liquids as wine, cider, ec.; it contains acetic acid; used as a rinse to remove soap curds from the hair.
violet-ray (vī′ō-lět rā): high-frequency; Tesla; an electric current of médium voltaje and médium amperage.
virgin hair (vûr′jĭn hâr): normal hair which has had no previous bleaching or dyeing treatments.
virulent (vĭr′oo-lênt): extremely poisonous; disease producing micro-organisms.
virus (vī′rûs): poison; the specific poison of an infectious disease.
viscera (vĭs′ẽr-ă): plural of viscus.
visceral (vĭs′ẽr-âl): pertaining to the internal organs; the heart, lungs, intestines, etc.
viscid (vĭs′ĭd): sticky or adhesive.
viscosity (vĭs-kŏs′ĭ-tē): the quality of being viscid so that a fluid flows with difficulty.
viscus (vĭs′kŭs): pl. **viscera** (vĭs′ẽr-ă): the internal organs, such as the heart, liver, intestine, etc.
vital (vī′tāl): relating to life.
vitality (vī-tāl′ĭ-tē): the principle of life; the state or quality of being vital; power of enduring or of continuing.
vitamin (vī′tâ-mĭn): one of a group of organic substances present in a very small quantity in natural foodstuffs, which are essential to normal metabolism, and the lack of which in the diet causes beriberi and other deficiency diseases.
vitiligo (vĭt-ĭ-lī′go): milky-white spots of the skin, common in Blacks.
vitriol, oil of (vĭt′rĭ-ŭl): a common name for sulphuric acid.
vocation (vô-kā′shŭn): regular employment; profession.
vogue (vōg): fashion; custom; style.

fāte, câre, ăm, finâl, ärm, àsk, sofă; ēve, évent, ěnd, recênt, evẽr; īce, ĭll; ōld, óbey, ôrb, ŏdd, cônnect, sŏft, food, foot; ūse, ûrn, ŭp, circŭs

vola (vō'lă): palm of the hand or the sole of the foot.
volatile (vŏl'ă-tĭl): easily evaporating; diffusing freely; not permanent.
volatilize (vōl'ă-tĭl-īz): to convert a solid or a liquid into vapor.
vitiation (vĭsh-ē-ā'shŭn): act of spoiling or injuring the substance or quality of.
volt (vōlt): the fractional unit of electromotive force.
voltage (vōl'tāj): electrical potential difference expressed in volts.
volume (vŏl'ūm): space occupied, as measured in cubic units.
voluntary (vŏl'ûn-tā-rē): under the control of the will.
vomer (vō'mẽr): the thin plate of bone between the nostrils.
vulgaris, acne (vŭl-gā'rĭs): common principle.
vulnerable (vŭl'nẽr-ă-b'l): capable of receiving injury.

W

wall plate (wôl plāt): an apparatus equipped with indicators and controlling devices to produce various currents.
wall socket (sŏk'ĕt): a wall receptacle into which may be fitted the plug of an electrical appliance.
walnut stain (wôl'nŭt stān): one of the wood extracts used as a hair coloring.
wart (wôrt): verruca; a circumscribed hypertrophy of the papillae of the corium, usually of the hand, covered by thickened epidermis.
water (wŏ'tẽr): a compound of oxygen and hydrogen.
water softener (sŏf'nẽr): certain chemicals, such as the carbonate or phosphate of sodium, used to soften hard water to permit the lathering of soap.
watt (wŏt): the electrical unit of energy.
wattage (wŏt'âj): amount of electric power expressed in watts.
wave, cold (wāv kōld): a method of permanent waving requiring the use of certain chemicals rather than heat.
wave, croquignole marcel (wāv, krō'kwĭ-nōl mär-sĕl'): a wave produced with the marcel iron, using the croquignole winding.
wave, finger (fĭn'gẽr): arranging waves into the hair, that has been wet, with fingers and comb.
wave, hair (hâr): the art of putting a wave into the hair.
wave, marcel (mär-sĕl): resembles a perfect natural wave, produced by means of heated irons.
wave, permanent (pûr'mâ-nênt): a wave given to the hair which is of permanent duration.
wave, push (po͞osh): a wave given by pushing waved hair into place.
wave, water (wô'tẽr): arranging the waves into the hair, that has been wet, with fingers and comb, and holding in place with water waving combs until dry.
weft (wĕft): an artificial section of woven hair used for practice work or as a substitute for natural hair.
weight control (wāt kŏn-trōl'): the maintenance of normal body weight by means of proper diet and exercise.
wen (wĕn): a sebaceous cyst, usually on the scalp.
wet winding (wĕt wīnd'ĭng): pertaining to permanent waving, winding the hair that has been saturated with a permanent waving solution on the permanent wave rod.
wheal (whēl): a raised ridge on the skin, usually caused by a blow, a bite of an insect, urticarial, or sting of a nettle.

fāte, câre, ăm, finâl, ärm, ȧsk, sofă; ēve, évent, ĕnd, recênt, evẽr; īce, ĭll; ōld, ŏ́bey, ôrb, ŏdd, cônnect, sŏft, fo͞od, fo͝ot; ūse, ûrn, ŭp, circŭs

white corpuscle (whĭt kôr'pŭs-'l): leucocytes; white blood cell; cells in the blood whose function is to destroy disease germs.

whitehead (whīt'hĕd): milium.

whorl (whûrl; whôrl): a spiral turn, in general; hence a hair whorl or cowlick, a spiral turn causing a tuft of hair which goes contrary to the usual growth of the hair.

wig (wĭg): an artificial covering for the head, consisting of hair interwoven or united by a kind of network.

winding, croquignole (wīnd'ĭng krō'kwĭ-nōl): winding the hair from the hair ends towards the scalp.

winding, helical or spiral (hĕl'ĭ-kâl or spī'râl): winding the hair from the scalp to the ends.

windpipe (wĭnd'pīp): trachea.

witch hazel (wĭch hā'z'l): after shaving lotion; an extract of the bark of the hamamelis shrub, also widely used as a remedy for bruises, sprains, and other similar ailments.

wool crepe (wōōl crâp): a substance used to fasten hair when winding in permanent waving.

wrapper (răp'ẽr): that in which anything is enclosed or wrapped, thus in permanent waving, the pad that covers the curl during the steaming period; that in which the curl on the rod is wrapped.

wringing (rĭng'ĭng): a massage movement in which the flesh is twisted firmly against the bones in opposite directions.

wrinkle (rĭnk"l): a small ridge or a furrow.

wrist electrode (rĭst é-lĕk'trōd): an electrode connected to the wrist.

X

xanthoma (zăn-thō'mă): a skin disease characterized by the presence of yellow nodules or slightly raised plates in the skin, especially of the eyelids.

x-ray (ĕks'rā): the Roentgen rays; these rays were discovered by the German physicist Wilhelm Roentgen and were called x-rays by him.

Z

zinc (zĭnk): a white crystalline metallic element.

zinc sulphate (sŭl'fāt): a salt often employed as an astringent, both in lotios and creams.

zinc sulphocarbonate (zĭnk sŭl-fô-kär'bôn-āt): a fine white powder having the odor of carbolic acid used as an antiseptic and astringent in deodorant preparations.

zygoma (zī-gō'mă): a bone of the skull which extends along the front or side of the face, below the eye; the malar or cheek bone.

zygomatic (zī-gő-măt'ĭk): pertaining to the zygoma; pertaining to the malar or cheek bone.

zygomaticus (zī-gő-măt'ĭ-kûs): a muscle that draws the upper lip upward and outward.

---

fāte, câre, ăm, finâl, ärm, ȧsk, sofă; ēve, ĕvent, ĕnd, recênt, evẽr; īce, ĭll; ōld, őbey, ôrb, ŏdd, cônnect, sŏft, fōōd, fŏŏt; ūse, ûrn, ŭp, circŭs

www.ingramcontent.com/pod-product-compliance
Lightning Source LLC
Chambersburg PA
CBHW081811300426
44116CB00014B/2324